High Performance HR: Leveraging Human Resources for Competitive Advantage

DR. DAVID S. WEISS

WILEY

John Wiley & Sons Canada, Ltd.

Toronto • New York • Chichester • Weinheim • Brisbane • Singapore

John Wiley & Sons Canada Limited
22 Worcester Road
Etobicoke, Ontario
M9W 1L1

Canadian Cataloguing in Publication Data

Weiss, David S. (David Solomon), 1953–
    High performance HR: leveraging human resources for
    competitive advantage

Originally published under title: High-impact HR.
Includes bibliographical references and index.
ISBN 0-471-64385-8

1. Personnel management. 2. Strategic planning. 3. Organizational
effectiveness. I. Title. II. Title: High-impact HR.

HF5549.W43595 2000   658.3   C00-932373-2

Production Credits
Cover design: Interrobang Graphic Design Inc.
Printer: Tri-Graphic Printing
Page layout: Heidy Lawrance Associates
Author photo: Sparks Studios

Printed in Canada

10 9 8 7 6 5 4 3 2

CONTENTS

ᘒ

PREFACE

☙ॐ

HR professionals have a tremendous thirst for information and techniques that will help Human Resources to be recognised as a valued business asset. This book, *High Performance HR: Leveraging Human Resources for Competitive Advantage*, was written to respond to that need. It challenges the traditional view of Human Resources with a new vision of HR as an internal business accountable for the return on investment of essential corporate assets, people, and organizational processes.

This book provides practical strategies for transforming HR's role, priorities, accountabilities, and organizational design. It reinforces what HR professionals are beginning to realize—that they must shift their focus to the company's strategic direction.[1] The challenge to HR is to unleash its own potential to seek the most effective way to proceed.

High Performance HR focuses on the work that HR can abandon and the new strategic business process outcomes on which it should concentrate. By shedding traditional "core" responsibilities, HR will be free to focus on more strategic business processes that contribute significantly to the company's competitive advantage. Many executives will welcome HR's new value-added position in the company with its competitive mindset and focus on adding value that benefits the external customer.

Based on extensive work and research in this field, this book clearly defines the changes required of HR and the practical strategies necessary for achieving these changes. The research and work is derived from several sources:

---

[1] The comments about companies in this book can also be applied to non-profit organizations and to government agencies and departments.

- Best Practices research conducted in the areas of HR services and how it delivers strategic value to the company, learning organizations, outplacement services, and collaborative labor-management relations.

- Extensive experience in the implementation of organizational change and the transformation of HR for many companies. In these situations, the ideas were tested and validated.

- Watching, thinking, and reflecting on other areas that have shown success and identifying how to apply their successful practices to the field of HR. For example, exploration of the success in marketing and external customer service led to many ideas of how practices can be applied within HR for internal client service.

A Description of This Book

This section presents a brief overview of the four parts of this book and a description of each chapter. It also provides questions that can help you assess the readiness of your company's Human Resources function to be a *High Performance HR* department.

Part One consists of three chapters that describe the challenge to HR to add strategic value to the company and the customer.

Chapter One articulates reasons for HR's existence and helps executives and HR leaders understand how HR can be positioned in the future. It also explores the different phases of company development and the kind of HR services that will best fit each phase.

Some questions to help you assess your readiness to deliver *High Performance HR* services are:

- At what phase on the growth curve is your company?
- What are the risks the HR department can reduce and the opportunities it can develop for the company?

Chapter Two argues that HR (and all company functions) should focus on delivering value to the external customer to insure alignment and competitive advantage for the company.

Some questions to help you assess your readiness to deliver *High Performance HR* services are:

- How focused is your company on servicing the external customer?
- To what extent are the executives open to viewing HR professionals as strategic partners?
- How effective is HR at enabling managers to be better leaders?
- Who is HR's customer?

- How would the priorities of HR change if it would focus on work that eventually delivers value to the external customer?

Chapter Three defines the work of HR and how HR can abandon specific work skillfully or "with discipline." It explains what HR can "dump" because it does not fit with the company's strategic objectives, what can be "delayed" to a later time, what can be "distributed" to others internally and externally, and what can can be "diminished" in scope so that HR can assume a more strategic role.

Some questions to help you assess your readiness to deliver *High Performance HR* services are:

- What percentage of HR's work is focused on the core HR roles and what percentage is focused on business transformation?

- What are the percentages in each of those areas?

- How can HR abandon (dump, delay, distribute, diminish) some work and accept more strategic work into its portfolio?

Part Two consists of two chapters that describe the first two areas of work for HR professionals. These are the core people processes and the organizational value-add processes.

Chapter Four explores approaches to delivering HR's traditional "core people process" work. The focus is on the employment cycle at work. Senior HR professionals can use this chapter as a way to organize the traditional work of HR. Less experienced HR professionals can use this chapter to understand the core work of HR.

Some questions to help you assess your readiness to deliver *High Performance HR* services are:

- What is the top priority core people process that is essential to the competitive advantage of the company?

- What are some approaches you can use to enhance the value of your company's core people processes?

Chapter Five explores the second area of HR's work. It explains the organizational value-add processes with a particular focus on technology deployment, organizational learning, and organizational consulting.

Some questions to help you assess your readiness to deliver *High Performance HR* services are:

- How can your company leverage the deployment of technology to contribute value to the clients and to enable managers to lead people more effectively?

- How can the company improve the learning environment that exists currently and enable employees to continually learn?

- To what extent is HR able to contribute value to clients through executive coaching and organizational consulting?

Part Three consists of five chapters that focus on the strategic value work for HR professionals—how HR can transform the company through strategic business processes. It explores four highly leveraged strategic business processes for HR. These are 1) cultivating a flexible culture, 2) championing strategic alignment, 3) implementing change and transition, and 4) insuring a return on investment in human capital.

Chapter Six introduces the third area of HR's work. This chapter is the overview for the next four chapters, each of which describes a business transformation strategy that HR can lead. The assumption is that HR professionals can choose the business transformation strategy that is the best fit for their company.

Some questions to help you assess your readiness to deliver *High Performance HR* services are:

- What is your company's competitive position?
- What implication does your company's competitive position have on the selection of an HR business transformation strategy?
- To what extent is HR perceived to have the ability to contribute to strategic business processes?
- Which one or two of the business transformation strategies would best fit your company's needs?

Chapter Seven explores how to cultivate a flexible culture through creating and living shared values, through leadership dialogues, through organizational "elasticity," and through rewards and recognition programs.

Some questions to help you assess your readiness to deliver *High Performance HR* services are:

- To what extent are your company's values defined and to what extent do they shape your employees' behavior?
- How effective are leaders at communicating to employees the real meaning behind the challenges your company is facing?
- How capable is your company at modifying its organizational design to fit the challenges of the moment?
- How do your company's rewards and recognition initiatives reinforce the culture that you are trying to create?
- To what extent is HR perceived to have the ability to contribute to this strategic business process?

Chapter Eight explores how HR can champion the alignment of strategic initiatives. It explains five areas of alignment: 1) to the vision, 2) with other strategic initiatives, 3) with customers, 4) with suppliers, and 5) within the strategic initiative team itself.

Some questions to help you assess your readiness to deliver *High Performance HR* services are:

- How aligned are each employee's performance objectives with your company's direction?
- To what extent are each of the strategic initiatives within your company aligned with each other?
- How aligned is your company with the needs of customers and suppliers?
- To what extent are each of your strategic initiative teams operating with internal alignment?
- To what extent are the core people process, organizational value-add, and strategic business processes aligned within HR?

Chapter Nine explores HR's role in implementing change and transition. It presents a model consisting of eight elements that will help HR professionals contribute to the challenges of change and transition.

Some questions to help you assess your readiness to deliver *High Performance HR* services are:

- How effective is your company at selecting the right changes on which to focus?
- How effective is your company in implementing changes that they selected and rejecting changes they can discard?
- How effective is your company in dealing with the human transition elements of change?
- How do you measure the success of each change initiative?
- To what extent is HR accepted as a resource to help your company effectively implement change and transition?

Chapter Ten describes a new area of contribution to business transformation. It describes how HR can enhance the company's return on investment in human capital. It suggests that HR has a financial accountability for the human asset and needs to identify ways that it can appreciate that asset.

Some questions to help you assess your readiness to deliver *High Performance HR* services are:

- To what extent is the issue of return on investment in human capital important to your company's executives?
- Is there a measure of human capital in your company?
- How can HR enhance the value of human capital through HR people and organizational processes?
- To what extent is HR perceived to have the ability to contribute to this strategic business process?

Part Four focuses on HR's future. It explores an HR structure and its associated roles and relationships and discusses the next HR evolution within companies. The book concludes with a brief epilogue that advises HR professionals to take the leadership role in leveraging Human Resources for competitive advantage through their work as "high performance HR professionals."

Chapter Eleven describes the preferred structure, roles, and relationships for HR to be able to deliver the core people processes, the organizational value-add processes, and the strategic business process outcomes presented in this book.

Some questions to help you assess your readiness to deliver *High Performance HR* services are:

- What segments of HR's work need to be delivered with a great deal of customizing to the needs of specific internal clients?
- What segments of HR's work can be delivered on a company-wide basis?
- How can HR create a balance between the need for economies of scale and the need for customized services to the client?

Chapter Twelve proposes a more visionary organizational design that describes various levels of integrating internal service businesses within the company to serve internal clients more effectively. The service businesses focus on collaborating in order that their clients can better meet the external customers' needs.

Some questions to help you assess your readiness to deliver *High Performance HR* services are:

- What is the readiness of your company's internal service businesses to collaborate with each other?
- What is your current level of integrating internal service businesses?
- What would be the benefit to your company to move to the next level in integrating internal service businesses?
- To what extent is HR prepared to take a leadership role in aligning its services with other internal service business within your company?

Who Will Benefit from This Book?

The book has been written for those hungry for information, ideas and proven techniques to advance HR's role in organizations. *High Performance HR: Leveraging Human Resources for Competitive Advantage* is very helpful both conceptually and practically. In particular, the following groups will find the book beneficial:

- Human Resources professionals, internal and external to the company, interested in understanding and applying a new role for HR.
- Executives and managers seeking to understand HR's changing role, the new value that HR will provide, and how they can make this change an integral part of their organizations.
- Associations for HR, training, organizational development and strategy and other groups that are concerned with people and organizational development and transformation issues.
- Members of the academic community interested in a text to teach their students about the changing role of Human Resources.
- Students in business school and HR programs interested in books to support their understanding of the field.

How to Read This Book

Most readers will benefit from reading this book cover to cover. However, others will find that they can dip into it for specific ideas and information, and it will add value. Here are some alternative ways this book can be read:

- Some readers—those responsible for the development of HR professionals—may want to use the book as a study guide to use in training. A suggested approach would be to ask the HR professionals to read Part One for the first discussion and Part Two for the second discussion. Part Three and Four can be read and discussed one chapter at a time. The readiness questions presented in the Preface can be explored after the completion of each chapter.
- If the readers are primarily interested in leading-edge roles for HR, they may want to focus on reading Part Three (Chapters Six to Ten), which describes the HR strategic business processes.
- Other readers may want to develop a model to understand and communicate HR's fundamental people and organizational work. These readers may want to focus on Part Two of the book (Chapters Four and Five).

- Still other readers may want to explore the topic of abandonment of work and how it is done, which can be found in Chapters Three and Four.

- Finally, readers may want to study a topic of their own interest. A detailed index has been prepared for referencing specific topics. For example, topics such as "teams," "motivation," "strategic partners," "coaching," and the "role of the executives," are referred to in several chapters. The reader can combine the ideas about a topic area to form their own analysis of the material.

Special Features Of The Second Edition

In the past eighteen months (since the publication of the first edition of the book), many HR professionals and executives contributed ideas and asked thoughtful questions to advance the discussion on strategic HR process outcomes. In addition, there have been numerous opportunities to apply these ideas for large and small organizations in the private and public sectors. To reflect these developments, the second edition includes the following:

- A new article appears in an appendix, which IRC Press of Queen's University first published. This appendix is an interview with the author by Mary Lou Coates on "Strategic Human Resources Management: Challenges and Opportunities." It provides direct and succinct answers to often asked questions that arise from reading the book.

- The "Comprehensive Reading List For HR Professionals" has been updated with important books published in 1999-2000.

- The questions in the "Preface" have been updated to reflect many of the challenges for HR professionals as they implement the ideas in each chapter.

- The title of the book has changed from "High-Impact HR" to "High Performance HR" to reflect the realization that HR work does not always yield visible impact. Rather, through its high level of focused performance, HR enables its company to achieve the competitive advantage it requires.

The hope is that this book will be a road map for executives and HR leaders who are considering how to leverage Human Resources for competitive advantage. It will also help create an understandable story of what HR is and how it contributes value to internal clients and the customer. And most important, it will provide HR professionals with an approach to guide them in their aspirations to becoming *High Performance HR* professionals.

ACKNOWLEDGMENTS

⊗

This book has been the product of over three years of writing and eighteen years of work. In the process of writing this book, I have had numerous opportunities to work with other individuals to whom I want to express my appreciation and acknowledgment.

A great deal of the development and refinement of my ideas for the book came from my association with the clients with whom I have worked. They stimulated thought by presenting intriguing issues and by their willingness to try out new ideas. With special gratitude, I want to thank Myles Harrigan for his unceasing focus on alignment and people processes; to Georgina Wyman for her experimentation with integrating internal service businesses; and to many other outstanding professionals and leaders including Greg Anderson, Haim Benjamini, Lynn Evans, Ruth Kemp, Graham Herbert, Corey Jack, Elena King, Paul Lucas, James Marchant, Harriet Stairs, Colleen Teed, Doug Tipple and Sue Ellen Wiles.

I also want to express appreciation to the entire team in the firm of Geller, Shedletsky & Weiss who have worked with outstanding commitment and competence and with excellent results to service our customers. We have built a marvelous professional community that has the openness and trust to share learnings with each other and to collaborate to meet our customers' needs. In particular, I want to thank my GSW partners for their support for this initiative: Malcolm Bernstein, Shel Geller, Ralph Shedletsky and Marijane Terry. A special thank you to Janet Burt for her work on the change and transition model and to Bob Harris for emphasizing the transition elements in the change and transition process. Special thanks to Malcolm Bernstein for his untiring work in the field of HR and for terms he uses often such as "organizational elasticity" and "employee resilience." Also, thank you to the rest of the organizational consulting team at GSW for their encouragement and for reviewing this manuscript: Joanne Berry, Richard Dubuc, Judy Hemmingsen, and Francoise Morissette, and to the administration professionals who helped with this initiative: Susan Beckley and Sandra Kane.

I also thank the many other professionals who contributed to this work. Of particular note are Dr. Jagdish Sheth for his wisdom and concepts about strategy; Dr. Bill Davidson for introducing me to the equation of "company equals business plus organization;" Ira Grussgott for his

"Hatch, Match and Dispatch" anecdote; Dr. Bruce Phillips for introducing me to the application of Bartlett and Ghoshal's work to companies; and Moshe Gilat for his major contribution to thought development in Chapter Ten concerning the return on investment in human capital.

I have also had many opportunities to speak publicly at conferences about these topics. All of the conference organizations that gave me the forum to speak about these ideas are very much appreciated. In particular, I extend great appreciation to the Industrial Relations Centre staff at Queen's University. For the past five years, they have supported and encouraged my work in these areas. Of particular note are Dr. Bryan Downie, Dr. Carol Beatty and Brenda Barker. Also, thank you to Mary Lou Coates of IRC Press who conducted the interview that appears in the appendix of the book.

The refinement of the manuscript is a very special area of development of a book. Every set of ideas can be broadly communicated, but writing eventually comes down to the details. Do the ideas fit together, are the concepts clear enough for the reader, and are there enough examples to help ground the concept in reality? A very special thank-you to Mary Jo Beebe for her ongoing support in this regard. Her challenging comments, attention to detail and exceptional patience have helped this project become clearer and more tightly formulated. Also, special thanks to Sylvia Odenwald for her ongoing support and confidence in me and this project.

A special thank you is extended to Karen Milner and the John Wiley & Sons team for their confidence in this project and for their comments on the manuscript. Also, I offer my thanks to the Wiley team for their promotion and continued support throughout the initial publication of this book. They were very instrumental in helping make this book the *Books For Business* number one best selling Human Resources book in Canada for 1999. The hope is that the second printing, under its new title "High Performance HR," will continue to be successful and reach an even larger audience throughout North America.

One friend in particular, Dr. David Bakan, has commented on this document from time to time, listening to my ideas about the project and, assisting me in thinking through the overall concept of the book. I thank him for his ongoing support, encouragement, insights, and friendship.

Finally, my family has been there throughout. My wife, Dr. Nora Gold, has been a major inspiration, encouraging me to write my thoughts and share them with the world as she has so marvelously done through her research and short stories. My young son, Joseph Weissgold, has been an outstanding energy source for me. I thank him for his humor and his insights. Not much would be possible without their love and support.

PART ONE

The
Challenge

CHAPTER ONE

෨෨

The Irish Elk

*Through many generations, the Irish elk became
the victim of an evolutionary quirk that led to its
demise. Each year its antlers grew longer, eventually becoming so heavy that it was unable to
lift its head and forage for food. It became weaker and weaker and eventually starved to death.
The antlers that had helped the elk survive in the
first place became exaggerated over time, leading
to its extinction.*

Consider the president of an organization in which the Human
Resources (HR) department is suffering from the "Irish Elk Syndrome."
HR is exaggerating what helped it survive by continuing to focus on
what the department has always done. While the company has been
transforming, HR has not kept pace. The president points out that without radical change HR will not be able to help the company achieve its
strategic goals.

In the past the HR department attempted to meet the company's
needs without actively focusing on the company's direction and the
return on investment. Today, however, the conditions under which HR
needs to operate have changed. The company expects an increase in the
return on investment in people. As the company reengineers, HR must
transform.

The new challenge to HR is to take accountability for the return
on investment of essential corporate assets, people and organizational

processes. Just as the Finance Department is responsible for overseeing the financial assets of the business, Human Resources' role is to oversee and be accountable for the investment in human capital (the money it takes to cultivate people and their talents). The company will maximize its return on this investment in human capital when HR maximizes the contribution people make to the company's strategic direction. The HR leader who can say, "I know the investment in human capital our company makes...," gets the attention of senior executives. But the HR leader who can follow up by saying, "...and I can tell you how to secure an even better return on human capital," may have an even more gratifying response. Executives may be surprised that HR refers to people in business and strategic terms, but they also will be very interested in hearing more.

In today's brutally competitive marketplace, many companies are searching for a new direction and are attempting to transform their businesses. Human Resource departments are also striving to transform.

The Focus For HR's Transformation

Transforming HR involves changing HR's priorities, accountabilities, roles, and organizational design. This transformation emphasizes the following focuses:

- *Strategic value*—the extent to which people and organizational processes provide competitive advantage.
- *A competitive mindset*—rather than the idea of being a monopoly service provider without competition.
- *Process outcomes*—creating a balance between excellence in process and the delivery of specific measurable outcomes.

A Focus On Strategic Value

Ten years ago I spoke at a conference[1] about why HR should focus on the company's strategic direction and how this would increase HR's value and help it gain a seat at the executive table. (Note: The comments about companies in this book can also be applied to non-profit organizations and to government agencies and departments.) Since that time, major changes have occurred in the global marketplace with

---

[1] A joint conference of the Human Resource Professional Association of Ontario and the Ontario Society of Training and Development, 1989.

implications for industry, technology, customer loyalty and organizational effectiveness. The changes in expectations held by companies and HR have been extensive. Some companies have transformed their HR function, giving it an important position in the corporate strategy. However, most have not achieved that transformation. Even the definition of the word strategy has assumed a new meaning. In the past, *strategy* often meant a high-level game plan with a long-term focus. Companies were willing to invest heavily in strategic initiatives because they felt confident of a return on investment several years later.

Today, two problems emerge with that definition of *strategy*. First, most companies are unwilling to have a long-term investment perspective. They do not believe the world is stable enough to insure that a long-term investment will pay off. Long-term strategies assume a stable or predictable business environment. In a radically transforming environment, the future is unknown and almost unpredictable. Executives therefore demand a shorter-term focus and a more immediate return on their strategic investment.

The second problem is that some managers work the system to their own advantage at the expense of the company. They do this by finding a way to be promoted three to six months before the revenue from the implemented strategy is realized. Moving to a new position *before* the revenue kicks in is a no-lose proposition for them because, if the revenue exceeds the expense, they will receive credit for developing the strategy. On the other hand, if the revenue does not materialize, they can always blame their successor for implementing the strategy inappropriately.

In today's market, companies expect a strategy to increase revenue almost immediately and simultaneously decrease expense. The new operative definition of *strategy* focuses on gaining sustainable competitive advantage. It can be expressed as "***a plan to achieve relative advantage against the competition.***" Initiatives that provide strategic value achieve relative advantage against the competition; all other initiatives are tactical.

Traditional HR activities such as recruiting, employee relations, compensation and training are necessary but not sufficient to help the company thrive in the new business marketplace. If this is HR's only focus, many executives may discount its strategic importance. HR's redefined role is to concentrate on providing strategic value that helps the company gain relative advantage against its competition.

A Focus Based on a Competitive Mindset

Some HR professionals view themselves as monopoly service providers and believe that managers and executives will not consider using external sources for HR services. This perception may be shared by line managers who either do not know they have this choice or who are not authorized to exercise choice. Alternatively, when HR delivers outstanding service, managers may not feel compelled to explore other options. Many companies have found that HR professionals become complacent if they think they have a monopoly on providing HR services. Rather than proactively fostering change, they wait for change to be imposed on them. They may react well to requests but lack initiative.

It's important for HR to develop a competitive mindset. For this to occur, HR must do the following:

- Set high standards for delivering quality service and conduct benchmarking initiatives against their competition.

- Develop people and organizational strategies to help the company deliver value to its customers.

- Emphasize HR priorities that help the company gain competitive advantage.

This *competitive mindset* is directed to achieving competitive advantage, and its measures of success are external business standards. It is entirely different from *operating competitively* with internal functions in the company, which can be dysfunctional. The complexity of transfer pricing, internal battles of process ownership, and internal HR competition can be destructive to HR's strategic value to the company. It is essential for HR to create an internal working environment that fosters collaboration and partnerships and, at the same time, a mindset directed to developing competitive advantage for the company.

When Human Resources operates competitively, it focuses on strategic value, takes initiative and becomes a catalyst for change. It also directs its efforts to maximizing the value of people to the company. As the name *human resources* implies, human beings are recognized as resources that can appreciate or depreciate. It is HR's business to ensure that the people asset appreciates in value to the company.

A Focus on Process Outcomes

In the past few years, many companies have focused on process improvements and process reengineering. An important outcome has been the recognition that demanding better results with the old processes is ineffective. Instead, the processes have to be changed for better results to follow.

The same process orientation has been embraced by internal service functions. Since these functions tend to be process-oriented already, the emphasis on process has been music to their ears. For example, the Information Technology functions have seen process improvements as their domain of strategic value contribution to the company. They know how to deploy technology to radically redesign processes, improve efficiencies, and reduce cost.

HR has also emphasized process improvements, which have led it to explore alternative ways of delivering service. For example, in the past many companies have perceived HR as an administrative function rather than as a profession with its own knowledge base and excellent processes. It was rare for HR to lead the company change process. Today, most senior executives know alternate delivery mechanisms exist to administer many traditional HR processes. In some cases, these processes can be performed by external resources in a more efficient and economical manner. Rather than viewing these resources as a threat, HR has changed its processes to distribute work it formerly did, allowing it to focus on investing in human capital for strategic advantage.

In some companies HR has been able to change its work processes and sustain higher ratios of HR professionals to employees (1:100 and even over 1:200 in a few cases). This has been accomplished by distributing activities to other functions that have the capability to perform some of the traditional HR processes. HR has also abandoned processes that met needs in the past but have limited usefulness now.

From our best practices analysis of many HR organizations (Geller, Shedletsky & Weiss, 1998)[2], it appears that the HR functions that are successful in process improvements are focusing on process outcomes. They do not improve "process for processes' sake." Rather they clearly define specific outcomes that are needed and identify processes that need to be recreated in order to achieve those outcomes. Unfortunately, some HR functions have lost sight of the outcomes in their work on process. They change processes to conform with benchmarks without focusing on the process outcomes that must guide the change.

HR's challenge is to focus its process improvements on process outcomes. When the expected outcomes are clearly defined and the results are measurable, the process improvements are evident. HR holds the accountability for the specific outcomes even if it does not deliver all

[2] Geller, Shedletsky & Weiss. 1998. An unpublished study completed on behalf of a client in the financial sector.

the parts of the process. A focus on process outcomes also helps HR leaders speak the language of their senior executives. Many executives become confused when HR speaks of people and organizational processes. Most are more concerned about the business outcomes than elegant HR processes.

The Growth Curve

HR's strategic contribution will vary depending on the company's stage of development. It is therefore important to understand a company's growth phases and the demands they place on HR. Knowing about these phases will also help define how HR can add strategic value as well as remove the people-related risks that can block the company from achieving its strategic direction.

Many years ago, Greiner (1972)[3] introduced a growth curve describing the evolution and revolution in businesses. The growth curve concept was further developed by George Ainsworth Land and was applied to many areas, including product development and its life cycle. A company's growth curves and patterns have direct implications for HR. Figure 1.1 presents a modified growth curve for a company's life cycle.

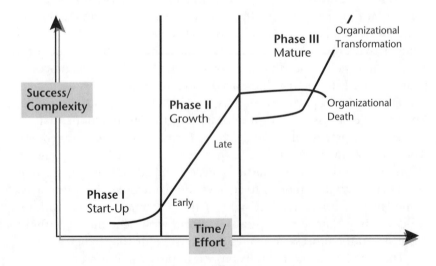

Figure 1.1: The Growth Curve

[3] L. E. Greiner, *Evolution and Revolution as Organizations Grow*. Harvard Business Review, July-August, 1972, no. 4, p. 37-46. Also see Ilan Meshoulam and Lloyd Baird, *Proactive Human Resources Management*. Human Resources Management, Winter 1987, 26, no. 4, 483-502.

Phase One—The Start-up Phase

In Phase One, the start-up phase, the enterprise leader has an idea for a business. The business' initial return on investment is often low. The enterprise survives because the leadership and employees have a passionate and determined interest in making it successful. The leaders are entrepreneurial, aggressive, and visionary. Employees are often highly committed and aligned with the leader's direction for the enterprise.

The customer is known to everyone. He or she is the person outside the enterprise who "pays the company's bills." Everyone focuses on delivering value to the customer, which helps the successful Phase One organization develop a culture in which everyone is responsible for innovation and quality.

The effective Phase One company concentrates intensely on the strategies to insure they are implemented. Costs associated with all activities are known, and actions are taken based on this knowledge. The leaders and employees foster a flexible culture that is typified by the comment of a leader in a Phase One organization, "We do whatever it takes to get the job done." The primary risk to the Phase One company is survival. Many start-ups do not succeed. They long for the luxury of sustained growth to secure their business and maximize their shareholder value.

Another characteristic of the Phase One enterprise is that often it does not have internal organizational support departments. One of the senior executives may be responsible for finance, and all managers are entrusted with the development of the people they manage. Frequently, the leader is very reluctant to invest in overhead costs associated with HR since all investments are devoted to the primary risk of survival. In Phase One, the company invests only to add value to the customer. The leader often perceives HR as an unnecessary cost because it does not appear to reduce any major risks. The leader believes either that managers can perform HR responsibilities themselves or that they do not have to be done at all.

Astute Phase One leaders recognize that avoiding the investment in HR is shortsighted. For example, a very successful cellular company invested heavily in HR at the outset, and it paid great dividends. Early in its development, the company had a major recall of cellular phones that could have jeopardized their credibility in the marketplace. HR leadership responded quickly and effectively to the crisis. Their professionalism was recognized as one of the reasons the company was able to overcome the many challenges associated with people and the organization.

Recently, Phase One companies have drawn considerable attention from executives in companies at Phase Two (growth phase) and Phase Three (mature phase). These companies like what they see and remember of Phase One and ask, "Can we recreate the Phase One environment in a mature organization?" These companies hope to harness the energy in Phase One without the threat to survival. They want all employees to focus on the external customer, have a very flexible and adaptive culture, align all activities to the strategic direction, and implement strategies in a cost-effective manner. They realize that if their organization has these capabilities, they will have relative strategic advantage against the competition.

Phase Two—The Growth Phase

Entering into Phase Two, or the growth phase, the company discovers its growth formula and finds that it has a winning "recipe for success." The Phase One company's dream of surviving and achieving business security appears attainable. For many companies, reaching Phase Two is a major achievement and a deserved cause to celebrate. For some companies, reaching Phase Two is an evolutionary process and not that clearly evident. They only know they are in Phase Two after they have been there for awhile. In other companies, it is marked by a major event such as when the company goes public, its ethical drug receives regulatory approval, or it secures a major account.

Entering Phase Two is a very positive development for an enterprise. However, as with all good developments, associated risks may appear. The company often evolves into a pattern similar to that of the person who makes dinner for friends and creates a delicious dessert. The person knows everyone likes the dessert, so he or she makes it over and over again. Companies in Phase Two develop their own recipes for success from which they are frequently unwilling to vary. As they succeed with their recipes, however, companies begin to realize that this phase has its own risks, and they can be considerable.

For example, a Phase Two company decides that a rigid culture that ensures growth and success is more important than the previous flexible culture that got it to this level of success. As a result they make some changes in the organization such as establishing control mechanisms to ensure decisions reinforce the success formula, creating departments that allow the executives to control where and how innovation occurs, establishing a centralized marketing department with a formula the sales force must follow, selecting people based on their willingness to follow rules, and choosing a leader who has strong administrative and bureaucratic skills and experience.

At some point in the middle of Phase Two, the senior executives realize that the new risks in their company relate, in part, to people and organizations. Their concern may be that the repetitive work of Phase Two is affecting motivation, and managers may not know how to respond to these challenges, employees may organize to secure better terms of employment and better working conditions, and they (executives) may not know how to handle new legislative requirements. After much angst (and only when the pain of inaction is greater than the pain of action), the senior executives recognize that they require an overhead investment to reduce the people and organizational risks. It is often at this phase that they hire someone to be responsible for Human Resources.

With a centralized Human Resources role, the right people are hired. This enables the enterprise to be managed the way the senior executives prescribe—managers will insure that employees follow the rules and procedures of the Phase Two success recipe. The executives convince themselves that they have discovered one of the antidotes to failure and that they have reduced another significant risk to their success.

Unfortunately, as the company continues to grow, the atrophy of success starts to set in. Eventually, the enterprise becomes yesterday's success, and it loses the foresight to see alternative ways to perform in the future. Employees arrive for work at the dictated time, managers do their jobs, bills are paid, and customers seem happy—until late one evening, the senior executive realizes all is not well. The enterprise's market share is flattening out, and it is becoming stale. The leadership recognizes that its approach to Phase Two is a problem—the approach has lasted too long, creating stagnation.

Companies become so pleased with themselves that they evolve into "legends in their own minds." Ultimately, this narcissism is their demise unless they recognize this failure early enough. They need to avoid getting stuck in their approach to Phase Two and the early development of the Irish Elk Syndrome.

Intel is an example of a company that appears to be unwilling to settle into Phase Two. The company is regularly creating breakthroughs and repeating the Phase One curve to achieve growth. As it grows rapidly, it emphasizes making its own technology obsolete before the competition can do it. Intel's Phase Two growth curve looks like a series of Phase One curves spiraling up the value chain instead of one line of growth.

A company needs continuous change and consolidation to survive. Becoming stuck in Phase Two without change can be a source of problems such as loss of market share and shareholder value. Eventually, if the Phase Two company does not change (as the growth curve in Figure 1.1 shows), it becomes a mature company and enters Phase Three, which appears as a flat line that eventually slopes downward. The HR role is to foster continuous, managed change to help the company avoid entering Phase Three. If it does enter Phase Three, the company will have one more chance to introduce dramatic change, or face eventual extinction.

A Phase Two growth company can incur many risks, which is a compelling reason to motivate the executives in this phase to invest in Human Resources. The list that follows, while not exhaustive, illustrates the people and organizational process risks in Phase Two.

People Risks in Phase Two

- *The company may not recruit, develop, retain, and remove employees effectively as the company grows:* The company must develop the knowledge and skills to recruit, develop, retain, and remove employees, and to fulfill legislative requirements appropriately. These are the major challenges in Phase Two that frequently motivate leadership to hire an HR professional.

- *Managers may make people-related mistakes that could place the company in jeopardy:* The company often trains their managers and institutes management controls to reduce risk in areas such as selection, employee relations, and terminations.

- *Employees who have been innovative in Phase One may not be willing to follow the new success recipe in Phase Two:* This is a challenging issue. The implicit employment contract in Phase One is based on initiative and innovation. Employees are expected to be enterprising, adventurous, and innovative. In Phase Two the employment contract is often based on following the rules. Employees who can adhere to policies and procedures are required. Motivating employees who are innovative is a challenge for a company in Phase Two. The company either promotes the Phase One employees to positions in which they can be enterprising, or these employees may leave to join the competition.

- *The entrepreneurial leader, the founding partner, may not be the right person to lead the Phase Two growth company:* Often, the founding leader does not have the right personality and leadership style to lead the company into the next phase of development. A leadership change is a common result of the transition to Phase Two.
- *Line management may not handle financial matters effectively:* Frequently, in response to this risk, the Finance Department establishes tight controls for line managers, including low spending limits for managers, multiple signatures and approvals, and centralized payables and receivables.

Organizational Process Risks in Phase Two

- *Phase One and Phase Two cultures may not mix well:* The challenge will be to change a Phase One culture that is flexible, adaptive, and entrepreneurial into a Phase Two culture that is precise and focused. Since Phase One employees are more entrepreneurial, they often clash with the rules-driven Phase Two employees.
- *The proper policies and procedures may not be in place to insure that managers and employees follow the recipe for success:* The emphasis on policies and procedures is a method used to control behavior (as suggested by the similarity of the words "policy" and "police"). At this point, the enterprise wants control, so it asks for tight policies and procedures and auditing systems to police and track them.
- *Potential opportunities may be missed by the sales force without a marketing department to identify the sales strategy for them:* This risk is a very common one in Phase Two organizations. The autonomy of the sales department is often reduced when a marketing department is introduced. Essentially, the salespeople are expected to be the go-getters, and the marketing department becomes the brains behind the salespeople. This change may be difficult for more independent-minded salespeople who worked in Phase One.
- *Information technology is an ongoing expense that often gets away from leadership:* Proper investments in information technology must be made, which also involves hiring employees to provide the necessary internal intelligence. Managing the cost of the technology and the human capital invested to benefit from the technology is an executive concern.

HR's role is to ensure that the above risks are reduced and at the same time to balance the Phase Two company's need for control with the constant need to help the company and its people recreate themselves. HR professionals must help the company avoid reaching a crisis point at which change will be an imperative. Their work is to steer the company away from entering Phase Three.

Phase Three—The Mature Phase

"The writing is on the wall. Change is no longer an option—it is an imperative," a senior executive announces. The reality sets in that the old vision is really tunnel vision, a modern version of the Irish Elk Syndrome. Success has blinded the company to the fact that it has fallen into a cyclical pattern with a certain performance yielding success that results in gratifying rewards, which leads to the same performance again and again (Figure 1.2).

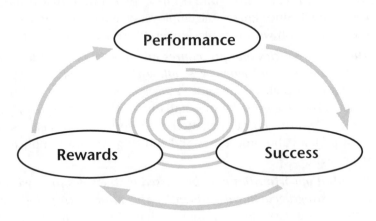

Figure 1.2: Tunnel Vision

The Phase Three pattern is difficult to break. The market and the customer have changed, yet the company wants the old success cycle to continue. Its winning pattern begins to lead it to impending disaster, yet it is hesitant to abandon its success recipe and urge the workforce to make the necessary change. Many of the work patterns in Phase Two stifle the Phase Three company's ability to create organizational renewal. These include:

- An inability to see the customer's changing wants and needs.
- A lack of awareness of competitive forces in the industry.
- Creation of an inflexible organizational culture.
- Development of rigid policies, procedures, and systems.

An Example of a Phase Three Company

Consider an example of a Phase Three company leadership that realizes customer focus is a "new idea." Blinded by an arrogant mindset that customer focus means "if we build it, the customers will come," the company's engineers are cloistered in their labs creating models. They apply Phase Two solutions to Phase Three risks and unveil their ideas to front-line workers who respond that the approach will not work.

The leader of the company, who sees the organization reaching a plateau, envisions a corporate nightmare—as the company walks to the edge of the cliff, the only way to go is downhill to organizational death. New risks are very evident. The leader needs to recreate the environment that existed in Phase One but create it in a mature company that has reached a plateau. The resistance to change is great, but the unwillingness to take this arduous journey can mean the death of the organization. Recognizing this, the leader and the senior executives isolate themselves in off-site retreats, choose new directions for the company, and assume their directives will create a desire in their employees to implement the new strategy. They know the company should focus on the customer, but their strategy does not include a serious effort to do this.

The executives encourage employees to break out of the "tunnel vision" so that they can see the light at the end of the tunnel. Employees respond by saying that all they can see is "the tunnel at the end of the light." Nevertheless, the employees succumb to the executives' wishes because they believe the only real customers of importance are the senior executives themselves. Eventually, some of the changes are implemented but only in a halfhearted fashion. The change effort is moderately successful but falls far short of the anticipated results.

The enterprise's leader now faces some difficult choices. Realizing that the enterprise is mature and that it needs dramatic change, he decides to downsize the organization. He asks the middle managers to take the initiative to reduce management layers from the current eight layers to five within six months. Unfortunately, his Phase Two managers do nothing.

Six months pass without the goal being reached, and the president announces that he is eliminating three layers of the company regardless of the talent within each targeted layer. The managers are furious and question his judgment. The president responds that he had asked them to implement the change, and since they had not done their job, he had to "shake the building until people fell out!" The damage to the organization is devastating. However, the president believes that since the managers did not make the requested changes, he had to make them himself.

This high-risk tactic, which has become common in many companies, is a final attempt to start a revolution and transform a Phase Three mature company. It indicates a major inadequacy of the executive leadership and HR. When a company requires massive layoffs, it signals leadership's failure to manage change. First, if the company had engaged in continual renewal during Phase Two, it might not have reached the mature phase. Second, the leadership and HR could have anticipated the changes needed in Phase Three so that resorting to such drastic action would have been avoided.

Executives in Phase Three need to be thorough in their assessments of the challenges and risks they face as mature organizations. Positive change does not come by assuming a facade of customer focus or by radical delayering. The organizational systems and the culture have to change so that everyone supports efforts to meet the customers' needs. Executives have to "walk the talk of quality thought." It is not just the talk that has to be implemented—their thoughts must also be well-developed.

It is common practice that the Phase Three transformation necessitates a change in executive leadership. One organizational leader explained the plight of the executive team during this phase with a story: "A hiker strolling along high cliffs that overlook the ocean stumbles over some rocks at the edge and tumbles over the cliff. As he falls to his death, he grabs a vine hanging from the side of the cliff. Clinging to the vine, he shouts to the heavens, 'Is anyone up there to help me?' He cries out several times until he hears a voice, 'Do you believe?' The hiker calls back, 'I believe, I believe.' Then the voice from above says, 'Then let go of the vine.' To which the hiker replies, 'Is there anyone else up there I can talk to?'"

The individual in the story represents the company in Phase Three. Sometimes the solution for the company is to find "someone else up there to talk to." This may mean releasing executives who do not have the skills to effect the change and bringing in new ones to turn the company around. It may also include hiring experts in the field of process reengineering or other specialists, including HR leadership, who can leverage HR for competitive advantage.

If the executive leadership's strategy is to tell the company to "let go of the vine" by ignoring competitive pressures and continuing the status quo, the company may, like the Irish elk, become extinct. Companies that do this are often targets for takeovers and acquisitions. Others simply disappear.

HR's Role in Phase Three

In the process of transforming the company from a mature company to an enterprise that is vibrant and can adapt to changing markets, the senior executives face many risks. These risks are so significant that, if not overcome, they may limit the company's ability to implement the changes it needs.

The risks and potential crises of Phase Three often encourage leadership to focus on what their business is really about, which means the basics—such as price, customers, service, and their market niche. They realize they have to de-emphasize bureaucracy. They look to HR as the group with the capability to make a unique contribution. In order to do this, HR must shift its focus to the company's strategic direction and the business. At the same time, HR needs to reduce (or remove) the organizational and people risks that may limit the company from implementing its strategy.

HR also may attempt to capture the energy and motivation the company once had at Phase One of its development. HR professionals realize, however, that it is much easier to create the needed organizational systems and culture in a Phase One start-up enterprise in which you hire people who have the style you want. Most companies that move to alternative working models, such as self-directed work teams, succeed when they are "greenfield" start-up sites, where people can be selected for that environment and culture. Attempting to transform an existing, mature Phase Three organization is much more difficult and often takes many years.

In an intensely competitive market, taking several years to change is too big a risk. The executives and HR professionals have to discover ways to make the changes occur much faster and as early as possible on the growth curve. Some companies have decided that the best way to change is to acquire start-up or growth companies that already have the culture and leadership they desire. Many others have become determined to change and transform their Phase Three company so that it becomes vibrant again. This pressure to change often means that HR needs to transform as well. HR will have to assess whether its professionals have the knowledge and expertise to solve strategic challenges and gain the credibility in these areas in order to achieve acceptance by the company and its leadership. HR will also have to engage in more intense analysis and discipline as it implements changes. HR professionals will need to continually learn and seek exposure to techniques and alternatives that will help them choose intelligently how to respond to challenges.

The chart (Figure 1.3) summarizes four strategic business risks. It also presents the recommended process outcomes to reduce exposure to the strategic risks and deliver high performance HR services to the company.

Table 1.1: Strategic Risks and the HR Process Outcomes

Strategic Business Risks	Process Outcomes
As leaders introduce changes, the employees may not be flexible enough to adapt.	HR cultivates the context for an adaptive and flexible culture in the organization and therefore enables change.
In the frenzy of Phase Three survival, energetic employees will have many initiatives but may be unaligned to a common direction to benefit the company.	HR champions the alignment of all initiatives to a common strategic direction.
Even if the environment is flexible and aligned, people may not accept and implement the strategic changes in a timely and high-quality manner.	HR insures that change is implemented by involving people and helping them transition to the changed environment.
The costs of labor may continue to escalate and, therefore, may make the company non-competitive in this time of dramatic transformation.	HR knows and communicates the cost and the return on investment in human capital. It helps determine costs and productivity of labor and helps guide resourcing decisions and investments.

Even if HR has the capability to reduce the above strategic business risks, it may not be able to emerge from its administrative load in order to transform itself and to provide the company with competitive advantage. The HR leadership will need to abandon work that is not strategic and find alternative delivery mechanisms for those administrative and core HR activities that still need to be done. It will then be able to focus on the strategic process outcomes and deliver high performance HR services to the company.

Respond to Company Risk with HR Professional Discipline

Risk taking in all phases has its complexities. The company needs to make the required changes and still feel confident that the probability of success is reasonably high. Also, enough time to work through a cultural transformation is often not available. If the company engages in a slow transformation, the competition may run away with the business. The competition will not wait for the transition to occur.

A metaphor may help explain the necessary approach to risk in all the phases: A young woman wants to learn how to scuba dive. Some friends teach her enough about diving so that she can experience the sport in some shallow waters and under their close supervision. She is thrilled at seeing an unknown world and wants to see it again. Because her first experience seemed so easy, she thinks lessons are unnecessary. "I know how to dive," she says. Then she has an opportunity to dive in deeper waters. Her friends, who include a licensed diving instructor, tell her that only under perfect conditions does she know how to dive and that she needs diving lessons if she is going to dive in deep water. Taking the advice seriously, the young woman takes instruction in diving. She learns about the equipment, to always breathe, to watch out for her buddy, to check air and depth, and to stay within her comfort zone. Only with a professional discipline does she risk the next dive. She enters the deep waters, is controlled in her approach, succeeds at overcoming the risk, and emerges delighted with her new experience.

The same is true for a company's response to risk at any phase of the growth curve and especially in the Phase Three transformation. Because of the increased exposure to risk, the company needs HR leadership to have greater professional discipline in order to succeed.

The challenge to HR is to unleash its own potential to seek the right way to proceed on behalf of the company. It must go beyond simply breaking the past mold, which is useful but is a reaction to the former ways of doing things. An enlightened HR leadership is not limited by past assumptions or molds. Rather, this leadership investigates the current situation without constraint or assumptions and seeks wise ways to implement strategy. Past models do not govern decisions about how it needs to transform in the future.

HR professionals need to focus on strategic value with a competitive mindset and an emphasis on process outcomes. They also need to modulate their contribution based upon the company's phase of development on the growth curve. As HR becomes more business focused, the company and HR receive many benefits:

- The company leverages its human capital more effectively.
- HR becomes essential to the implementation of the strategic direction of the company.
- HR delivers more strategic value and thereby increases its contribution and importance to the company.
- HR becomes responsible for far more intriguing work than it has had in the past.

HR's role is to step up to the challenge to champion the people and organizational strategies necessary to help the company succeed in today's changing market. This book will help HR professionals learn how to deliver competitive advantage and how to achieve the corresponding professional discipline and performance techniques needed to actualize this new business role successfully.

Summary

- The new challenge to HR is to take accountability for the return on investment of essential corporate assets, people, and organizational processes. The company's return on this investment will occur when HR maximizes the contribution people make to the company's strategic direction.
- Human Resource departments that refuse to transform are suffering from the "Irish Elk Syndrome," by focusing on what the department has always done. As companies reengineer, HR must transform or they may become extinct.
- Transforming HR involves changing its priorities, accountabilities, role, and organizational design. This HR transformation will focus on:
  - providing strategic value
  - working from a competitive mindset
  - people and organizational process outcomes
- How HR transforms will vary depending on the company's phase or state of development. Knowing about these phases will help HR determine how to add strategic value and remove risks that can block the company from achieving its strategic direction.
- The Phase One start-up company is characterized by leaders and employees who are passionate and determined to make the

company successful. The leaders are entrepreneurial, aggressive, and visionary. Employees are often highly committed and aligned with the leader's direction for the enterprise.

- A characteristic of the Phase One enterprise is that often it does not have internal organizational support departments. Astute Phase One leaders recognize that avoiding the investment in HR is shortsighted.

- In Phase Two, or the growth phase, the company discovers its growth formula and finds that it has a winning "recipe for success." Entering Phase Two is a very positive development for an enterprise. However, as with all good developments, associated risks may appear.

- Unfortunately, as the company continues to grow, the atrophy of success starts to set in. The leadership recognizes that its approach to Phase Two is a problem—the approach has lasted too long, creating stagnation. Companies need to avoid getting stuck in Phase Two and the development of the Irish Elk Syndrome.

- Executives in Phase Three mature companies need to be thorough in their assessments of the challenges and risks they face. The organizational systems and the culture have to change so that everyone supports efforts to meet the customers' needs.

- The risks and potential crises of Phase Three often encourage leadership to focus on what their business is really about, which means the basics—such as price, customers, service, and their market niche. They realize they have to de-emphasize bureaucracy. They look to HR as the group with the capability to make a unique contribution.

- HR must shift its focus to the company's strategic direction and the business. At the same time, HR needs to reduce (or remove) the organizational and people risks that may limit the company from implementing its strategy. HR focuses on the following strategic processes to reduce the risks:
  - Cultivate the context for a flexible culture that can adapt to change.
  - Champion the alignment of all initiatives to a common strategic direction.
  - Insure change is implemented by involving people and helping them adapt to the change.

  – Guide decision making based on a return on investment in
    human capital.

- The challenge to HR is to go beyond simply breaking the past
  mold, which is useful but is a reaction to the former ways of
  doing things. It needs to unleash its own potential to seek the
  right way to proceed on behalf of the company.

An HR Business within a Business

The changing nature of Human Resources is reflected in the following story: A company executive had a problem concerning an external customer and asked a Human Resource professional to perform a service in order to solve the problem. He dutifully implemented the solution the executive provided. Unfortunately, the action did not resolve the problem for the executive's customer, and, to the HR professional's surprise, the executive blamed him! Seeking a reason for the censure, the HR professional scheduled a meeting with the executive. He said, "I don't understand. You asked me to do something, and I did it precisely the way you requested. Why are you blaming me because it didn't work?" The senior executive replied, "I told you what I thought we should do about the problem, but I'm not the expert in the solution. That's your business. Unfortunately, you didn't question my solution. You accepted the wrong answer and delivered it exceptionally well. Now I have a dissatisfied external customer on my hands."

Human Resource professionals like the one in the story are being required to change their methods of solving internal client problems. They are finding that they must know who the external customer is in order to identify the correct business solution to internal problems. The HR professional in this scenario did not recognize his business accountability to analyze the implications for the external customer. If he had, he could have considered alternative solutions and recommended a more appropriate approach. By implementing solutions that do not meet the needs of the external customer, HR may become known in a company as the department that "does the wrong thing exceptionally well."

Businesses and Organizations

Davis and Davidson (1991)[1] in their book *20/20 Vision* describe a company as being divided into the *business* and the *organization* (that is, Company = Business + Organization). The *business* as they describe it corresponds to the elements in a Phase One company. It exists to exploit the opportunities in the marketplace and includes the basic functions that must exist to deliver value to the external customer such as manufacturing, promotion, and sales. The *organization* consists of the support functions (usually created in the middle of Phase Two) that are needed to provide internal service to the business.

Davis and Davidson suggest companies ask themselves the following question in regard to the purpose of organizational support in a company: "Do you have a business that exists to support the organization or do you have an organization that exists to support the business?"

Early in Phase Two on the growth curve, the organization and support roles often exist to **control** the business. The risk for a Phase Two company is lack of control. The reason for the organization's existence is that it helps to reduce the risk that the business may not be able to manage itself effectively. Only later in Phase Two, as the organization approaches Phase Three, does it consider how it can **add value** to the business.

Here is an example of a software engineering company in the middle of Phase Two: The company's executives are required to pay for the services of central office support departments such as HR, Information Technology, and Public Relations. The executives complain because they do not see the value in this arrangement. They feel that central departments inhibit rather than enhance their performance. Senior line management calls these departments "overhead," meaning the cost they have to pay over and above their normal costs to cover each "head" in their organization. Essentially, their analysis is correct. In this company these organizational departments are control functions designed for a central office purpose and are not designed to add value to the line managers' business.

Not until later in Phase Two are HR and other organizational departments challenged by the company to add value to the business. When

---

[1] Stan Davis and Bill Davidson, *20/20 Vision*, Simon & Schuster, 1991.

this occurs, the concept of the business as the organization's *internal customer* is established. HR is measured by the extent to which it satisfies its internal customers (all business as well as other organizational departments). For several years, the concept of the *internal customer* has helped HR and other organizational departments make the transition from a "control" mindset to a "service" mindset. It has enabled them to respond positively to the question of whether or not the organization provides added value to the business.

The term *internal customer* is often used to describe the internal service relationship. It can be modified as illustrated in this example: A company in the business of food manufacturing recognized the confusion that could be caused by using the term *customer* to describe both internal and external groups to be served. They wanted to emphasize that the ultimate customer is the external customer and that no one else should be referred to by the term *customer*. They called the internal customers (departments within the company) their *clients,* the external customers (the supermarkets) their *customers,* and the external customer's customer (the public who purchases their product), their *consumers.* (The terms *clients* and *customers* will be used in the remainder of this book.) A similar exploration of words can be done in every business. The focus should be on words that are precise so that they have value. If *customer* refers to everyone, then the word has no value. Another message in this example is that to add maximum value, the focus must be on satisfying the external customer.

HR departments have to develop beyond the control function to at least the added-value level. While it is appropriate to be concerned with specific internal responsibilities such as hiring, training, and development, HR also has an important role in enabling the company to deliver value to its customers.

When the company is trying to avoid risks and wants a control-oriented HR function, it is even more risky to forget who the customer is. HR must provide added-value client services to enhance the customer's satisfaction. To help achieve that result, it must create new kinds of relationships with its clients.

Becoming an HR Business within a Business

HR's contribution as a value-added organizational support is not sufficient in these times of dramatic change. The current and future challenge to HR is to raise its value contribution to a higher level of competitiveness. HR can accomplish this by expanding beyond the "organization" side of the company to deliver value from the "business" side of the company as well. This means that HR is taking the first step to become a "business within a business."

Some HR organizations have erroneously applied this idea by adopting what they refer to as a 50/50 vision. This means that HR becomes a revenue-producing entity with 50 percent of its services supporting the company and 50 percent supporting external companies. Unfortunately, this approach has been a dismal failure. This vision has resulted in a divided focus for HR in which most of the HR professionals have found it more gratifying to work with the external companies than to elevate HR's service to the internal company. As a result, the notion of "HR as a business" has been rejected by some as a failure.

This failure needs careful analysis. Where is the source of the failure? I suggest that the idea of HR moving from the organization side of the company to the business side is a valuable and important idea. The source of the failure is the focus on providing service to external companies. The proper redefinition is to position HR, as well as most other internal service functions, as a business with a focus on external *customers* rather than external *companies*. HR's new standpoint will be to function as an HR business within a business, focused on the strategic competitive interests of the company. As a business, HR works with its business partners to establish key performance indicators that can be measured and operates with the expectation that HR will deliver its part of those commitments.

Align HR to Deliver Value to the External Customer

The company and HR (as a business) should be aligned with a common strategic direction to deliver value to the customer.

The diagram in Figure 2.1 illustrates the concept that all areas of the company should concentrate on delivering value to the customer (shown in the center). Many HR professionals find this to be a novel idea since they frequently have little understanding of the external customer's needs. A secret of a company's success will be the value contribution HR makes to the external customer by taking a leadership role in the transformation of the business, investing in human capital, and partnering with their clients to meet the customer's needs. The latter requires that HR understand the internal client's needs and reflect on how internal solutions contribute value to the external customer.

Figure 2.1: The External Customer-Focused Company

Consider a situation in which an executive asks HR how many customers the HR department employees have seen in the past year. HR indicates employees don't visit customers. To which the executive replies, "Then why would I want to hear your opinion if you don't know what our customers think!" Or said another way—why should an executive be interested in HR's opinion about the business if HR has no idea what the customers' needs are and how they affect what the client requires from HR?

HR must know the "voice of the customer." This means HR will have to see customers and work closely with marketing to understand customer needs. HR can then:

• Help align internal initiatives to support customer initiatives.

• Work with senior executives as a strategic partner to develop clear priorities about how to add value to the customer.

To discover solutions to problems, HR collaborates with clients and concentrates on the question, "Are the HR solutions in the best interest of the customer?" By doing this, HR is more apt to resolve the customer's problem and also satisfy the needs of the clients. When HR assumes this role, it shifts from a value-added organizational support to a competitive business advantage for the company.

Redefining HR's Internal Client Relationships

Redefining HR's relationship to internal clients can be challenging. Consider a business unit leader who, in a casual conversation with an HR professional, mentions a difficult problem and the action she took to solve it. The HR professional tells her he would like to know why she took that action. With a surprised look, the unit leader replies, "What do you mean you want to know why?" The HR professional points out that he has some information that may be helpful to the executive in making her decision. He explains that he would like to collaborate with her in the future to serve external customers. After some reflection, the unit leader says, "All right, you don't agree with the solution—then what should we do?" To which the HR professional responds, "We work together to determine the best solution for the customer."

The change in relationship that HR is proposing is not often easy for internal clients to accept. Here are some reasons:

- *HR may not have credibility with senior managers:* Many executives do not view HR as a business. They are used to thinking of HR as an organizational support department and accustomed to telling them what to do. HR will need to achieve the credibility to be accepted in the new role.

- *Managers may be unwilling to take on people responsibility:* Managers are not accustomed to taking responsibility for people management and may not view HR professionals as enablers for this new role. HR will need to support managers and provide ongoing consultation as they take on additional people roles.

- *Employees may feel they are being neglected:* Employees may think they will lose an important ally if HR does not service them directly. HR will need to develop alternative ways to provide the necessary support and represent employee interests.

HR's relationships with these three internal client groups will change if HR emphasizes its contribution to the customer and introduces changes in the way it invests in human capital. These changes will require HR to adopt a sensitive approach in order to influence clients to change their roles and expectations of HR.

HR Client Relationships with Executives

It is very difficult for HR to avoid the trap of thinking that the executives are the real customer. After all, many HR changes are driven by senior management expectations to deliver service, cut costs, and become more efficient. HR is required to be responsive to those expectations. Nevertheless, HR must understand that the ultimate customer is the external customer.

Once, in a discussion with an HR professional, I explained that the customer was the "person who pays the bills." His reply was that the senior executive paid his bills—not the customer. Obviously, I was referring to the company's bills not the individual's, but the exchange is meaningful. Many people feel the power rests with the executives and that to oppose their requests could be a "CLM" (Career Limiting Move). HR professionals need to have extensive fortitude to position their relationship with executives as a strategic-thinking partnership and not as a relationship between an organizational supplier and a customer.

The terms "strategic" and "partner" have implications for this role:

- *Strategic* implies that HR will deliver competitive advantage (or at least competitive parity) as described in Chapter One.

- *Partner* implies that HR professionals will be able to have meaningful strategic and customer-related conversations from a business perspective (and not just an HR perspective). HR will be able to partner with internal clients to deliver value to their external customers by doing the following:

  - integrating and assimilating information about the business

  - foreseeing the implications of the business information as it impacts people

  - formulating people and organizational solutions that increase the probability that the business will implement its strategic objectives and meet customer needs

Many HR professionals are attempting to develop their capabilities as strategic partners. Often, the Human Resource VP initiates this by developing a strategic partnership with the company's president and becoming an equal member of the senior executive team. In this way, he or she has the credibility to be a mentor for the other HR strategic partners.

Often, these executives (usually business unit heads) have a wide sphere of influence. HR professionals need to team with them to focus on planning and implementing strategies. Their work will be to discover and implement ways of delivering value to the customer and gaining competitive advantage.

Matching the intellectual capacity of HR professionals to senior executives will increase the probability of HR's acceptance as a strategic partner. As Jaques describes in his book, *Requisite Organization* (1989)[2], different executives operate at various levels of complexity and "time horizon" (refers to how far into the future they can envision change). In order to have meaningful conversations that add value, HR professionals must have a similar level of intellectual ability to add value to their internal clients. They need to be able to intrigue internal clients with ideas, connections, and links to other experiences, etc.

In this sense, HR strategic partners are "idea merchants" who can stimulate conversations with their clients. As HR professionals, they must have a large "mental database" that enables them to help their clients see their problems and opportunities from different perspectives. They are then able to help their clients discover business solutions that make sense for the business and the people within it.

HR strategic partners must also have the strength of character to respectfully oppose executive suggestions if necessary. They must be able to question a request if it does not enhance customer value but do it in a professional manner such as, "I need to understand what problem will be resolved by the approach you are suggesting." Most executives, if they respect you, are very willing to answer this question.

When an HR professional is at the executive table, he or she is not wearing an "HR hat" exclusively, but rather, a "business hat" as well. He or she adds value to all issues, not just those directly related to HR. In essence, the HR professional is a strategic thinker who has an HR specialty.

HR professionals' ability to add value through their partnership with senior executives includes the following:

- *A broad understanding of the business:* This helps HR contribute value about the overall direction of the company.

- *A knowledge of how all the activities need to align:* This knowledge helps the company maximize the success of strategic initiatives and eventually deliver value to the customer.

- *A professionalism in investing in human capital and HR processes:* With this ability, HR can help guide people and organizational decision making.

- *A unique perspective:* This perspective allows HR to be an "idea merchant" to enable strategic advantage through people and organizational process outcomes.

---

[2] Elliot Jaques, *Requisite Organization*, Cason Hill and Co. Publishers, 1989.

Rogers and Peppers in their book, *The One To One Future*[3], refer to the fact that companies need to gain "customer share" rather than "market share." This means they need to maximize their percentage of a customer's lifetime business. One of their examples that illustrates this idea is about a large bank that wants to increase its customer share. The bank realizes that a customer who has a large mortgage should not have to go through a credit check if he or she requests a credit card. Unfortunately, the company's mortgage and credit card departments are not aligned so that this can occur.

The bank decides to change its focus so that it adds value for its current customers. It does this by restructuring its systems and services with an emphasis on the customer rather than its products. The customers respond positively to the coordinated attention, and they increase their use of the banking products. Over time, the bank finds it is easier to introduce new products, and it increases the percentage of its customers' financial business.

Similarly, HR maximizes "client share" with executives through strategic thinking partnerships. In this role HR professionals have the opportunity to increase the potential work, guidance, and support of their partners through their expertise both as business people and human resource professionals.

A clear signal that HR has "arrived" as a strategic partner is when senior executives are as interested in partnering with HR as HR is in partnering with them.

HR Client Relationships with Managers

Consider an HR Vice President who is committed to the principle that every manager must take as much responsibility for the workforce (people management) as he or she does for the work. She argues that there are really 250 HR representatives in the company. Two hundred and forty of them are the line managers in the company and the remaining ten are HR professionals who work in a center of excellence to support the line managers.

The VP is not surprised that she encounters resistance from managers to this idea of changing their roles and expectations. What does surprise her is that the resistance is attributed to her style of influencing people. Many managers feel she is "controlling." They see her vision of HR as a power play to enhance her position in the company.

---

[3] Don Peppers and Martha Rogers, *The One To One Future*, Doubleday, 1993.

Quite astutely, she realizes that the managers are willing to manage people, but they need to be influenced by the right person. She finds a highly respected senior line manager who partners with her to be the champion of this change in the manager's role. The senior line manager champions the change. The line managers respond with greater openness and willingness to reconsider their approach to people management.

HR needs to find the path of least resistance to influence managers to change their role so that they take primary responsibility for attending to employee needs. To achieve this end, HR must be skilled at enabling managers to manage their direct reports. HR creates the environment to help managers become people managers and motivates them (in whatever way that works) to recognize that their people responsibilities are equally as important as their functional, product, and process responsibilities.

Consider another situation in which a person is promoted to the role of manager because he is the most skilled of all the employees. The reason for the promotion (as in most promotions) is threefold:

1. A job needs to be filled, and this person is selected and wants to do the job.

2. A hope exists that this new manager will leverage his or her knowledge and talents for the benefit of direct reports.

3. Promotion gives the company an opportunity to put more money and benefits in the hands of a valued key resource.

The new manager begins his new job, but instead of teaching others what he knows, he focuses on handling more complex problems and dilemmas. In essence, he does not teach others his professional knowledge but instead becomes a higher-level individual service provider. He misses a primary reason for receiving the promotion. HR needs to help this manager create a learning environment in which other employees learn what he knows.

HR can take a proactive role in seeing that managers can accomplish the function of trainer/educator by:

- Creating an ongoing learning environment in which managers can develop people management skills, in either formal or informal settings.

- Instilling in managers the excitement and spirit of Phase One in managing their employees and business with a focus on customer needs.

- Providing ongoing support and coaching to help managers work with their employees.

Perhaps the most difficult challenge for HR is to learn how to enable the managers to be people managers rather than step into the void to take over their responsibility—in other words, help them do it rather than do it for them. As Peter Block suggests in *Flawless Consulting*[4], HR should not be "an extra pair of hands" for managers but rather enable them to manage their employees effectively. As Robinson and Robinson (1997)[5] suggest, HR professionals have become performance consultants to help managers manage people effectively.

HR Client Relationships with Employees

In some companies, HR is expected to be the employee conscience, or the champion of employee needs. This role may be appropriate in companies where the employees are not represented by an association or a union. In these companies, the HR department may be the only place where employees can express concerns if they are not satisfied with their work situation. HR is then expected to function as an employee representative and to be an advocate for their collective needs.

However, in most cases, HR does not have the time or capacity to handle that role anymore. This is not to say that HR professionals should abandon their responsibility to employees and leave managers to their own devices to manage employees. HR has a major responsibility to provide managers with the necessary tools and training to manage their employees effectively. HR reaches employees through enabling managers to be excellent people managers.

This change of relationship with employees may be uncomfortable for some HR professionals to hear for a variety of reasons:

- HR often enjoys and is gratified by helping employees directly.
- The mindset in some companies is that managers are the subject-matter experts and HR takes care of the people, or as one manager said, "Managers manage the work; HR manages the workforce."
- The HR professional often has the skills and knowledge to handle employee-related issues.

In some companies, HR spends a great deal of time on all matters related to employees. Managers deal with the good news to employees, and HR deals with the bad news. Managers come to HR for signatures of approval for people issues. The message, as one HR person describes

[4] Peter Block, *Flawless Consulting*, Pfeiffer & Company, 1981.
[5] Dana Gaines Robinson and James C. Robinson, *Performance Consulting*, Berrett-Koehler Publishers, Inc., 1995.

it, is that the "people belong to HR, while the products, work and results belong to management." In the Phase Two growth environment, in which a primary risk is the ineffective management of employees, this focus may have some merit. However, in the transformed Phase Two or Phase Three environment, HR is expected to recruit employees who are more self-reliant. As one manager says, "If you want me to have people-management responsibilities, don't send me people who do what they are told. Send me people who can figure out what to do without being told." Managers become the employee champions in this environment, and HR works with the managers to help them manage and lead their employees.

A high-tech company once used an interesting approach to bridge the gap for managers who did not have people skills. They paired every line manager of a technical unit with a people manager. At the general manager level, co-leaders were established—one for business and the other for people. This approach, although expensive, made it clear that a centralized HR did not have the responsibility for the employee.

The challenge for HR is to enable managers to be people managers and at the same time create the context for employees to flourish and have their needs met. Their work is with the managers as their coach and organizational consultant. HR professionals provide their specialized expertise to help the managers lead their teams, manage performance, and communicate with their workforce. Of course, HR retains its role in employee relations to resolve difficulties that are beyond the manager's competency level.

One way in which HR can support the change in relationship with employees is to implement a very employee-friendly *call center*. The call center is used to respond to employees' questions and issues of concern that, in most cases, managers can not answer directly. On occasion, managers will ask questions to know the best way to respond to employee questions directly.

On a macro level, governments are realizing the potential of giving their customers (the public and businesses who pay taxes) access to their central database. In this way they will enable users to become self-reliant, and they will save costs. A recent report entitled, "Preparing Israel for the Information Era," suggests that a majority of the public will conduct business with government authorities over the Internet in the near future. The public and businesses will "mine" information from public databases. The report indicates that giving access to the end user to access the central database will "improve human capital and preserve Israel's ability to compete economically."

The same pattern will take place within companies as well. To the extent it is possible, HR's responsibility to employees is to create an environment that supports employee self-reliance. Using new technologies for communicating information helps create that environment. However, when employee self-reliance is not feasible, employees want to be managed by their manager. HR has to transfer the role of managing employees to managers, and motivate them to be accountable for people management.

All Roads Lead to the External Customer

The foundation of the company's transformation starts with the focus on the customer. If all executives, managers, employees, and departments, including Human Resources, focus on the customer, the company will have the following:

- A focused strategy to meet and exceed customer expectations.
- Alignment of all clients to the customers' needs.
- Implementation of the strategy to gain competitive advantage and delight customers.

HR's value to the customer is based on its internal client work, which is a direct result of its new perspective as a business that partners with the clients to deliver competitive advantage for the company. HR also aligns with other internal service functions (such as information technology, finance, and communications) to help bring the client the best solutions to add value to the customer.

Overall, as a business within a business, HR will be in a position to know what is and what is not important within the company. HR professionals will be able to make business judgments about how they will deploy their services and people within the company. Eventually, HR's work will enhance the ability of the company to make the strategy work and to deliver enhanced value to the customer.

Summary

- Human Resource professionals are expected to recognize their business accountability to understand the external customer's problem.
- The concept of the *internal customer* has helped HR and other organizational departments transition from a "control" mindset to a "service" mindset.

- HR has an important role in enabling the company to deliver value to its external customers. To do this it must establish new relationships with its internal clients. The terms, *clients* (internal customers) and *customers* (external customers), will be used in this book.

- HR must expand from the "organization" side of the company to deliver value from the "business" side of the company as well. HR's new standpoint will be to function as an HR business within a business, aligned with the company in a common strategic direction to deliver value to the customer.

- It is very difficult for HR to avoid the trap of thinking that the executives are the customer. Nevertheless, HR must understand that the ultimate customer is the external customer.

- Redefining HR's relationship to internal clients can be challenging. The changes are not always easy for clients to accept because:

  – HR may not have credibility with senior managers.

  – Managers may be unwilling to take on people responsibility.

- HR strategic partners must have the intellectual capacity to add value to their internal clients.

- HR professionals' ability to add value through their internal client relationships includes:

  – A broad understanding of the business.

  – A knowledge of how all the activities need to align.

  – A professionalism in investing in human capital and HR processes.

  – A unique perspective.

- The HR emphasis is on collaborating with clients to deliver enhanced value to the external customer.

 ත

The Discipline of Abandonment

Abandonment is frequently associated with a negative event such as a parent leaving a family. However, in business, abandonment takes on a positive context when it is done in a disciplined, responsible, and professional manner. Consider the executive team that takes stock of its workload to find it has ninety-six projects. After further analysis, the team realizes it does not know why it is involved in some of the projects, how or if the projects fit together, or even of what value the projects are to the external customer.

In the past, the ten executives on the team developed five strategic objectives for their company. They decide to engage in an experiment to see how or if the projects fit with the five strategic objectives. To make the exercise more challenging, they add a sixth objective—to relinquish or abandon projects that do not contribute meaningfully to the other strategic objectives. Although they argue as to whether the sixth "abandonment" objective is strategic or not, they still proceed with the exercise.

They divide the team into five pairs and give each pair a set of ninety-six cards, each with a name of one of the projects. Each pair of executives sorts the project cards into the five strategic objectives and identifies which projects should be abandoned. They decide to abandon those projects that:

- do not fit with the strategic objectives of the company
- can be delayed to a later time

- can be done by resources outside the company

To add drama to the event, they place a garbage pail on the table in which they can "trash" projects they will abandon. After they complete the sorting, the executives review the piles of cards and identify the projects. The executives find that some of the projects appear in more than one strategic objective category and discuss the implications of this. They find that there is benefit in the alignment of thought to a common understanding.

Next, they empty the garbage pail, which contains 20 percent of the project cards. They decide to abandon ten of the projects—either to delay them or not do them at all. After a heated discussion over the remaining nine projects, they finally agree to delay five. The remaining four do not align with any of the five strategic objectives, but they have to be done because of legislation requirements.

The abandonment exercise has an excellent return on investment. The executives redeploy employees to meaningful work, advance the implementation of the strategic objectives, and create greater focus for the entire company.

Why Disciplined Abandonment Is Important

Both Human Resources and companies have to learn the discipline of discarding certain responsibilities so that they can take on new ones. Many of the books executives are reading tell them *what* to do, but few tell them what *not* to do. Leadership's new discipline will be the skillful abandonment of initiatives on an ongoing basis to adjust for new strategic directions.

Abandonment involves risk, which makes it very hard to let go of the old. To be done successfully, it must be "disciplined," meaning that the focus is on the strategic direction and maximizing the value to the external customer. Personal vested interests or antiquated beliefs are not allowed to affect decisions.

Using human personal experience as an analogy, think about how difficult it may have been for you emotionally to let go of something you created. People tend to love what they create. When they build something, they are very reluctant to be the one to dismantle it. Consider the system in a family in which mature sons and daughters return to their parent's home for a family visit. It's a cold, snowy day and before they leave the house, a parent reminds them to put on their boots before going out—as if they were still little children. It is very natural to want to keep the system they built alive and well, even if it is not reality anymore.

In the work context, the ability to abandon in a disciplined manner is a precondition for the creative mind. To creative thinkers, what they did yesterday does not tell them how they are to behave today or tomorrow. If they are stuck in yesterday, they may never get to tomorrow. A process or project is not sacred to them but simply a means to an end.

Many companies have engaged in a disciplined abandonment process without calling it that. Some call it "blank sheeting" the organization, in which they ask, "How would we create the organization today if we were to start all over again?" This process can only be done with people who are willing to relinquish what they have. They clean the slate to consider new ideas they have not thought about before. The process of reengineering also involves a similar disciplined abandonment capability.

Disciplined abandonment is essential to add focus to the development of the company's strategic direction. It is a foundation piece in the creation of meaningful change. Without discarding previous work, employees will dispense with new ideas as not doable because of the lack of time or resources to achieve both the new and old objectives simultaneously.

Consider the company that decides it needs cross-functional teamwork to develop new products. The problem is that the cross-functional work must be done in addition to each employee's "day job." Essentially, the company has assigned additional work to employees who already have a full workload. Quite naturally, they complain. The company has not recognized the necessity of abandoning at least a portion of the employees' workload to allow them to devote energy to the new responsibilities.

Abandonment with discipline also appears to be the underlying theme behind General Electric's initiative called "Work-Out." Essentially, GE was very successful in the 1980s in reducing cost by removing people from the company. However, they still had the same work but with fewer people. The challenge in the 1990s was to get the work out of the system. The strategy consists of abandoning the work that is extraneous to the company's strategic objectives. Many other companies have used a similar "work-out" process to abandon work of lower value to the customer. Disciplined abandonment is also essential to the future success of Human Resources and the implementation of its strategic process outcomes.

Leadership and Abandonment

Chapter One described how Phase One executives are often replaced when the company moves to the next phase of the growth curve. This does not have to be the case if the executives are capable of disciplined abandonment. Most excellent leaders are able to develop a big idea and harness their employees' commitment to a common direction. The higher-level challenge for leaders is to know when to give up on their original idea and move to the next way of doing things. In "growth curve" terms, the discovery of the Phase Two growth formula is the leaders' success. Their failure is that they don't recognize the need to discard the previous growth process for a new one, to avoid reaching the mature phase (Phase 3).

For some leaders, the investment in past success blinds them to the need for a new direction. When this occurs, the only recourse the company has is to find new leaders who can more easily give up the old and commit to change. Of course, bringing in a new leader does not guarantee successful new directions. In some cases the new leader appears to have a new perspective, but in reality it is the perspective developed at the previous company. The new leader has not abandoned his or her old mindset but rather is trying to force fit an old paradigm onto the new company, which in many cases results in failure.

In one mature company, the executives realized that they were having difficulty relinquishing the processes and models they had created. They were proud that the processes had brought their company success, but they realized that as their company was maturing into Phase Three, they would not be the ones to move the company into a new direction. Instead of stepping down, however, they chose a different path.

They challenged a group of seven "next generation" executives, who were viewed as the future key resources of the company, to develop the company's future strategy. The senior executives gave this group the chance to design the company they would eventually lead. They viewed this approach as an excellent leadership transfer process and as a method to insure that the next level of management would take ownership of the future direction.

The next generation leaders took the challenge very seriously and developed a plan for sweeping changes and strategies. To the surprise of many, the senior executives accepted all the recommendations and put the next generation leaders in charge of the strategic objectives they identified. This event took place over five years ago, and, today, as the former leaders retire, the leaders of the next generation team are running the company and implementing the plans they developed five years earlier.

The easy part for leaders is to develop the strategy. The hard part is to let go of the previous strategy to make room for the new. The process of disciplined abandonment and renewal has become a key success factor for leadership and often is a distinguishing factor between success and failure. It also has broad implications for all the systems in the company as well as for Human Resources' future directions.

Abandonment and Removing "Noise" From the System

Companies need to be aware of the "noise" in their systems. The term "noise" is used to represent the low-level irritants that most people ignore. For example, in most office buildings, the ventilation system is constantly emitting a low level noise. However, in some situations, the noise is so loud that it becomes intolerable.

The same occurs within organizational systems. Often, a low-level noise in the system is ignored or tolerated. However, in times of dramatic change, the noise can be the cause of problems, and it may need to be targeted and removed. HR can have a major role in dismantling and abandoning the noise in the system when it is a barrier to effective performance.

A common area of noise in companies is the systems that perhaps were once useful but currently function as barriers to the effective implementation of change. For example, the "rewards and punishments" in a company can be a source of noise because they can motivate people to do things that are against the desired strategic direction. In essence, they can be "negative motivators" that motivate people in the wrong direction.

Once a company identifies the noise in the system, it needs to remove it quickly so that the company can follow an alternate path. People resist change because strong motivators stimulate them to behave in a counterproductive way. In most cases, if the company removes the noise, people are willing to move in the direction the company desires.

Many companies invest heavily in positive motivation programs designed to stimulate employees to behave in a certain way. When they do not get the desired response, they add more positive motivators to the equation to outweigh the negative motivators. Unfortunately, this effort is frequently a waste of time and money. Once the companies remove the positive motivators, the employees revert back to the old way of working because the negative motivators still exist.

The alternative and recommended approach is to target the negative noise, remove it from the system, and then implement a gentle positive motivator. This will often be sufficient to motivate people to move in the desired direction (if the direction desired is a reasonably good idea).

How Can the Noise Be Identified?

The noise in the system can be identified in a number of ways:

- *Determine whether the leadership has to work too hard to motivate people to move in a certain direction:* Invariably, if the positive motivators have to be excessive, some other equally strong motivator is blocking people from proceeding in the desired direction.

- *Conduct a SWOT analysis (usually part of a strategic planning process) in which the internal weaknesses are identified:* In a SWOT analysis (that is, Strength, Weakness, Opportunity, and Threat), the company identifies the external opportunities and threats (the risks for the business). Then they ask the following:

  - What are the internal strengths that will help the company capitalize on the opportunities and reduce the threats?

  - What are the internal weaknesses that will block the company from capitalizing on the opportunities and allow the threats to take effect?

  The internal weaknesses are often within the control of the company to reduce and are often the noise HR can help the company abandon.

- *Examine systems instituted during Phase Two that may need to be dismantled because they are no longer relevant:* While Phase Two systems require control and restriction, the need in the Phase Three transformation process is flexibility and empowerment. The company can analyze the systems and abandon those that are barriers to the new way of operating. Otherwise, these barriers become negative motivators—once useful but now contradictory to the new flexible culture the company wants to create.

  Consider the high-tech company in Phase Two that introduces controls by requiring multiple signatures (often three or more) on documents before approval. This procedure helps control decision making but also slows down change, which is advantageous to the leaders in the traditional Phase Two environment. However, the company recognizes that the system that worked in the past has become an albatross, stifling progress. The company introduces a "Sign No More" campaign, which means no form will have more than two signatures. If employees feel they need more signatures, they must ask an executive for approval. With this one elegant move to abandon an irritating noise in the system, people are compelled to answer these questions:

– Who must sign the document?
– Can both an employee and someone several levels higher in the organization give their signatures?
– Who is accountable for the work?

• ***Determine what is "negatively reinforced" in the company:*** What is negatively reinforced often has more power than what is rewarded. For example, most companies have published "values" that reflect what the company wants people to consider important as they do their work. In most cases, the values do not shape the way employees behave. If you ask employees to name the company values, sometimes they will know the answer. However, if you ask employees what behaviors get people into trouble in the company, they immediately have a strong opinion and response. Upon further exploration, employees agree that the real values in the company are the behaviors for which they are "punished."

For example, one company was promoting employee risk-taking. The employees continued to be risk averse. When asked, one employee jokingly summarized the reason with the following line: "To err is human; to forgive is not company policy." These real or perceived negative reinforcers can become the noise in the system that will block employees' willingness to change.

Examples of Noise In The System

• ***Example #1:*** A pharmaceutical company recognizes that it needs a cross-functional team approach in order to service the needs of customers more effectively. The executive team encounters resistance from employees and managers to the new approach. Upon reflection, the team discovers that the reward system recognizes individual performance rather than team performance.

If the company changes the reward system to emphasize team-work, most employees will be willing to work in teams. To do this, they must first remove rewards that drive motivators of unwanted behavior and then establish rewards that encourage behaviors supporting the new team culture. Next, they need to build in measures to keep the focus on the advantages of working in teams.

- *Example #2:* In a bilingual school system, the leader develops a vision of an integrated curriculum for the two languages. His plan is to teach all subjects using both languages. This is in contrast to the traditional approach in which the second language focuses on language acquisition only and almost all educational content is taught in the primary language.

  The leader encounters major resistance from the teachers to the new idea. Teachers are unwilling to change the curriculum and adjust their style of teaching. Upon investigation of the noise, the leader discovers that the teachers of the various languages are from different cultures, do not know each other, and are not familiar with each other's curriculum.

  The leader believes that if he removes the barriers that keep the teachers from learning about and appreciating each other's cultures and curriculums, the teachers will abandon their negative mindset and welcome the new curriculum ideas. The leader creates opportunities for the integration by putting the two language classes side by side, creating forums for the teachers to get to know each other, and having teachers do some team teaching. As the barriers are removed, the curriculum integrates successfully.

- *Example #3:* In a large manufacturing company, the HR department requires extensive documentation of every management and employee action. Although the HR professionals try to convince the managers that the forms deliver value to clients, the managers resist. They view HR as a control function that takes its greatest pride in developing another control form rather than in enabling the managers to do their jobs.

  After realizing that it has actually created noise in the system by requiring excessive documentation, HR professionals engage in an exercise to determine which of the forms are necessary. They begin by posting all their forms on the walls of a large training room. To their shock, they fill all the walls.

  They set a target to reduce the number of forms by 50 percent. Their exercise involves asking what risk to the external customer the documentation reduces and, therefore, which forms employees really need. In examining the forms, they find many that people are required to complete even though they do not know why and in spite of the fact that in some cases no one uses the information. By the end of the exercise, they discard over 75 percent of the forms. Most of those remaining are put on-line for ease of use by the managers and employees. After an effective internal marketing plan, HR is recognized for its efforts to remove the internal barriers to the company's success.

People, Organizational, and Business Processes

Consider the triangle diagram (Figure 3.1) that allocates HR's work into "Core People Processes," "Organizational Value-Add Processes," and the "Business Transformation Processes." While it may be argued that some of the items can be categorized differently or even that some elements are missing, that is not the essential point. The message is that HR's work can be divided into these kinds of value contributions to the company and eventually to the customer.

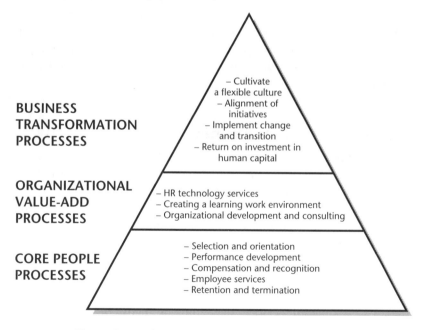

BUSINESS TRANSFORMATION PROCESSES
- Cultivate a flexible culture
- Alignment of initiatives
- Implement change and transition
- Return on investment in human capital

ORGANIZATIONAL VALUE-ADD PROCESSES
- HR technology services
- Creating a learning work environment
- Organizational development and consulting

CORE PEOPLE PROCESSES
- Selection and orientation
- Performance development
- Compensation and recognition
- Employee services
- Retention and termination

Figure 3.1: HR's Value Contribution to the Business

The core people processes are typical of many HR organizations and consist of service roles associated with the employment life cycle—staffing, performance development, employee relations, compensation, terminations, etc. These are all important functions. However, in many cases, they are not sufficient to add value to the strategic direction of the company nor to the external customer. These activities are core HR activities, but they won't resonate for executives as the deliverables that will reduce the risks that concern them.

The organizational value-add processes include the following:

- Enabling the people and the organization through the deployment of technology systems.
- Creating a learning environment that reflects some of the bigger concerns of senior managers of many companies.
- Providing expert coaching and organizational consulting services to the line when the line manager has a problem. HR must help the line manager deliver more value to the external customer.

At the "business transformation" level, HR professionals partner with the senior executives to establish and achieve their strategic objectives and to plan the people and organizational strategies before the problems arise. In the process HR reduces strategic risks of an inflexible culture, the misalignment of strategic initiatives, an inability to implement strategy, and a lack of knowledge about the return on investment in human capital.

An Exercise in Abandonment

To help HR professionals identify work that can be abandoned, I often ask them to individually allocate their current work time to the three levels (i.e., people, organizational, and business) in the triangle. I then ask them to do the same exercise for the "preferred future," which means identifying how they would divide their work time to add maximum value to customers and advance the strategic direction of the company in the future.

The individual responses are aggregated to form a group score. The overall results tend to show similar patterns when this exercise is done. Variations are sometimes evident depending on the HR organization, how advanced they are, and the phase of the company on the growth curve.

The graph in Figure 3.2 shows an example of the "current situation" for an HR department. Approximately one half of the work is in the core people processes level, about 35 percent in the organizational value-add level, and the remaining 15 percent in the business transformation level. The example of the "preferred future" for HR's work shows about 15 percent in the core people processes level (the rest is abandoned), 50 percent in the organizational value-add level, and the remaining 35 percent in the business transformation level. The graph (Figure 3.2) depicts the results from the sample HR department.

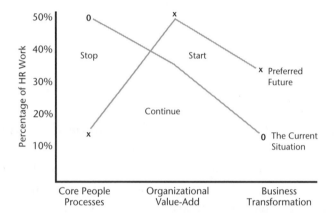

Figure 3.2: Example of the Current and the Preferred Future Distribution of HR Work

The following are some important points about the graph:

- The area on the right labeled Start is the value-add and transformation work that needs to be achieved to reach the preferred future. However, to simply add Start activities without abandoning others is irresponsible.

- The area on the left of the graph labeled Stop reflects the core work that needs to be removed to make room for the "start" activities. In some cases, HR's inability to stop what it believes it does well, will make it difficult for it to discard activities. Other HR organizations are explicit about the need to abandon as much work as they start.

- The area marked Continue represents the current work that can continue to be done.

The "Start, Stop, Continue" chart tells the entire transformation story with the detail left out for later commentary. As Saul Alinsky indicates, "People do not argue with their own data." The chart may indicate that

HR needs to relinquish some of its current activities in order to accept new strategic initiatives into the HR repertoire. The HR professional almost always concurs and can identify some examples of what needs to be given up and what needs to be done. Of course, additional analyses are then undertaken to identify precisely what work will be abandoned.

Four Kinds of Abandonment for HR

Often, most of the work HR abandons is at the core people processes level of the triangle chart. However, the abandonment must be disciplined. The work has to be done—people have to be hired; they must be paid; and training, employee relations, and terminations still have to take place. The work will continue to be done—but not necessarily by HR.

Conveniently, the four types of abandonment are four D's: dump, delay, distribute, and diminish.

1. *Dump the work so that HR does not do it anymore, nor is it done by anyone else:* This includes the following:
   - The removal of any "noise" from the system as described above.
   - Abandoning the HR "parenting" roles such as tracking systems—for example, reminding managers to complete employee appraisal forms, tracking attendance at training programs, focusing on the job as the unit of activity versus work, or requiring multiple signatures on forms (set the goal of no more than two to three signatures for any form).
   - Eliminating work of little value such as letters to unsolicited applications, many job descriptions, duplications of performance management on both electronic and paper forms.
   - Eliminating counterproductive work. For example, one company started a customer service campaign called "ABC" or stop "Annoying our Best Customers." In addition to being humorous, it stopped many activities that created customer dissatisfaction and added little value to the company (e.g., telemarketing calls during dinner time, etc.). The same idea can be applied within HR to stop "Annoying our Best Clients."

2. *Delay the activity and perform it later:* This type of abandonment can include the following:
   - Delaying revisions to policies and systems that are not essential. For example, delaying the revision to the employee survey or the company insurance coverage and benefits.

3. ***Distribute the work to others:*** This is a very popular approach for HR and can be done in a number of ways:

- ***Employee Relations:*** Some work, such as most employee relations work, can be distributed to the line manager. As described in Chapter Two, HR does not fill the vacuum to meet the employee's needs directly. Doing that will lessen the manager's ability to manage his or her employees. As the classic "fish" maxim goes, "Feed them fish and they eat today; teach them to fish and they will eat forever." Teach the managers to manage people and distribute the responsibility to them rather than do it for them.

- ***Transactional HR Work:*** Some work such as payroll, compensation, benefits, and much of the administrative work can be distributed to external suppliers or internal resources to deliver the activity. At the same time, HR must vendor manage these activities to insure quality performance.

- ***Shared Services:*** Larger organizations have the size and economies of scale to build their own shared services for HR distributed work. Shared services essentially is client driven work, that could have been outsourced, that is done internally. When the organization is large, shared services are a better solution than outsourcing for several reasons:

  – It can be less expensive than outsourcing.

  – It can customize services better.

  – It does not distract HR from its focus on the strategic needs of the company.

  – The knowledge gained about the work performed in the shared services remains in the company.

- ***Technology Based Distribution:*** By allowing employees to access information electronically, HR distributes the work to the employees on-line and does not have to manage so many activities. When HR insures that all managers and employees have access to the central database, many benefits can occur. For example:

  – *Employees* are able to update personal information, research training information, sign up for courses, identify job and work opportunities, submit applications, identify career opportunities, change flexible benefits, manage their own money, and find information about company developments.

  – *Line managers* are able to access the system in their role as employees. They are also able to do activities such as information analysis, performance development and review, research, reports, and electronic signatures.

– *Executives* are able to access the system in their roles as employees and managers. They are also able to use it to get cost of labor information (described in Chapter Ten) to help them make decisions on the deployment of people and allocation of resources.

A more detailed discussion of how technology can enable people and organizational processes appears in Chapter Five.

4. ***Diminish the scope of the work***: Simplify the process to its essentials that deliver the value needed. This includes:

• Activities that can be reduced in scope and partially delayed such as new job evaluation systems, some generic training programs, or competency-based analyses.

• Some work can be simplified through better designed information technology systems. Technologies, such as the Intranet (an internal Internet), enable ongoing communications and the distribution and updating of HR policies and procedures with the most efficiency.

The Discipline of the "Tie Goes to the Runner" in Abandonment

In baseball, if the defensive team throws the ball to first base and the offensive team's runner reaches the base at the same time, a "decision rule" is called. The logical answer is that it should be a tie, but a tie means that it has to be replayed. So baseball developed a rule that would enable the game to go on called the "tie goes to the runner."

There are many "ties" in determining who will do the work that HR abandons. Here are some decision rules that are part of the discipline of abandonment:

• If the management of people can be done equally well by HR or the line manager, who should do it? In this chapter it is argued that the "tie goes to the line manager" so that HR can help every manager become a people manager.

• If the work is not strategic and can be done equally well at a similar cost by HR or by an outsourced service provider, who does the work? The suggestion is that the "tie goes to the outsourced service provider" to create the focus for the internal HR resources on providing strategic value to the company and the customer.

- If the work can be done on-line (on the computer) as well as on paper, how should it be done? The answer is that the "tie goes to using the computer" because of the benefit of shared learnings and of the efficiency of employees and managers accessing the central database themselves.

- If the work can be done as it is now or it can be eliminated, what should be done? The approach taken is the "tie goes to not doing it." In this way, HR avoids doing the low-value work and can focus on strategic initiatives.

Life after Abandonment

Disciplined abandonment means HR dumps, delays, distributes, and diminishes non-strategic activities and removes the "noise" in the system that limits progress. It can then focus on aligning all efforts to add value to the external customer. When HR has discarded non-strategic work, its focus can be on organizational value-add and business transformation processes that contribute to the company's strategic direction. With this focus, HR can help create a company with an outstanding state of readiness to achieve its strategic direction as quickly as possible and repeatedly (as initiatives change) to its customers' satisfaction.

Summary

- Both Human Resources and companies have to learn the discipline of discarding certain responsibilities so that they can take on new ones.

- To be done successfully, abandonment must be "disciplined," meaning that the focus is on the strategic direction and that the value to the external customer is maximized.

- The process of disciplined abandonment and renewal has become a key success factor for leadership and often is a distinguishing factor between success and failure.

- Companies need to get rid of the "noise" in the system that blocks the company from transforming and moving forward. HR can have a major role in dismantling and abandoning these barriers.

- HR work can be divided into work that is business transformation, organizational value-add and core people processes. Core people processes, while important, often do not add strategic value for the company or for the external customer.

- There are four kinds of disciplined abandonment choices that conveniently all start with the letter "D." These are:
  - Dump the work entirely.
  - Delay the activity and perform it later.
  - Distribute the abandoned work to others.
  - Diminish the scope of work that is not strategic.
- Disciplined abandonment can help HR create a company with an outstanding state of readiness to achieve its strategic direction as quickly as possible and repeatedly (as initiatives change) to its customers' satisfaction.

PART TWO

People and Organizational Processes

CHAPTER FOUR

ဆဝ

Core People
Processes

The story goes that a church member asked his minister if he could tell him what his strategic objectives were. Without hesitation the minister said, "It's clear to me I'm in the hatch, match, and dispatch business." Surprised by the response, the church member asked the minister to explain. He said, "The reason I'm here is to help people at their birth (hatch), at their marriage (match), and at their funeral (dispatch)."

Ironically, HR's "core people processes" role is not that different. HR is there at the recruitment (hatch), the development (match), and the exiting (dispatch) stages of the employment life cycle. These processes are the core expectations of a well-run HR department. However, they do not make the HR role a strategic asset for the company. The strategic question HR must answer is, "Which of HR's employment life cycle services give competitive advantage and which can be abandoned with discipline?" This chapter will explore the answer to this question.

In this process of abandoning some core functions, HR needs to be cautious about the following:

- If HR abandons parts of its "hatch," "match," and "dispatch" employment life cycle services, and they are not performed well, HR may not be asked to contribute at the organizational value-add or at the business transformation level. HR must insure that the company excels in these core people processes, whether they are performed internally or externally.

- In addition, HR must have excellent communications skills to capture both the spirit and the intent of abandoning parts of these roles. It needs to clarify that these changes are essential for the future of the company and determine how the changes will enhance (or at least not reduce) service quality and contribute to achieving the company's strategic direction. HR then needs to work with line managers to define both HR's and line managers' roles and accountabilities for managing people.

HR must insure that the core people processes are performed in a quality manner, in a timely fashion, and at a reasonable cost. HR is not necessarily the deliverer of the entire process. For example, even in a traditional work environment, the people process of "selection and orientation" of new employees involves many players. These can include the line managers (who identify the need and conduct some interviews), the HR professional (who may develop the approach to sourcing the candidate and do some interviews), the search firm, other employees (who may participate in the selection process), and internal trainers (who may not even be part of HR but who may orient the new employee to the new job).

Parts of each of the people processes are delivered by internal resources other than HR or by external resources. Of course, some portions of the people processes will continue to be delivered within HR, but the focus for HR is on insuring that the outcomes of the people processes occur, not on delivering all of the people process elements.

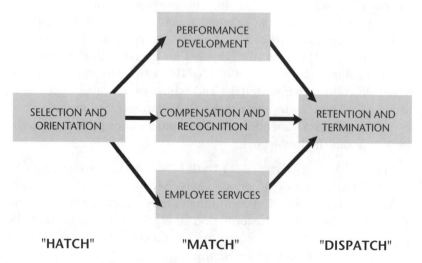

"HATCH"   "MATCH"   "DISPATCH"

Figure 4.1: The Core People Processes

The primary areas in the core people processes are presented in figure 4.1. The figure illustrates the employment life cycle from employee selection to termination. The terms "hatch," "match", and "dispatch" are used to make the stages in the employment life cycle more memorable.

Essentially, at the hatch stage (at the beginning of the cycle), the employee is selected and oriented. In the match stage (at the middle of the cycle), the employee is developed and compensated and ongoing employee services are offered. In the dispatch stage (at the conclusion of the cycle), the employee either leaves the company or attempts are made to retain the employee so that he or she does not leave.

The "Hatch" People Processes

HR's core "hatch" people process includes selection and orientation. Selecting excellent talent has become critical to organizations, especially during the growth phase of their development. Companies have resorted to some aggressive measures to recruit talent. For example:

- One company has recruited teams of senior employees around the globe to fit their culture.
- Another company has found it very difficult to recruit for some of their high-tech positions. They have realized that candidates for employment at the university level have a very different mindset and use a very different language than recruiters of a different generation—the result being difficulty in assessing the candidates' software development skills. The company has hired university students to recruit other university students so that candidates will be talking to peers who understand their language.
- Another company has hired entire teams of M.B.A. graduates.
- Yet another company has hired an entire graduating class of software engineers to respond to the current shortage of expertise in that area.

Some companies have discovered that it is much easier to recruit at the senior levels where they can assess the candidates' values, the type of culture they work in, and their management style. The specialist roles require more involvement by the specialty areas to both attract and orient these candidates.

Enhancing the Selection and Orientation Process

Consider a company's hiring process when a shortage of software engineers exists. The position is a very strategic one. The market for engineers is very competitive, so HR may want to keep the role of recruiting engineers. Whether HR continues its role in hiring people for less strategic positions should be based on: 1) whether it can be done more effectively and economically internally and 2) if doing it internally will not distract HR from focusing on its primary strategic tasks. A great deal of the traditional hiring that HR does can be enhanced by abandoning parts of this role to external service providers and to the line managers.

HR can also enhance its "selection and orientation" process by doing the following:

- Anticipate selection needs even before there is a request for a new employee. This enables HR to forecast skills requirements based on anticipated recruitment needs.
- Change the perception of the company in the marketplace so that it attracts candidates even before the recruitment need is identified.
- Teach managers to be more consistent in how they specify needs and how to interview, select, and orient.
- Develop a recruiting process that identifies more precise needs of the work and therefore better potential candidates.
- Expect candidates to provide information beyond a simple resume so that parts of the selection process can be automated.
- Apply technology solutions, such as software that helps identify high-probability candidates.

Measuring Return on Investment for Selection and Orientation

HR professionals can measure the extent to which they are fulfilling the selection and orientation people process. For example, HR can measure the time it takes from when the internal client identifies a need for a new employee to when the employee arrives at the company. Then, they can identify the speed with which they are able to orient and assist the employee to work at an acceptable level of effectiveness. The return on investment for the HR effort in the "selection and orientation" process is shown in Figure 4.2.

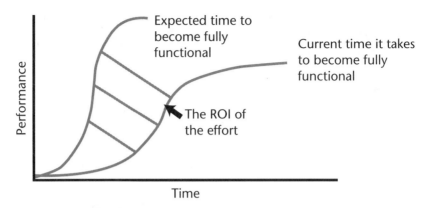

Figure 4.2: The Selection and Orientation Process Outcome

HR's role is to discover ways to reduce the time required for this process in order to deliver the best possible outcome. HR identifies the best process "means" and is accountable for the process outcomes on which its performance is measured.

Employer of Choice for Key Resources

One strategy that has been popular in the hatch area is for companies to focus on making their company an "employer of choice," which means that the company positions itself to be the most appealing employer in its field so that it can attract and retain the best talent. In order to be particularly attractive to possible employees, the company pays close attention to how it recruits, how it pays people, what benefits it provides to attract and retain employees, and the nature of the work and the work environment.

Unfortunately, although the idea is wonderful in theory, most companies have failed at the employer of choice strategy because of lack of focus. Often, the strategy is applied to *all* employee positions. This is often unnecessary and a poor investment of resources and time, which HR professionals can abandon. Investing a great deal of energy in becoming an employer of choice for *all* employees can dilute the necessary emphasis on key resource employees who directly add value to the strategic objectives of the company.

Key resource employees are those who give your company a strategic advantage against the competition. The "employer of choice for key resources" approach is more precise and far less expensive overall. HR can focus on recruiting key talent that is in short supply and consider outsourcing the recruitment of less "strategic" employees.

HR needs to assume some other roles in relation to key resource employees:

- Define key resource employees' competencies—those skills that they must possess in order to provide competitive advantage for the company.

- Insure that executives participate annually in talent reviews to identify the key resources and the nature of their work.

- Find ways to ensure that key resource employees are extremely loyal to the company so that they will be less likely to leave.

The short supply of key talent also challenges HR to expand its strategies of how to attract and retain key resources. Most HR professionals focus on creative compensation models as the prime motivator. However, research supports other compelling motivators, including marketing an exciting employment brand, providing meaningful challenges, supporting personal career growth opportunities, insuring that key resources are managed by admired leaders and accommodating work and personal "life balance" requirements. The competition is fierce for key resource employee talent; therefore, the focus should be on becoming the employer of choice for key resource employees, rather than all employees.

Orientation as Part of the Selection Process

"Orientation" is in the beginning stages of the employment life cycle rather than in the performance development part of the life cycle. The decision to include orientation as part of the selection process has been taken after some careful thought. The basis for the decision is driven by the needs of the hiring manager rather than by the activities undertaken during orientation.

When a manager has a need for an additional employee, he or she senses that the hiring request is fulfilled when the person is selected and oriented, and not simply when the person arrives on the job for the first day. HR, on the other hand, may view orientation as a training function because it has characteristics that are similar to training and performance development. Orientation is often done in a classroom, it has a particular design, and it can be offered in a repeated fashion.

HR should define processes based on the client's perception. Therefore, orientation should be part of the selection process and not part of the performance development process. At minimum, in the absence of any compelling reason to put it in selection or in performance development, my preference is that the "tie goes to selection" because of the above reasons.

The effective orientation of new managers and employees will allow you to gain more immediate value from the new hire. New employees are typically more open to instruction during the first few weeks in their new role. Managers should be using that time to work closely with new employees, building relationships, and creating a common language that they can draw upon as the employees becomes more independent in their responsibilities. They should spend extensive time after people are hired working with them, having conversations about work, and building their relationships.

HR also has a role in orchestrating the orientation process through more formal means. For example, one company emphasizes a new employee orientation process which lasts for the first three months on the job. Another company has an orientation program that includes presentations from all areas of the business and is held four to six times a year. This same company orients new managers through a 1:1 intensive session with their HR representative to review all elements of their new role and to begin the process of building a relationship with HR as an added-value resource. They receive a *new manager survival kit* and also participate in an assimilation process to discuss the work environment and the preferred company management style.

The "Match" People Processes

HR's core "match" role typically includes performing all HR services from the time the person joins and is oriented until the time the person considers leaving or is about to leave the company. It should be (although often it is not) the most important challenge to HR, since it reflects the full term of employment for employees.

The "match" role includes the following three processes:

1. *Performance Development:* This includes matching the employee's performance and career to his or her capabilities. The following are some of HR's responsibilities in performance development:

   – Identifying the competencies needed for the work to perform at an acceptable and at a differentiating level.

   – Developing employees so that they remain competent in their work areas as they accept new responsibilities and advance in their careers.

- Enabling the career development of employees to help them fulfill their potential and developing succession planning approaches to ensure the talent is available as managers retire or leave the company.

2. *Compensation and Recognition:* This includes designing compensation and recognition programs to create a desirable environment and eliminating motivators that encourage people to do things that are not desirable. Compensation and recognition includes:

- Direct pay such as base salary, benefits, payroll, and executive compensation.

- Other indirect recognition approaches.

3. *Employee Services:* This includes all services that enable two-way communication between the company and the employee. For example:

- The role of the manager and HR in employee relations.

- Alternative ways for employees to access information when they have questions and deal with sensitive matters such as harassment issues.

- Being the voice of employees and to know what are their concerns.

- Nurturing the relationship with employee representatives such as with unions and associations, to create a climate that is mutually beneficial to the employees and the company.

Performance Development

This section explores how HR contributes to the performance development process in relation to the employment life cycle. The performance development issue of creating an ongoing learning environment is part of the next chapter, which focuses on organizational value-add processes. Without question, it is highly desirable to foster and build an ongoing learning environment. However, HR can still deliver the core people processes of performance development without proceeding to the larger-scale organizational intervention of creating an ongoing learning environment.

From the company's perspective, the process outcome of performance development is to ensure that employees stay competent throughout their career with the company. Some variability in performance is expected. New technologies may be introduced that will require employees to learn new ways of working. The external customer may change demands that will challenge employees. Some employees will advance in their careers and the expectations will change.

HR assumes the accountability to build the mechanisms that ensure employees and managers remain competent as the expectations and demands of the work change. HR does not fulfill this responsibility alone. Line managers develop their employees, peers contribute to their learning, and employees are expected to self-learn as well. In addition, external resources are often used as experts to teach employees and managers how to perform in the desired manner. HR's accountability is to insure that the employees have the opportunities to stay fully competent. The process outcome measure is the time, quality, and cost of the process to restore employees to full competence in their new or adjusted work responsibilities.

Identifying the Competencies Needed for the Work

Many companies have been driven by creating the broadest possible jobs to enhance flexibility of work assignments. This desire has created a focus for performance development on identifying how employees could be multi-skilled beyond the specific demands of the job. They have bypassed the job family, looked at the nature of work, and defined the required competencies. In some companies, people with more differentiating capabilities have been rewarded more than those who are not as multi-skilled.

Unfortunately, in many cases, competency development has become a laborious process. Often it is time-consuming, and the competencies are not defined until they are obsolete (e.g., after the work has changed). From experience, the most successful and meaningful competency-based initiatives have had the following four characteristics:

1. *Have an Immediate Application:* Set a deadline for completing the competency analysis and putting the results to immediate use. One company uses competencies to help determine a performance review process. Another uses them to assess which employees will be part of a strategic project. In yet another, the competencies help identify which employees will be able to work with a new technology, who will need to be trained, and who will need to be moved to another area when the technology is introduced. The important characteristic is that the competencies are put to immediate use.

2. *Don't Demand Perfection:* The time urgency will help people real-ize that the competencies have to be good but not perfect. Develop the competencies you can live with and modify them as they are implemented. Stay away from elaborate theories, and make them practical.

3. *Work from a Menu of Competencies:* Competency menus exist to help line managers in selecting competencies. HR can assist man-agers in using these menus to choose competencies that are most appropriate to the work (expect to recycle existing competencies that have already been developed by vendors). Using menus simplifies competency development and speeds up the process.

4. *Involve Line Managers in the Process:* HR needs to involve line man-agers in selecting competencies. Line managers can participate in the following:

   – Selection of the more general managerial competencies.
   – Taking a lead role in developing the technical competencies.
   – Evaluating employees on the identified competencies.

Developing Employees So That They Remain Competent in Their Work

This part of the performance development process focuses on develop-ing people through educational and experiential means and providing honest feedback through performance review sessions. Some companies have been linking performance closely to compensation.

Consider the HR organization that boasts it has a training depart-ment with approximately 200 courses and 500 staff members to manage and deliver the programs. They believe they are doing a great service to the company. The employees who attend courses are pleased with the education and training. However, the senior executives see limited value and return on this large investment. All they see is a large number of courses that look more like a school than a professional development process.

They undertake a study of the training department. Many of the courses have fewer than ten people in attendance. Intense tracking and fee transfer efforts frustrate managers who send employees to the cours-es. The training area is viewed as an expensive school that is not focused on what the company needs to be doing.

The review includes interviews with the company's 30 senior executives, most of whom are new hires in newly created positions with recent experiences at other major companies. The executives are asked how they would design a training department from "scratch" if they had the opportunity to start over. The overwhelming majority of the senior executives, including the veterans of the company and the newcomers, recommend the following:

- Focus internal training and development on strategic objectives. This means they design and deliver internally only the programs that will give the company strategic advantage against the competition.
- Create an environment in which people will be able to learn on their own.
- Have the HR/Training Department broker the remainder of the courses to external preferred service providers.
- HR keeps the client contact role to identify needs and source the suppliers.

By focusing on planning, client contact, and strategic service delivery, HR frees up a great deal of time to invest energy in new business process outcomes. In the above example, they redesign the training area so that it focuses on performance development. Eventually, they are able to run the training department with fewer people and they are able to deliver more value with their programs.

Performance Measurement and Feedback

Many organizations use a performance management process to provide employees with performance feedback. Although HR professionals describe the performance management process as important, it has uneven success in shaping and motivating behavior. Many reasons are offered including skill deficiencies by managers, the unwillingness to have negative and potentially demotivating conversations with employees, the bureaucratic nature of evaluating and completing forms, and the lack of meaningful measures of performance.

In one company, the managers had a standing joke about how they conducted their annual performance appraisals. The managers in this company rarely gave negative feedback to employees. The only time they spoke to employees about negative performance was when they were about to terminate them. The joke about the performance reviews was that they were the meetings in which you were told that "you're great, you're great, you're great, you're gone!"

Some organizations have been more successful with feedback in performance reviews if performance is anchored in company-wide objectives that focus on the company's major stakeholders. The performance measures are also linked in a quantifiable manner to the overall business planning process and, therefore, executives view it as a business tool. Many have been calling this anchored performance review a "balanced scorecard.[1]" For many, the term "balanced scorecard" has become part of the lexicon and has practically replaced other descriptors for performance appraisals. The enhanced profile of the "balanced scorecard" approach has motivated managers to develop more skills in performance feedback and take the performance review process more seriously.

Here are some examples of how companies have anchored their "balanced scorecard" in company-wide metrics of key stakeholders:

- One company has tied executives' bonuses to employee satisfaction scores, customer satisfaction scores, and productivity improvements in addition to financial measures such as revenue generation and profitability. This same corporation also pays for "hot skills" and the successful completion of a project to increase retention of key "high-technology" staff.

- Another company has adopted an approach in which all performance reviews are linked to the same financial measures, customer satisfaction scores, employee satisfaction scores, and productivity improvement targets. The variable pay of their managers is based 50 percent on the financials (revenue and profitability), 30 percent on the customer survey, and 20 percent on the employee attitude survey.

- Many companies establish employee measures as part of their "balanced scorecard." In terms of measurement of this performance expectation, one company is using a 360° feedback device as their data source. Bonuses are based on behavioral measures included in the 360° feedback device. This company started using 360° feedback for developmental purposes a few years prior to using it in the performance review process. They recently decided to motivate managers to give attention to the results by measuring management behaviors and linking them to their bonuses.

---

[1] Robert S. Kaplan and David P. Norton, *The Balanced Scorecard,* Harvard Business School Press, 1996.

Enabling Career Development and Succession Planning

Many employees are highly motivated by career opportunities and ways they can fulfill their potential. Companies are also sometimes concerned with the identification of potential successors for the current leadership. Consequently, HR professionals have devoted attention to career planning and succession planning.

Jaques in *Requisite Organization* (1989)[2] gives an example of how managers can take on new accountabilities in career development. He suggests a new role for the manager of the employee's direct supervisor or as Jaques refers to this position–the manager once removed (MoR). The new role of the MoR would be to mentor employees in their career development. Jaques' approach is that the MoR can add value to employees' career development in a more meaningful way because he or she has broader perspectives on career choices. In implementing this approach, the MoR and the employee set up sessions at least annually. A downside is that MoRs may have too many employees to mentor and may not be able to see all of them. An alternate approach is for the MoR to mentor only the key resource employees as recognition for their contribution to the company.

If the company has an effective career-planning process, it can be linked to the company's succession plans. Succession planning can be an issue for any company. There is often a need to plan for the future leadership, but some companies do not see the patterns of an aging leadership and do not recognize the need for a plan to address the development of the future leadership of the company.

The problem appears to be most severe in owner-operated companies. The owners' emotional ties can sometimes block their ability to see the need to pass the leadership to the next person. Also, they often select one of their children to be the next leader even when they may not be the best qualified or their selection process may create family problems that carry well beyond the workplace.

The process of succession in owner-operated companies follows a different model than in non-owner-operated companies, which see succession as a need to fill the leadership boxes on the organizational charts with competent people. The choices are linear. People climb the corporate ladder, and, if they are chosen, they can succeed the former leadership. Otherwise, someone from the outside is brought in to fill that position.

---

[2] Elliot Jaques, *Requisite Organization,* Cason Hall and Co. Publishers, 1989.

Owner-operated companies also may have organizational charts with boxes and reporting relationships. However, succession planning operates with a model of concentric circles. The owner is in the center. The immediate family is often in the next circle outside the center. In the third circle are the trusted long-standing staff (regardless of the position in the company). The other circles are for the rest of the employees. Usually, those in the inner circles are considered for succession for senior positions before those in the outer circles.

When I explained this concept to a frustrated VP of HR, she began to understand why she felt excluded from the inner circle conversations. It also clarified why her opinions as well as some other executives' ideas were ignored and some more junior directors' ideas were listened to. It shaped her understanding of the owner's desires for succession and how he would most likely want to proceed. She confirmed this impression with the owner and discovered that candidates for succession were primarily from the inner circles.

Compensation and Recognition

When the HR professional in a brokerage services firm asked the executives what they wanted from Human Resources, their answer was very clear. They said "compensation, compensation, compensation." In this environment, the HR professionals need to ensure that they get the compensation right and that the systems they introduce respond to compensation as a key driver of performance.

The compensation and recognition process provides the mechanisms to motivate employees and teams to focus on the company's strategic direction and to compensate them for their contributions to the company. The performance development process described above illustrates some ways companies are linking compensation to a "balanced scorecard" to support the strategic direction.

Other companies use compensation and recognition as a method of incentive pay. For example, one company is using compensation and recognition to motivate people to the desired behaviors without a direct link to performance reviews. The key to their incentive compensation is driving the required behaviors and making sure senior managers are aligned as to what those behaviors should be. Senior managers must communicate clearly and reinforce the desired behaviors and end results. The big question that HR needs to address is whether the incentive pay actually drives the desired behaviors.

Another company provides annually each employee with a total compensation statement to increase their knowledge of their total compensation package. This package includes training costs, salary, benefits and vacation. Yet another company has asked managers to distribute variable pay according to their own criteria. Although this approach may be attractive in theory, the managers are looking to HR to help them with guidelines so that employees will not blame them if and when the employees do not receive the pay or bonus they believe they should receive.

Here are some approaches to compensation and recognition that may be of interest to the reader. Some of the methods include:

- *"Compensation" examples:* flexible total compensation, paying above the median, higher pay for performance that is exceptional, stock options, bonuses, incentive pay (e.g., based on earnings, productivity, etc.), profit share, paying for hot skills, flexible benefits, and pensions.

- *"Recognition" examples:* perquisites, training and development, time off, casual dress, and recognition that is particular to the individual or teams for actions they have taken or for contributions to the company.

Abandoning Parts of the Compensation and Recognition Process

HR can also abandon some of the roles in the compensation area. For example, most of the technical components of the pay and benefits management process are streamlined through electronic means and outsourced to experts in this area.

In a more extreme example of the need for abandonment, one company had a policy that managers had to hand deliver pay checks to employees as a way to build relationships. To the senior executives' surprise, employees communicated that they felt disempowered by this activity. The employees preferred having their pay automatically deposited to the bank of their choice and handled through external service providers. The executives had to abandon their erroneous belief that employees preferred having their payroll checks hand delivered.

Other streamlining methods of compensation are currently being explored and implemented. The most popular approach is to outsource the entire compensation process. HR retains its role in the development of the overall compensation strategy and in vendor management. The outsourced firm handles all the transactions associated with compensation according to the plan developed with HR.

In addition, with the advent of total flexible compensation (employees put together their own pay package with a fixed allowable sum), some companies have distributed much of the compensation services directly to the employee. The employees can adjust their total compensation as well as their flexible benefits within specific guidelines. If employees need financial guidance, they often have resources available to them for advice up to a specific budgetary limit. The flexibility to adjust their compensation and benefits allows employees to allocate the financial assets to their individual needs (e.g. dental care for families with young children versus life insurance and pension plans for older employees).

One company applied this flexible compensation approach to executive perquisites as well. The company put all of the money allocated to an executive into one "bucket" so that each executive could select the combination they would like, whether they joined a club or moved some of these dollars into a retirement plan. It also removes HR from the transactional role of managing these perquisites for the executives.

Employee Services

The employee services are the direct services HR provides that insure employees are able to access information and advice about the people services available in the company. Methods used include call centers for questions and advice and a drop-in center for personal communications and issues. Also, some companies utilize technology to give managers and employees direct access to the central database. They can input and extract information they need for their work and for managing their careers.

The employee services role sometimes can be all-consuming for HR and ultimately dysfunctional for the company. In some companies HR sees the employee as its customer and has responsibility for all aspects of the employee's personal and work-related matters. It is still common to find HR professionals who are responsible for social service activities such as event management, buying flowers for special events, buying the Christmas presents, etc. Often the HR professionals are frustrated by these requests but do them anyway.

The best person to handle these kinds of social service requests are often the executive assistants of the senior executives. Not only do they have more interest in these kinds of tasks, they are often better at it than their HR colleagues. In addition, if HR no longer does these time-consuming social service tasks, they will have more time for strategic activities.

HR can focus attention in the employee services area on the following:

- Enabling the line managers to fulfill their role in employee relations.
- Creating a response center to address issues of concern to employees directly.
- Being the voice of employees to know their attitudes and beliefs on an ongoing basis.
- Nurturing a collaborative relationship with employee representatives and union leadership.

Enabling the Line Managers to Fulfill Their Role in Employee Relations

The role of the manager is changing to include accountability and responsibility for employee relations. Some companies have proceeded down this path and transformed the employee relations role substantially. HR's role is to help line managers work with their employees rather than HR working with the employees directly. HR does not fill in the void created when managers do not handle situations that they should be able to handle. Rather, they educate and support the manager in fulfilling this role. One company has defined this expectation clearly in a workshop on "Employee Relations" in which they outline the role of the manager and explore which issues can be escalated to HR.

The principle is that managers are the primary contact on employee relations issues. HR works with the managers as performance consultants to enable them to become effective leaders of people and to handle the employee relations issues. Rather than doing it for them, HR professionals coach managers so that they can be the leaders and the champions of their employees' needs. HR professionals add value as the manager's "shadow consultant" (in a way that is not always visible to the employee) and through direct intervention in high-risk situations.

High-risk situations in which HR assists directly include:

- Specific coaching for select key resources and for senior executives.
- Coaching in severe cases (such as harassment or legal cases) in which HR professionalism is needed because it is beyond the level of capability that could be expected of a line manager.

- Intervening in a topic area that is very sensitive (such as harassment cases, management abuse, human rights situations, illegal acts by employees) and that can not be handled as effectively and without legal risk by line management.
- Handling legal and compliance issues that are legislated for the workforce.

Creating a Response Center to Address Issues of Concern to Employees Directly

Many organizations have introduced call centers or response centers for customers regarding their product lines and services. The technology has worked well with customers and it is now being applied to employees within the company. The response center is necessary to balance the expectations placed on the line manager to engage in employee relations conversations. Many of the issues for employees are informational or specific technical advice requests. Line managers cannot be expected to take that role because of time constraints and they may not know the technical answers. As a result, a response center approach makes sense for employees as the alternative vehicle they can use to get answers.

The response center can be accessed by all forms of communication vehicles, including telephone, internal and external e-mail, and fax. Usually, the response centers are able to screen calls and implement a triage system to prioritize calls according to importance. Although there is a priority system, the triage is designed to insure that simple calls are not slowed down for the more complex problems.

In one financial organization, the response center contacts are divided into three areas: 1) information needs, 2) career opportunities, and 3) case management. "Information needs" clarifies all the questions about programs and processes related to employees. "Career opportunities" assists employees in identifying the potential career opportunities in the company and what to do if employees have concerns about their career development. "Case management" deals with more complex problems such as harassment cases and personal issues. These issues are referred to someone within the response center with expertise to advise on these issues.

Being the Voice of Employees

An important expectation of HR is to be the voice of employees. HR professionals develop a high profile with employees. They function as the "voice" for employees if they cannot be satisfied through their managers and help executives know what employees think and feel. They also assist employees to access information and consulting help from HR and other sources.

In some cases the "voice of employees" is selected by employees when they choose to be represented by a collective body such as a union or an association. In the absence of those groups, HR is the group that has that accountability.

The next section describes ways HR can nurture the relationship with representative bodies so that they can still hear the voice of employees through other people. HR also has other direct ways to learn about the feelings and perceptions of employees such as through employee surveys. Many surveys are very useful. However, recently, some alternative creative models have been explored. For example:

- One organization introduced an employee attitude survey that was conducted twice a year using an interactive voice-messaging system. It takes employees about ten minutes to answer the survey questions, which address key factors such as leadership, work environment, pay packages, and challenging work. The survey results were compared to other external organizations. These results were discussed with the CEO and broken down by function and by manager. Each survey was followed by a meeting between executives and groups of employees to discuss the results.

- Another company decided to use sampling theory to collect data from employees more frequently. Their usual method of gathering data was through an employee survey conducted annually. They wanted data quarterly and decided to conduct a survey with a random sample of 25 percent of the population four times a year. The sample was large enough to give a reliable prediction of the entire workforce population. They were able to collect data quarterly and have a better pulse on employee attitudes and beliefs without burdening employees to complete a survey four times a year.

  This approach is particularly useful for companies undergoing rapid change. The executives need to know often what the employees feel and how they are responding to the change. The executives should anticipate that the employee survey results will be uneven.

Employees may not receive changes well even if they are in the best interests of the customer and/or the company. However, if the executives know the response to changes regularly, they will have a better chance to respond quickly to rebuild employee motivation.

Nurturing a Collaborative Relationship with Employee Representatives and Union Leadership

In many companies, the effort and cost to do the "core" work of negotiating with employee representatives can be substantial. Some companies have specific industrial relations departments devoted to this role because of its unique nature and requirements.

What has become evident is that the traditional adversarial way of approaching employee representatives creates internal conflict and a dysfunctional organization. Companies that have made sincere attempts to forge new relationships with employee associations and unions have made significant gains. My first book entitled, *Beyond the Walls of Conflict: Mutual Gains Negotiating for Unions and Management* (1996)[3], describes how to change the nature of these relationships. Companies and unions that have used the principles and techniques proposed in this book have been able to move from an adversarial relationship to a constructive relationship.

The topic of collaborative negotiations has stirred interest in mutual gains problem solving and how this approach can be used. A recent Canadian Institute conference that I chaired on "Best Practices in Mutual Gains Negotiating"[4] revealed many best practices that illustrate how this "core" activity can become added value and potentially a strategic advantage for the company and the employees.

Public stories of success came from companies and unions such as Saturn and the UAW, AT&T and the CWA, Nortel and the CAW, and Noranda and the Steelworkers. With labor-management strife increasing in many jurisdictions, these stories are important to guide organizations desiring a change in the way union and management negotiate and work together.

An essential element of success is the "hard wiring" of systems to support the change in the relationship between union and management. This means that committees or planning groups are built in to

---

[3] David Weiss, *Beyond The Walls Of Conflict: Mutual Gains Negotiating For Unions And Management.* Irwin Professional Publishing, 1996.
[4] *Best Practices in Mutual Gains Negotiating.* Canadian Institute. November 1996.

the way the organization does its work. The result is an integrated planning, problem-solving, and dispute resolution process that becomes part of organizational systems and gives joint problem solving the attention it needs to be successful. The way in which these groups work may differ from one another. Some may have joint work at very high levels, others at the grass roots level. The best practices emerge when the different methods are combined. The following are the planning groups and descriptions of their roles.[5]

- *Union Representatives on the Senior Cabinet:* In some companies, the union president sits on the senior executive cabinet as an ex-officio member and is part of the discussions to hear all the challenges facing the company. At any time, the union president may decide not to hear certain information, or the senior executive may decline to offer it if confidentiality will be compromised. Although these are options, the union president attends almost all meetings of the senior cabinet.

- *Joint Senior-Level Steering Committee:* A joint senior-level steering committee establishes the direction for the union and management relationship. In essence, it is a policy committee for how the groups work together and solve problems, and it sustains a positive union and management relationship in the organization. This committee can also contribute as a consultative committee on a broader range of HR issues and processes.

- *Joint Exceptions Council:* A joint union and management "exceptions" council approves variations to the collective agreement. On a pilot basis, they experiment with changes to increase flexibility during the contract term. The council allows for non-precedent setting activities to take place.

- *Ongoing Joint Problem-Solving Groups:* An organization cannot wait three years to resolve problems, and some specific issues are dealt with better outside of contract talks. Therefore, joint problem-solving groups are created to study and resolve complex issues during the term of the contract. They attempt to resolve problems at a local level before escalating the issue to higher levels.

- *Joint Planning and Training for Negotiations:* In preparing for collective bargaining, union and management representatives become

---

[5] This section is based on an article written by the author, Dr. David Weiss, "Best Practices in Mutual Gains Bargaining" in *Labor Alert*, Carswell, 1997.

accustomed to working together. Jointly, they develop educational programs on the process of joint problem solving, an analysis of the company's competitive situation and external surveys of potential solutions to problems. They negotiate using the principles and approaches described in *Beyond the Walls of Conflict (1996)*.

The potential is there to elevate the relationship with employee associations and unions to a level that adds value to the company. HR has the capability to transform what may be perceived as a strategic liability into a strategic asset. If HR can contribute to making that kind of change, then the company and employees will benefit. They will help the company to change its direction and to stop competing with each other and start competing against the competition.

The "Dispatch" People Processes

The dispatch role for HR typically includes retaining and terminating the employee relationship. Retention refers to the avoidance of early exiting and unwanted terminations. Terminating the relationship includes retirement, outplacement, and career transition (to insure that people who leave do so with dignity). In recent years, the dispatch role has become a focus of many HR departments. Phase Three transformations have included massive downsizing with many people asked to leave to reduce costs and to create more efficiencies. Simultaneously, retention strategies have been developed to keep key employees in the company.

Key Resource Retention

HR must develop strategies for retaining key resource employees—those who are instrumental in providing competitive advantage for the company. When other companies are raiding key resource employees, retention strategies take on an even higher degree of importance.

Recently, a high-tech company had an urgent need to develop a retention plan for highly coveted program developers because of the aggressive nature of recruiting practices by its competitor. The competitor placed newspaper and radio advertisements that compared its benefits plan with the company's plan (the competitor's package was considerably better than the company's) and concluded with a strong message to call the competitor.

The company's senior executive saw the risk and appealed to HR for a better way to retain employees. He went on to say that his program developers were "complaining with their feet and leaving the company." The competitor's strategy was very aggressive, and the counter strategy HR developed to retain the talented employees was equally as strong. Their strategy was for the company to become a key resource employer of choice. While the strategy was an expensive one, the investment proved to be of great importance against the competition.

Some of the retention tactics they used were:

- Financial incentives such as flexibility in pay and benefits to meet the personal needs of the employee.

- Workplace environment incentives such as personalized work space and flexibility regarding work and personal life balance, including working from home.

- Focus on achieving full potential of the employee by providing continuous development, additional autonomy to make decisions, and specific career advancement opportunities.

- Developing plans with the key resource "fast trackers." This approach included letting the fast trackers know they are fast trackers and that they would be given the opportunity to develop new skills through work transfers or playing leadership roles on committees.

The principle in retention is to have one-on-one conversations to discover the underlying motivators that will entice an employee to stay rather than leave. The HR professionals then provide a menu of choices from which they mass customize to the specific needs of the key resource employee. Alternatively, the employee can select from the menu of choices. In that way the employee is able to design their own retention plan that will precisely meet their needs.

For example, one company was populated by young, highly skilled software programmers and scientists. Many of these employees were coveted by their competitors. The company needed to develop a retention strategy. They quickly realized that these employees did not care about some of the traditional recognitions in the organization which were very important in other parts of their business. For example, the Christmas party, BBQ parties, and 10-year pins had little motivation for them. The leadership joked that it was probably more appropriate to reward their technology people with a one-year pin because that is about as long as they would stay.

This task was quite complex because what tends to keep younger employees (referred to as "Generation X") happy is very different from the "Baby Boomer" generation. Benefits and compensation were of course part of this retention strategy. However, they found that new ideas were required for Generation X. They decided to develop a menu of choices with a specific budget for the indirect methods of retention. They were able to fashion a retention approach that suited the individual needs of the key resources.

Some of the alternative choices they contemplated included:

- flexible work options and job-sharing possibilities
- more sophisticated technology at the desk top
- participating in high-profile professional conferences
- leaves of absence for educational or personal leave with a commitment to return
- provision of child care services
- enhancing remote access capability and the creation of virtual teams
- casual dress every day
- private space in the office for eating and socializing
- lunch menus chosen from the desk top and delivered to their work station.

Focus on Renewal During Downsizing and Terminations

HR's dispatch role in downsizing and terminations has become a major time consumer for many HR professionals in the past few years. HR's sophistication in this area has developed considerably.

A recent "best practices" research study in the area of downsizing was conducted by the HR consulting firm, Geller, Shedletsky and Weiss (1996).[6] They identified seven key features of best practices in downsizing that have been stated in the literature:

1. Provide early warning for employees and sufficient time for them to prepare and execute redeployment and re-employment initiatives.

2. Adopt aggressive redeployment efforts to minimize the need for layoffs.

3. Identify and secure alternatives to job elimination (e.g., job sharing, reduced wages, reduced work weeks).

---

[6] Geller, Shedletsky & Weiss. Unpublished best practices research on outplacement services. Prepared for a client in the financial sector.

4. Provide funds and/or opportunities for employees to develop skills or retrain and facilitate access to internal and external resources (e.g., colleges and universities) for these services.

5. Establish and maintain a job bank to proactively source internal and external job opportunities.

6. Provide ongoing outplacement and support services up to the time of termination and, preferably, to the point of re-employment.

7. Offer "options" to fully support external re-employment opportunities.

If massive staff reductions must occur, HR needs to be able to reduce the impact of the downsizing. HR achieves this through its involvement with the senior executives in the planning process and by having more time to plan the downsizing according to the best practices cited above.

When HR professionals are involved at an early stage in plans for downsizing, they have time to prepare for the following:

- *Selecting and using external vendors to manage the downsizing process:* HR identifies their preferred supplier list of outplacement service providers.

- *Managing the overall process outcome and abandoning the direct service delivery of the process to the external outplacement service providers:* HR lets the outplacement firm focus on the downsizing of the business while HR concentrates on rebuilding for the long-term and motivating the remaining employees. Essentially, HR manages the overall plan for the process outcome. HR is not as tainted by the layoffs and can put its energy where it belongs—toward the company's renewal.

Many ask why are layoffs so massive? When mass terminations occur that are not consistent with the above best practices, it often reflects inefficiencies in ongoing strategic thinking and a lack on the company's part of seeing the problems as they emerged. The amount of work required of HR to manage massive downsizing is often overwhelming. In some cases, HR can do nothing else but the downsizing work. Frequently, the company and the HR professionals are demoralized, and the employees who do not leave the company are de-motivated and despondent.

Companies in which HR and senior executives engage in continuous strategic thinking are able to see changes in personnel as a normal ongoing process. They are constantly managing a healthy process that enables people to leave the company in a positive way and bring in new people to stimulate new ideas and dynamics. A process that is ethical and ongoing creates a perpetual renewal that reduces the likelihood of a need for a massive downsizing.

In some situations, a massive downsizing is the enterprise's only alternative, and the suddenness is unavoidable. Most recently, this is occurring in government agencies and regulated monopolies. In many of these situations, HR is not ready to manage the process because it has not been expected to operate on a strategic level. However, the crisis may be useful in helping HR establish a more strategic position for the organization's renewal in the future.

Perhaps it would be helpful to understand why massive downsizing can occur in a large government agency or regulated monopoly environment (e.g., postal services, local telephone companies, public utilities). Consider the possibility that most large government agencies and regulated monopolies operate with an unwritten government employment policy. The policy supports over-employment as a method to create more job opportunities for the public. This means that, although there are many talented people in these enterprises, the government agencies and regulated monopolies are over-staffed by design to create jobs and employment opportunities. While some work could be easily automated, it is not done because the agency wants to keep the jobs for the employees. Reducing costs by introducing efficiencies is not encouraged because it will mean fewer jobs. In essence, according to this scenario, some jobs exist in government agencies and regulated monopolies as an alternate hidden employment tax on the public. In the case of the government, the hidden tax is paid by the taxpayer. In the case of the regulated monopolies, it is paid by the users of the services the utilities provide.

To illustrate this scenario, consider a telephone company that is a regulated monopoly. Assume the regulation specifies that the telephone company can not exceed a certain level of profit. When the telephone company exceeds that level, it has two choices: 1) either give money back to the customers or 2) increase their cost base. Most telephone companies prefer to increase their cost base by investing in better equipment and hiring more people. This results in an over-employment situation.

In the telephone company example, when the regulators decide to introduce competition and change the regulation to reflect controls on price (and not profit), the telephone company has to reduce major costs to stay competitive. One of these costs is the number of employees.

Massive layoffs ensue, which reduces costs and actually improves efficiencies. Essentially the company reduces the number of employees to the level it would have achieved had it not over employed. After the layoffs, HR begins focusing on abandonment and providing strategic business advantage.

The same is true when a government realizes (or more precisely, the public realizes) that it has an intolerable debt. The government decides to introduce new efficiencies. Knowing that by design it has been significantly over-staffed, it targets the cost of employment as an area to reduce. It needs to demonstrate that it can manage itself and bring down its costs. The quickest way (although not an appreciated approach from a political perspective) is to reduce the number of government employees.

The government claims they are acting in the "public interest" (the long-term good of the public) rather than in the "interest of the public" (meeting the immediate interests and needs of the public). The government then engages in massive layoffs that reduce costs and improve efficiencies. In this situation, HR can not prepare for this eventuality easily. Only afterwards can it re-invest human capital and contribute to the transformation and renewal.

The "dispatch" role of retaining strategic employees should be part of HR's work, whereas downsizing would be better done by preferred suppliers, who will take guidance from strategic-thinking HR professionals. HR can then concentrate on the renewal of the company, investing in human capital to enable the remaining employees to rebuild the enterprise, and delivering value to internal clients and the external customer.

Delivering Core *and* Strategic Process Outcomes

When HR is able to guarantee that the core people process outcomes will be delivered, the senior executives will be more willing to partner with HR for competitive advantage. One of the costs of partnership is being excellent in the core people process roles of *hatch, match and dispatch*. The core people process outcomes must be delivered with precision, quality, timeliness, and at the appropriate cost.

However, some HR organizations make the mistake of viewing success in the core people process outcomes as their only focus until they "get it right." Many executives are demanding more from their HR services. HR must deliver the core people process outcomes and at the same time deliver the organizational and business processes described in the next few chapters. The executives want it all, and many are becoming more impatient. Just as they want strategic value to mean higher revenue and at the same time lower cost, they want HR to deliver the core people processes *and at the same time* contribute to the organizational value-add and business transformation process outcomes.

HR will be able to handle the increased work load of the core, organizational and business process outcomes only if it becomes excellent at abandoning HR core work as described in Chapter 3. As HR adds new work and challenges, it needs to cull and abandon work of lower value. HR professionals must constantly ask themselves the following two questions:

1. Does this work contribute to the company's relative advantage against its competition?
2. Does this work eventually contribute added value to the external customer?

HR operates in a constant triage mode to manage workload and deliver value to the company. HR professionals must be rigorous in focusing on strategic value. At the same time they must be willing to distribute core work to other resources while guaranteeing the excellence of the process outcomes.

Summary

- The "core people processes" role of HR takes place at the recruitment (hatch), development (match), and exiting (dispatch) stages of the employment life cycle.
- The "core people processes" include the following: Selection and Orientation, Performance Development, Employee Services, Compensation and Recognition, and Retention and Termination Processes.
- The question for HR is which of its employment life cycle services are adding value and giving competitive advantage and which are core processes that can be abandoned in a disciplined way.
- At all times HR retains accountability for the process outcomes, even if the process is delivered externally, internally by people outside of HR, or by HR professionals.

- HR's core "hatch" people process typically includes staffing and orientation. HR recruits key resource employees and considers outsourcing the recruitment of other employees. HR must also excel in international recruiting and negotiating for key resource employees.

- The "match" role sometimes can be all-consuming for HR, which includes performance development, compensation and recognition, and employee services. HR can distribute to others some of the roles in the match area.

- The "dispatch" role for HR typically includes retention (the avoidance of early exiting and unwanted terminations), and termination from the company (e.g., retirement, outplacement and career transition). The emphasis in termination is to insure that people who leave do so with dignity.

- HR must develop strategies for retaining key resource employees—those who are instrumental in providing competitive advantage for the company. When other companies are raiding key resource employees, retention strategies take on an even higher degree of importance.

- In the past few years, the "dispatch" role for HR in downsizing and terminations has become a major time consumer for many HR professionals. A recent "best practices" research study in the area of downsizing was conducted by the HR consulting firm, Geller, Shedletsky and Weiss (1996). This study identified seven key features of best practices in downsizing.

- The "dispatch" role of retaining strategic employees should be a major HR focus, whereas the role in downsizing would be better done by preferred suppliers who will take guidance from strategic-thinking HR professionals.

- HR is expected to deliver the core people processes and *at the same time* deliver the organizational and business process outcomes described in the next few chapters.

CHAPTER FIVE

෧෧

Organizational Value-Add

Many Human Resource professionals contribute value to line managers and to the entire company through their organizational work. The organizational value-add work that HR does has broad impact on the entire workforce. It is often the building block on which major people process changes are built.

This chapter explores three areas of organizational work for HR that delivers value-add to the business. They are represented by the letters "TLC," the Tender Love and Care that HR can provide to nurture the organization. The organizational value-add processes are:

- Technology as an enabler to allow many of the new HR activities to occur as well as to enable many of the core people processes.

- Learning as a constant life-long experience for employees at work. This organizational process will also have implications for the people processes, especially performance development.

- Consulting to enhance organizational performance. The HR professional uncovers organizational needs that reflect the specific concerns of the line manager and then designs interventions that enable the line manager to run his or her business effectively.

T: Technology as an Enabler to Allow Many of the New HR Activities to Occur

Many companies used the problem of re-coding their information technology architecture to be Year 2000 compatible as an opportunity to abandon the old technology and invest in a new and more flexible system. Employees and HR are direct beneficiaries of the decision to "buy" rather than "fix" the system. Under normal conditions, many companies would not modernize. However, since they had to update the system anyway, modernizing was done for less incremental investment. As a result, the application of technology to enable HR practices took a giant step forward and will continue to do so in the future.

The investment in the new technology has enabled HR to escalate the delivery of a new kind of value to the organization that it was unable to deliver before. The technology has been useful to enable employees to manage some of their own information and benefits packages. This development will continue to be part of an exciting transformation that technology will enable.

In a recent benchmark study on HR (Geller, Shedletsky & Weiss, 1998)[1], the early benefits of introducing new technology were identified, including the following:

- *Increasing employee access and modifying the central database*
  - Many companies now have all employee files on line and electronically available. This allows employees to enter and retrieve information quickly.
  - Some companies give employees access to what they call the "tombstone" data. Employees can make changes to basic information such as change of address, dependents, benefits coverage, etc.
  - HR is able to update policies and communications regularly without the cumbersome problems of production and distribution of material.

- *Enhancing core people processes*
  - Many companies are exploring how to use technology for employee relations situations, diversity, compensation, benefits, human resources consulting, and training and development.
  - The Intranet is being used for job postings, listing HR policies and programs, and for training.

---

[1] Geller, Shedletsky & Weiss, 1998. An HR Benchmark Study. Unpublished study for a client in the financial sector.

- Some companies have developed web sites for recruiting and will accept only electronically submitted resumes.
- Technology is also used as another way to respond to employee questions by both providing easy access to information and through e-mail communications.
- The company's leaders are able to update employees on how work is being done, introduce new products, and share learnings on an ongoing basis.

• *Compensation and bonuses*
  - One company is using technology globally to harmonize HR compensation policies, processes, and practices across the company. This includes the calculation of bonuses to create one culture and increase efficiency.
  - Some companies have modified their compensation and benefits programs so that they can be run electronically. People sign up on their computer when they start with the company. They have flexible benefits, can self-initiate and change their own benefits, and are able to re-enroll on line. For example, in one company, employees can sell their vacation time for a dollar value and buy and sell other benefits into their personal account. They also save money according to a certain plan and then can invest this money. Employees are also educated on how to invest their money.
  - In a brokerage company, the HR department used to have 100 databases for bonuses. New technology was used to determine, calculate, and distribute the bonuses for all eligible people. Managers receive market data from compensation studies through the database so managers can make compensation comparisons directly. If a manager wants to adjust a bonus locally, he or she sends the adjustment to HR on a spreadsheet for input into the system.

• *HR financial management and reporting*
  - Technology has enabled some HR departments to directly charge line businesses for HR products and services. The charge-back process has helped HR to be perceived as adding more value to the company.
  - Some companies are using the system for quantitative HR reports for line executives. One financial organization has a designated strategic partner who links the financial MIS system to the HR software system. Another company has developed a number of

quantitative reports on HR that include demographics, total compensation, organization structure, and updates on key resources in the company.

• *Aligning HR systems with other databases in the company*
  – Some companies align their HR systems with the systems that are being used elsewhere in the company. This allows them to align HR data with the customer and financial data. It also helps align the HR reports with the reports from other areas of the company.
  – The HR system is also used by executives to access information and to determine the return on investment in people. Some executives have explored this possibility as explained later in Chapter Ten.

The Future Potential Contributions of the HR Technology

The potential of new technology in HR is much greater than how it is used today. It is likely that the customer service features that are offered to customers will start to be offered to employees as well. HR's more advanced technological services will also become a competitive advantage in attracting and retaining employees.

Many experts have identified that although employees want new technology, they want it to adapt to them rather than them having to adapt to the technology. HR will have the responsibility as a new kind of intermediary to adapt the technology to the needs of the employees. Some of the ways HR will need to be able to add value to employees through technological services are as follows:

• *As employee career agents:* Some companies are experimenting with linking career opportunities to personal competencies. Using HR systems, employees enter their personal competencies and are automatically notified if a career opportunity is available that is consistent with their competencies and their interests.

• *As packagers of content for employees:* As the information on the Intranet swells, there will be too much content available from which employees will have to choose. Helping employees and managers find and package what they want on the Intranet and the HR system will be an important role for HR professionals. They can provide the support to employees to let them know what is available. They can also tailor the mass of information to the needs and interests of individual employees. Just as the content packager in the external market place is likely to have customer loyalty and dominant access to the customer, HR has the opportunity to be the primary access to employees in this role as content packager.

- *As vendor relations representatives:* HR is expected to guarantee quality performance when it outsources services to external service providers. It is very difficult to insure quality control without the proper systems. Through its electronic capability, HR can monitor and manage its external service providers. The technology enables HR to know what the vendors are doing on an ongoing basis. HR can also share purchasing needs of many clients to standardize services and achieve economies of scale from their purchases. They also have the capability to gather information from their recruitment database, information from search firms, etc.

- *As builders of virtual communities:* Electronic technology is already enabling many employees to work from remote locations and from the home. New virtual teams are forming that share a common "cyber" space rather than a common physical space. The electronic communications become the new "water cooler" conversations where idle chat and social interactions take place. HR can deploy technology to support the development of virtual teams and virtual work communities, allowing people to work anywhere and connect with anyone anytime. The quality of life improvements can be vast for people who find this to be an attractive work alternative. HR can also help to create technology-based interest groups (perhaps with entrance requirements) that will link people with similar interests within and outside the company to share learnings and information with each other.

Some Challenges in the Approach to New Technology

Deploying technology in a company is not without its challenges. Here are some of those challenges (in addition to price):

- *Customer-centric vs. employee-centric technology:* Each company will need to determine whether their HR technology will be driven by a company-centric approach or an employee-centric approach. With the company-centric approach, the system will be designed to deliver information to management and to manage the human capital asset in the company. With the employee-centric approach, HR will be asked to be content packagers and will use the technology to enable employees to feel better about their work. These choices are not necessarily an either/or choice, but as the technology is employed initially, the emphasis on a specific approach will probably impact technology purchase and development initiatives.

- *Aligning technology choice with the technology used elsewhere in the company:* Eventually HR technology will be integrated with a larger database that exists within the company. Some companies are selecting suppliers that have systems that are incompatible with the dominant technology used in the company. The recommended approach is that the technology should allow for the possibility that in the future the HR database will be integrated with the financial database and other information sources.

- *Allowing access to the central database:* To what extent is the company willing to give employees and managers access to the central database? The suggestion is that whatever the decision on this matter, the company should design the system so that it can access the central database in the future even if access is restricted now.

- *Surveying employees to identify technology needs:* Surveys of employees about their technology needs often ask questions about a hypothetical capability that the employee will have. Unfortunately, surveys based on hypothetical technological situations are not precise predictors of the future behavior of employees. Employees sometimes indicate that they want capabilities that they do not use once they have them or they indicate they do not want capabilities that they welcome when they arrive. Perhaps the best predictor of employee behavior is to study past employee behaviors (as learned in behavioral interviewing for selection purposes) to predict how they are likely to behave in the future with the deployment of technology.

- *Who develops content, inputs data, and updates the information:* For the system to be current, people must input data and content and update the information regularly. Often that process is time-consuming. A method to simplify the inputting and updating of data will be necessary.

Notwithstanding the above limitations, the influence technology will have on HR and the services it provides to the business will grow. At this time, the HR technology capability is designated as an "organizational value-add process." However, if the technology fulfills the promise of its potential, it is likely that HR technology will be elevated to a business transformation strategic process within three to five years. When that occurs, HR will have another important reason to be discussing issues at the executive table with the senior executive team.

L: Learning—Building a Continuous Learning Environment

This section describes seven principles that emerge for HR professionals as they design a learning environment. These principles also will enable companies to transform the "core people process" of performance development to a higher level in which they can create an "organizational value-add" continuous learning environment.

Principle 1—The Primary Purpose of Training Is to Teach People How to Self-Learn and Not to Teach Content.

Imagine that you decide to landscape your home garden. As a result of your new interest, you are attentive to every conversation about landscaping. You read magazines and books about gardens. As you walk or ride down the street, you observe other people's landscaping, and you gather ideas. You are in a continuous learning mode about landscaping.

What would the work environment be like if all employees demonstrated the same passion for continuous learning? Employees would seek out new knowledge to improve things. Every person would be motivated and stimulated by the vibrancy of each day. Employees would be self-reliant and self-educated. As a result, leaders would need to create the forum to harness the learning for collective benefit, and HR would need to teach people how to learn continuously.

Over the past few years, some companies have identified life-long learning as a critical success factor. If people are always learning and are open to learning from others, the culture will be more flexible and change will be more readily accepted. Managers will also find that it will help them with decision making. Today's work environment is increasing in complexity and continuously changing. Managers and leaders must have the opportunity to learn continuously in order to be able to deal with the ambiguity and difficulty of making decisions.

For employees to survive in the new work environment, ongoing learning is essential. Job security has disappeared, making it important to be employable. Some companies are creating opportunities for employees to upgrade continually so that their skills do not become obsolete. In these companies, most employees reciprocate by taking advantage of the opportunities to learn. HR's role is central in helping companies create an environment in which employees are motivated and learn continuously. HR professionals must focus on teaching people how to self-learn, not on teaching content.

The company gains specific benefits from an environment in which employees can self-learn. For example, many large companies face a dilemma when they introduce a new approach or process. Consider a company that has introduced a new initiative. For the initiative to be effective, all 5,000 employees will be required to be knowledgeable about it. To train 5,000 people in groups of 20 will require conducting a course 250 times. In most companies, that could take one to two years to complete. Even with elaborate train-the-trainer processes, the time and cost involved to reach all employees is too high. Often, by the time the company trains all the employees on the new process, the content is obsolete. Companies need to reach all employees faster than this.

When companies create an environment that supports continuous learning, the nature of what people are taught changes. The purpose of the course is not to impart the content. People should be able to learn the content continuously and independently. The emphasis is to teach people *how* to learn—how to stay current and up-to-date on a day-by-day basis. They no longer have to wait for the course to be presented. They are taught the learning skills so that they can access the tools and learn by themselves. Most often, employees access these learning tools directly from their manager or through the company's Intranet and central database.

Principle 2—Managers Are Accountable for Creating an Ongoing Learning Environment.

While HR can be accountable for continuous learning in the company overall, managers are responsible for ongoing learning opportunities in their work units. Of equal importance to the manager's role as a technical leader is his or her responsibility to orient and educate new employees. I have often wondered why managers would relinquish the terrific opportunity to influence their new employees. As described in Chapter Four, new employees are often very highly motivated, and they do not know the way work is done in the manager's work setting. During the first few weeks of employment, the manager has the opportunity to teach, dialogue, share ideas, and explore the capabilities of the new employee. The manager can build a relationship and an understanding in those first two weeks that will last for the duration of the individual's employment. HR or a centralized training department can augment this learning with an orientation program, but the primary relationship starts with the manager, not with HR.

Managers also have the major accountability to educate employees. However, managers often avoid this accountability. Sometimes the reason is the lack of time to educate employees. In other cases it may be a more deliberate avoidance. For example, managers may fear that if they teach their employees what they know, the employees will be as knowledgeable and skilled as they are and no longer need them. Nothing can be further from the truth. As an ancient saying indicates, "I learn a lot from my teachers, more from my peers and the most from my students." Managers learn from the process of articulating knowledge to others. The process of teaching makes managers sharper and more knowledgeable in their areas of expertise. Managers should have no fear about sharing learning with employees.

Principle 3—All Employees Are Accountable for Their Own Learning.

The first and second principles set the climate for employees to recognize that in this company they are held accountable for their own learning. The company and the manager will do whatever they can to create the environment that will enable employees to learn. Employees will have access to the sources they need for learning (including the central database, their managers, HR services, other mentors in the company), but they will have to take responsibility for stepping up to the challenge and demonstrating continuous learning; no one can do it for them.

When HR removes the barriers that block learning, minimal effort is needed to motivate employees to learn continuously. Employees take the initiative to learn and the "core" role of training is transformed to ongoing learning.

Principle 4—All Employees Are Able to Teach as Well as Learn.

In the old working environment, knowledge was power. In the new working environment, knowledge is a shared resource. People have very little time to play the power games of withholding information and knowledge.

Since all knowledge is accessible, except perhaps specific strategic information, all employees have the opportunity to learn as well as to add value to the discussion. Information and understanding are distributed to line managers and employees both directly and through technology. The absolute respect for the intellectual capacity of every employee to grasp correctly and comprehend this information is essential to the flexible learning environment.

People's experiences are leveraged across the company. Cross-functionality of teams is encouraged because people can contribute ideas to other areas even if they are not experts in those areas. HR facilitates this environment by creating the group and learning settings in which all employees can participate, not just those people with the most seniority or the highest position in the company.

For example, when executives lead "question and answer" sessions to share directions, they can model the behavior to involve all employees. Many times after they deliver presentations, the leaders ask employees if they have questions. Frequently, they face an uncomfortable silence. They know the employees have questions, but no one is willing to speak up. The reasons vary. Sometimes it is a trust issue; at other times it's an insecurity issue on the part of the employees. For example, the employee may think, "Am I the only one who does not understand this?"

A simple way HR can help overcome this anxiety is to have people talk in table groups after the presentation to generate comments or questions. This accomplishes three things: 1) it gives people time to think of what they want to say, 2) it allows those people who are shy in large groups to have the opportunity to give their issues some voice, and 3) it validates that no question is silly but, rather, that many other people are struggling with it as well.

HR professionals use their knowledge of group dynamics, understanding of the big picture, and excellent facilitation skills to create an environment in which people feel they are all learners and teachers. This environment is one in which:

- The most senior person can learn from the most junior.
- People maximize diversity in the workplace through listening and learning from each other.
- The politics are less intense, and people can listen to each other and have more meaningful dialogue.

The message is that everyone has wisdom—that what employees need to do is pay attention and learn from each other, and the wisdom will be discovered and heard.

Principle 5—Learning Occurs "Just-in-Time" When and How It Is Needed.

Just-in-time learning means learning anywhere, anyhow, and anytime you need to learn it. The just-in-time concept has transformed manufacturing processes. It also has the capability of transforming the training and learning process. With just-in-time learning, people will be able to adapt more quickly to changes.

In many years of teaching and facilitating groups, I have found that the greatest use of learning is by people who have an immediate application need. For these people, the training and learning have the most impact. In the optimum situation, everyone would be in a learning experience, accessing information that is readily available when they have a compelling need for it.

Through the use of technology, shared information can be just-in-time. The prerequisite is that people are willing to share information freely and openly and have people self-learn. The principle of teaching people how to learn rather than teaching them content is based on employees getting information when they actually need to learn and not when they attend the course (which is rarely at the time employees need it—usually it's either too early or too late).

As an example, consider a manufacturing plant where an inventive plant manager decides to facilitate just-in-time learning. In this work environment, stopping the workflow for a brief period of time will not put a severe dent in efficiency. He places a flip chart in each work unit and then instructs the managers to stop everyone from working when something goes wrong and to gather around the flip chart. The plant manager uses the flip chart to illustrate the scenario and to facilitate a discussion about how to do it right the next time. Learning in this plant environment is designed to happen as the need to learn occurs.

Another important development in just-in-time learning is the effectiveness of *distributed methods of learning* in which the content is centrally developed and is distributed to interested parties. In some cases it is sent to those people who express interest. It can be made available with technology so that people can receive the knowledge without making a specific request for the information.

A distributed method is particularly effective for *instrumental learning*, which focuses on skill and knowledge development. In most cases there are better ways to obtain instrumental learning than in a classroom, such as:

- CD-ROM interactive training, which is now commonplace.
- Learning interactively through technology applications and content available at the employee's desktop.
- Learning on the job and from mentors.

On the other hand, *inspirational learning* focuses on changing the group's focus and mobilizing them in another direction by inspiring them. Ideally, this is done in a group setting and participants benefit from the social environment of a classroom. The peer discussions add value to the process of confronting difficult issues that are relevant to the new mindset. Some ideas to increase the urgency of inspirational learning so that it will be more of a just-in-time learning experience include the following:

- *Conduct formal training sessions with the full pyramid of leader, supervisors, and their employees in the room:* With the full range of employees present, the focus is on the system rather than on the individual, and it is more likely that changes to the system will be put into effect after the session. In situations when only one employee tier is present for training, that group of employees may be changed as a result of the training and then return to a system that has not changed. The barriers encountered may block those employees from implementing the changes they contemplated during the training.

- *Get the right groups in the room to learn together who can add value to each other:* In some contexts the right people are those who can make the decision so that the process does not have to be delayed for a follow-up meeting. For example, a group in one bank included leaders of another group to work closely with them on their strategy. HR also does this by including line managers as part of a planning team with HR to discuss the best ways to maximize HR's strategic contribution to the company.

• *Make the training available to people who need to learn the content and the processes:* The participants will then be more likely to apply what they learn as soon as possible.

Principle 6—Continuous Feedback Techniques Are Used to Measure the Effectiveness of Ongoing Learning.

To assess the effectiveness of ongoing learning, it helps to put in place some mechanisms that measure the return on investment. For example, some companies have their employees develop learning maps that outline what they need to do to develop and maintain their employability. Others develop performance contracts with employees based on their learning needs. Both of these techniques can help HR assess the extent to which employees progress.

Formal measurement devices can also be used, such as surveys of employees, leaders, customers, suppliers, shareholders, etc. However, some inventive informal measurement methods have also been developed that are worthy of note. For example:

• Using technology to conduct daily surveys on one issue per day for just-in-time feedback.

• Having a call-in telephone number for one-item surveys in which people vote "yes" or "no."

• Conducting "web-based" surveys regularly and providing immediate feedback to the participants.

• Creating attractive graffiti spaces for people to write their ideas about the learning environment on the walls.

• Using technology as a means to document ideas and to share ideas that do not work.

Principle 7—The Entire Organization Shares What Has Been Learned.

On a much broader scale, the entire organization has the capability of sharing what they learn about effective and ineffective practices. If everyone knows what others know, the organization will have a wealth of knowledge. Also, the organization loses a lot of knowledge when a person retires or leaves. It is important to discover ongoing ways to map what people know and insure that the intellectual capital remains with the organization as much as possible.

The idea of sharing information about ineffective practices may be even more important than sharing information about what is effective. Ineffective practices are those actions that the organization needs to *unlearn*. When these practices are shared with employees, it helps them avoid the pathway to the problems previously encountered. The work environment should support sharing what to abandon so that others know what no longer applies and should not be done. Sharing ineffective practices can help people avoid wasting time making someone else's mistake.

Traditionally, in most organizations knowledge is centrally controlled and developed by people in training or is imparted by leadership. Sharing information about practices, both effective and ineffective, can be decentralized and based on anyone's experience. Everyone is a developer of knowledge and can share it with everyone else.

While information can be shared in formal ways, such as conducting professional development meetings in which everyone teaches something they know, computer technology provides a way of reaching more people in the organization. The process of sharing information about effective and ineffective practices can occur from remote locations. By using a database, people are able to enter their information into a central area. Anyone can access this shared information even if it is not meant specifically for them. In addition, some empirical evidence exists that sharing information through technology allows people with junior status in the organization to be heard more effectively. These individuals are more willing to enter their information in a system than to speak at a meeting.

By following the seven principles, companies can help transform the "core" role of training and development. They can create an environment for continuous learning in which employees have the tools to adapt as changes occur and help set the stage for the implementation of the company's strategic direction.

C: Consulting to Enhance Organizational Performance

There are potentially many ways HR professionals can add organizational value. However, perhaps one of the most effective ways that contributions can be identified and value-add opportunities discovered is through excellence in consulting to internal clients. HR professionals add value to the client by tailoring consulting to their specific needs.

The consulting relationship seems to have a life cycle of its own. In some quarters the life span of the consulting relationship with a client is referred to as a five-stage process. To illustrate the five stages, here is an example of a hypothetical HR professional named David. As an HR professional, David has been assigned to a client in the company. The life span of the relationship can be typified by the comments of the client during the five stages of their relationship:

- At Stage 1 (when David is assigned to the client), the client says, "David who?"

- At Stage 2 (after David's first successful contribution), the client says, "I like David. He reminds me of . . . "

- At Stage 3 (when David is a centerpiece of the senior management team), the client says whenever there is a major issue, "Let's get David to help us with this problem."

- At Stage 4 (when David's value to the client is diminishing), the client muses, "Does anyone remember the old David?"

- At Stage 5 (after David has moved on to be a vital resource for another client), the former client says, "David who?"

It is important that HR professionals be capable of assuming a leadership position with the senior management team for whom they are providing organizational value-added consulting services. They also have to have the humility to know when they have outlived their welcome and need to move on.

One astute HR professional in a manufacturing business realized she had to move on to another business area when she found that she was being asked to implement changes in an area of the organization she had changed a few years earlier. It was time for someone else to contribute fresh ideas to add value to the situation. She moved to another business area in the company, and the transfer worked exceptionally well.

It is important that HR professionals know when to move on in order to continue to be successful in responding to client needs within the company. Internal clients need fresh ideas and the intellectual capacity to be intrigued by HR professionals on an ongoing basis. A change in HR professionals may be the way that fresh ideas and viewpoints may be sustained.

HR professionals are expected to work with clients in three kinds of consulting interventions. These are:

1. *Organizational consulting:* This kind of consulting focuses on assessing needs and facilitating a method of performing an activity. An example of this kind of consultation is when the HR professional assesses and designs an intervention to respond to a people or organizational challenge that an internal client is facing.

2. *Technical counsel:* HR professionals frequently rely on their technical expertise to support their clients. For example, if a business executive wants to hire a new vice president, the HR professional should have the technical expertise to manage this process so that the best person is found and developed in his or her new role. In this capacity, the HR professional may be a broker for services for others both internally and externally. Often the technical consultation is about an employee compliance issue for which the HR professional can offer expert counsel.

3. *"Walking-talking" consultant:* Often the HR professional is called upon for a quick word of advice. These interactions consist of giving guidance and providing insights by coaching the client. In essence, HR professionals offer value as they "walk and talk" at specific moments in their relationship with their clients.

Coaching vs. Consulting

HR professionals are called upon to consult with clients on many kinds of issues. During initial conversations about an issue, HR professionals need to diagnose the source of the problem. In some cases, the problem will require consulting to help the client achieve a certain desired result while in other situations *coaching* the client on more personal developmental needs may be required. HR professionals need the diagnostic skills to determine if an issue is a consulting need or a coaching need, or both. In many cases it is advisable to coach and then consult. If the client has coaching needs, those needs can be addressed either before or as the HR professional is doing organizational consulting.

A helpful phrase is that HR professionals should "solve the problem in the room (the manager with a personal developmental need requiring coaching) before solving the problem outside the room (the manager with an organizational challenge that requires consulting)." HR professionals "solve the problem in the room" first because that often helps them understand the context for the problem that is raised as an organizational consulting assignment.

Managers may present a wide variety of coaching-related problems at varying levels of complexity. It is helpful for HR professionals to be able to diagnose the source(s) of the problems and to be prepared to coach managers when the needs arises. This section identifies seven coaching needs for managers that HR professionals often encounter, each of which begins with the letter "C."

1. *Context awareness and fit:* The manager must understand how they contribute to the problem situation to know how to respond effectively. Some managers lack a full understanding of the context as well as the impact of their behavior and its consequences. HR professionals can coach and dialogue with managers to discover the real context and to help them understand the impact of their actions and beliefs. They can also help the managers learn more about what they are able to do and not able to do in the situation. When providing this kind of feedback, HR professionals can find objective management assessments very helpful.

2. *Competence and knowledge deficits:* The manager lacks the competence and/or knowledge to perform a certain role. For example, many managers seek help from HR professionals on how to coach employees who are having performance problems. HR professionals coach their clients on how to respond to the situation or how to access the skills and knowledge they need.

3. *Commitment deficits*: Some managers have the competence and knowledge, but they lack the commitment or motivation to do the job. They do not need skills training. Rather, their motivations for resistance need to be discovered. HR professionals need to discuss these issues with managers before engaging in organizational consulting initiatives.

4. *Conflicts interpersonally:* Sometimes the issue revolves around the relationship between the manager and another person (e.g., the supervisor, a peer, or an employee). The HR professional coaches the manager on how to address the conflict through interest-based problem-solving approaches (Fisher and Ury, 1981[2]; Weiss, 1996[3]).

5. *Credibility and trust gaps:* Some managers have the skill and desire but lack the credibility with their groups. This kind of conversation may be more difficult for the HR professional. Often, it is helpful to have objective data such as management assessments or 360° survey data to discuss the credibility issue. The data helps provide the conversational tool to proceed with this kind of coaching. In other

---

[2] Roger Fisher and William Ury, *Getting To Yes*, Penguin Books, 1981.
[3] David S. Weiss, *Beyond The Walls Of Conflict*, Irwin Professional Publishing, 1996.

cases, external specialists who have skills and experience in this area may be called upon.

6. _Career aspirations:_ The manager may be using the organizational consulting intervention as a career advancement opportunity. Some executives use organizational change to advance their career, while others have reached a plateau in their career, and they need to "jump start" their career to regain their motivation. It will be important for HR professionals to be aware of these aspirations and to understand some of their clients' behaviors as the organizational consulting assignment proceeds.

7. _Concerns of a personal nature:_ As the relationship builds between the HR professional and the manager, the manager may disclose personal concerns that require attention. HR professionals respond to these personal concerns as they would to any employee assistance situation. They need to know their limits in these cases, refer wisely, and maintain strict confidentiality and trust with managers.

Understanding the Value-Add of Organizational Consulting

If HR professionals are to become effective organizational consultants, they will need to learn about types of solutions, as well as actual solutions that clients often need. Their menu of choices must be varied so that they can add value to the internal client on an ongoing basis. They will also have to be very interested and astute about the market and competitive analysis of their client's part of the business as an important place to discover possible answers to their problems.

With this knowledge of their client's business and understanding of the possible solutions, HR professionals are able to ask their clients astute questions and intrigue them on the spot. HR professionals use their experiences as clues to what may be occurring in the client's situation. They then listen intently to the client to deeply understand issues so that they can design an organizational consulting process that best addresses the client's needs.

An important distinction exists between most external consultants and internal HR professionals who are in an organizational consulting role. External consultants are driven by ongoing contact and by discovering new opportunities to help their customers. In some cases, internal HR professionals do not desire to discover new opportunities to provide organizational consulting because it will dramatically add to their workload. As a result, some HR professionals engage in internal consulting activities with their clients on a reactive basis rather than on a proactive basis. This is an unfortunate development. Many opportunities to provide organizational value-add may be missed. Also, there are many opportunities to build relationships with the internal client that will be helpful as the HR professional continues to migrate toward business transformational activities that are described in the next four chapters.

As a result, HR professionals foster the relationship with their clients. They network with others to enhance their credibility and access to their client. When they meet with their clients they target an opportunity (e.g., recent event), have an issue in mind, and discuss it. If they see the opportunity, they start consulting on the spot as a "walking, talking" consultant and make a project out of everything. To be able to have these kinds of conversations, HR professionals will need to know their clients and know their own motivations as well. They should know the answers to the following kinds of questions:

- What are your client's interests and expectations?
- What are your interests and expectations?
- How can you align your approach to the "overlap" between the client's interests and your own?

Throughout the organizational consulting intervention, the HR professional is focused on delivering outcomes that enhance the overall performance of the client's business. The five variables that are most useful in assessing the quality of the outcomes the client receives can be described by the following:

1. **Wise Recommendations:** These are recommendations that reflect the "right" thing to do rather than recommendations based on political biases and who should win in a given situation.

2. **Efficient:** An efficient decision is the simplest possible recommendation for the need. It allows for economies of scale, it is easily communicated, and can be repeated with relative ease.

3. **Measurable:** Clients are often looking for opportunities to determine if a measurable difference occurred as a result of the organizational consulting. The direction chosen should be measurable so it can demonstrate the added value it provided.

4. **Educates and empowers the client:** The HR professional is not expected to do the same kind of consulting over and over. The process of consulting should be educational for the client so that

when that situation, or a similar one arises, the client will have a better chance of being able to respond to it independently.

5. *Enhances the relationship between the HR professional and the client:* The quality of the relationship between the HR professional and the client is important to both parties. A positive coaching relationship will mean that the client will seek out the HR professional the next time there is an issue and the client will also be more likely to be receptive to the HR professional's insights and observations.

A Process Orientation to Organizational Consulting

The approach taken to organizational consulting is a process orientation. This section identifies four processes in the typical organizational consulting intervention. Each begins with the identification of a client need and ends when the client has had that need satisfied.

The four processes of organizational consulting are presented in Figure 5.1. They form a total consulting intervention from "understanding" to "assessment" to "implementation" to "evaluation."

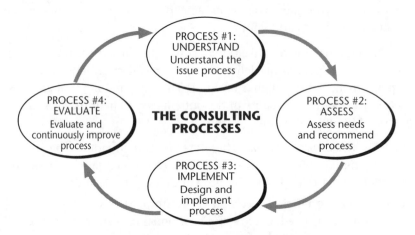

Figure 5.1: The Consulting Processes

Although the four processes of organizational consulting are presented in sequential order, the client and the HR professional may determine to proceed in any order. For example, in some cases there is no need for an elaborate "assessment" process. Rather, the understanding (Process #1) alone may be sufficient to determine what needs to be done. Therefore, they may choose to skip directly to implementation (Process #3). In other cases, the understanding process may identify that the need is to evaluate a previous intervention. If so, the HR professional and client would proceed directly to evaluation (Process #4). In most cases though, the HR professional begins with Process #1, so the organizational consulting intervention can be understood and defined with the client in a clear and precise manner.

At the conclusion of each of the four processes, the client and the HR professional have the opportunity to identify whether they are satisfied with the achievements of that process. At that time, they can determine whether to proceed further with the organizational challenge they are facing.

The Four Processes: Understanding, Assessment, Implementation, and Evaluation

The four processes in organizational consulting are described in detail below. After the description of each stage, the process is applied to a case example.[4]

> The case begins with the appointment of a new director, John, to a regional sales management team. While the "grapevine" has provided information that John is a very bright, aggressive, and skilled individual with excellent interpersonal skills and management experience, it has also revealed that he has no experience in sales. Because of his lack of sales experience, employees have the feeling he was "parachuted in" over the more appropriate potential candidates.
>
> John is joining a group in which sales are down in all product lines and even the last customer service survey showed a decline in customer appreciation. Conflict is passive, not overt. Sales manager meetings are lackluster and unproductive. John has tried to engage in problem identification and resolution discussions with his team. These efforts have been met with little enthusiasm or real commitment. Individual and team meetings to identify the issues and resolve them have produced little improvement. The region seems to be in a tailspin that John cannot control, so he decides to meet with an HR professional to discuss his dilemma.

---

[4] The case example was developed by Richard Dubuc of Geller, Shedletsky & Weiss, 1998.

- *Organizational Consulting Process # 1—Understand The Issue*

  If this process is accomplished satisfactorily, the client will understand the problem completely and will be able to determine an appropriate direction. The direction might be that further assessment is necessary, that something needs to be implemented, or that a continuous improvement intervention should take place. The process flow chart (shown in Figure 5.2) begins with the source of the problem.

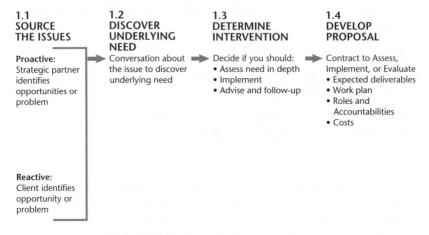

Figure 5.2: Understand the Issue Process

Sometimes HR professionals are able to identify problems even before they are evident to their clients. At other times, the problem is identified by the client. In either situation, the HR professional attempts to discover the underlying need and to determine the appropriate intervention. In some cases, there may be a need for a mini-assessment to understand the problem.

In the process of establishing client expectations, the HR professional and the client need to be totally candid in discussing the problems that may occur and in determining a realistic timeframe for the new changes to be implemented. Then they need to negotiate the expectations with each other. In the negotiations, the HR professional must ensure that the client's expectations are realistic and that it is within their capacity to deliver that service.

To document expectations the HR professional develops a proposal concerning the course of action to take. The proposal to the client usually summarizes the HR professional's understanding of the situation and is written in a brief one- to two-page letter format.

It usually includes the following elements:
- understanding the expected deliverables of the intervention and the metrics for evaluating success
- the work plan—i.e., what, by when, by whom
- roles and responsibilities for the HR professional, the client, and others
- fees and expenses associated with the assignment

The timing of the initiative and its pacing should be designed with an understanding of how much the clients and their employees can absorb at any given time. The pacing of the initiative should also consider the business pressures required to implement the changes in order for the company to achieve its strategic objectives.

In the case example, the HR professional meets with John. They have a conversation in which John describes the situation. They clarify that John wants the team to be working together and focused on common goals. They decide to engage in a series of interviews with the team members to discover what they believe is the problem. After the meeting, John feels somewhat relieved that someone is trying to help and he is not alone with this problem anymore.

Shortly after their meeting, John receives a one-page e-mail from the HR professional specifying what they agreed he will do. The HR professional will orient John's team to the process at one of John's team meetings. The HR professional will conduct the interviews over the next two weeks and report back to John shortly afterwards. They decide to proceed with the assessment process.

- *Organizational Consulting Process # 2—Assess and Recommend*

In many consulting situations, HR professionals will need to explore the issues further than the initial "understanding" meeting. A more detailed assessment will be required to determine the course of action. Figure 5.3 shows how the HR professional works with the client to identify the outcomes desired, compare the outcomes to the current situation, collect data, and then develop recommendations with the client of how to proceed. If this process is completed satisfactorily, the HR professional will undertake a precise analysis and it is probable that an intervention will be identified.

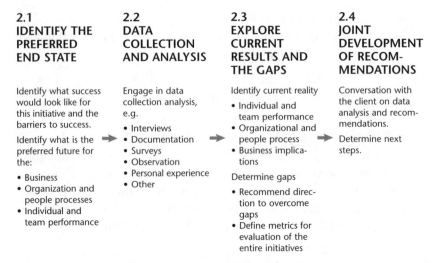

2.1 IDENTIFY THE PREFERRED END STATE	2.2 DATA COLLECTION AND ANALYSIS	2.3 EXPLORE CURRENT RESULTS AND THE GAPS	2.4 JOINT DEVELOPMENT OF RECOM-MENDATIONS
Identify what success would look like for this initiative and the barriers to success. Identify what is the preferred future for the: • Business • Organization and people processes • Individual and team performance	Engage in data collection analysis, e.g. • Interviews • Documentation • Surveys • Observation • Personal experience • Other	Identify current reality • Individual and team performance • Organizational and people process • Business implications Determine gaps • Recommend direction to overcome gaps • Define metrics for evaluation of the entire initiatives	Conversation with the client on data analysis and recom-mendations. Determine next steps.

Figure 5.3: Assess and Recommend Process

This process has the potential of being very expensive. There-fore, the astute HR professional will analyze the extent to which detail needs to be collected and tested. In some cases, especially where there is a desire to dispense with the current method of operating, it may be less important to do a detailed assessment.

After the data is collected, the HR professional develops joint recommendations with the client to explain the meaning of the data, and together they identify the directions to take. In many cases, they develop an implementation plan. In some cases, though, they may realize that the direction that is needed is different from the one they originally anticipated.

In the case example, both John and the HR professional participate in the orientation meeting. The team members are not very excit-ed about the interview process, but they agree to proceed after they are convinced that individual information will be kept confi-dential and only aggregate information will be reported back to John and the team. In this case, the sales managers are comfortable with the HR professional as the interviewer. (In other situations, an external consultant would be useful to identify the issues through the interviews and to prepare the aggregate report.)

During the interviews people do open up to the HR profes-sional. They discuss their preferred way of working and compare it to the way they are working now. They also consider what needs to be done to improve overall team performance. As the interviews are proceeding, it becomes evident that the interviews themselves are having a positive effect. People are feeling good about being interviewed and discussing their issues. They are also beginning to implement independently some of the ideas they suggest in the interviews. Although the changes are nominal, it is a development in a positive direction.

After completing all the interviews, the HR professional prepares a summary report of the aggregate data and meets with John. Together they identify that the most important issue for this team is that it has suffered through a very difficult time with their previous leader. The former leader was aggressive and in some cases people felt he was abusive. They are still suffering from that experience now. Most of the people feel that it is odd that John was appointed the leader of the team without extensive sales experience, but they are willing to give him a chance. Their bigger issue is getting over their previous boss.

John and the HR professional discuss how they will proceed. They agree that this team needs a safe place to have a meaningful conversation about what has happened and start to leave the past behind. They also need to specify their requirements from John in order to succeed in the future. They decide to plan an off-site session devoted to those issues.

- *Organizational Consulting Process # 3—Design and Implement*

The implementation process is where the real value from organizational consulting occurs. An effective assessment of the situation will be helpful, but it does not create meaningful change. The HR professional needs to carry the assignment through the implementation process to evaluation to insure that the problem is resolved.

This process requires HR professionals to have specific competencies in design, communications, and facilitation. Not all HR professionals can be expected to have all those skills. Therefore, many HR professionals have operated as organizational consultants with external experts who help them at different parts of the process. Astute HR professionals continue to play some role in the process even if an external consultant is used. They can maintain their profile and relationship with the client and the employees even when someone else is doing all the detail and analytical work.

If this process is completed satisfactorily, the client is assured that the intervention will proceed as assessed and that it will have a high probability of resolving the identified problem. The process (shown in Figure 5.4) involves designing the implementation and developing the communications plan. It includes communicating to and engaging others. It also implies that implementing the intervention will be done in the simplest manner. "Quick hits" that can be done immediately are identified and implemented to create momentum for change. The more elaborate aspects of the implementation are rolled out to the business so that it becomes the normal way of doing business on a daily basis.

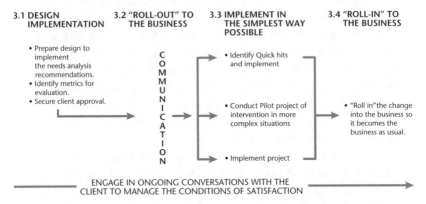

Figure 5.4: Design and Implement Process

In the case example, John and the HR consultant design the intervention with the team. They plan the off-site event and decide to build the session around the aggregate report they prepared. They also introduce some time in the schedule for people to get to know John better and to express their needs of him as a leader. The session proceeds as planned. The aggregate report functions as a conversation starter for the team to legitimize talking about sensitive issues. They do discuss the issues they had with the previous boss and how they would like to see John lead. By the end of the session, they agree to implement more of a professional team approach, and they set team targets for their performance. They also agree to meet every two weeks to discuss how they are proceeding and continually improve their working relationships.

- *Organizational Consulting Process # 4—Evaluate and Continually Improve*

Both the HR professional and the client often skip this process (shown in Figure 5.5) because of the pressure to proceed to the next initiative after implementation. If this process is performed satisfactorily, the benefits of the intervention will continue to be evident, and intervention shortcomings will be identified and resolved. In addition, the initiative will result in shared learning for the business so that others will be able to respond to future problems with less assistance from the HR professional.

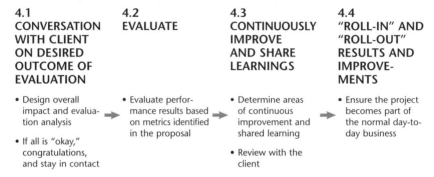

4.1 CONVERSATION WITH CLIENT ON DESIRED OUTCOME OF EVALUATION	4.2 EVALUATE	4.3 CONTINUOUSLY IMPROVE AND SHARE LEARNINGS	4.4 "ROLL-IN" AND "ROLL-OUT" RESULTS AND IMPROVE-MENTS
• Design overall impact and evaluation analysis • If all is "okay," congratulations, and stay in contact	• Evaluate performance results based on metrics identified in the proposal	• Determine areas of continuous improvement and shared learning • Review with the client	• Ensure the project becomes part of the normal day-to-day business

Figure 5.5: Evaluate and Continuous Improvement

In the case example, John and the HR professional meet after the session and discuss the progress they achieved on this initiative. They recognize that it was a good start, but more work is needed for this team. They agree to re-visit the situation formally in six months. At that time they will conduct informal interviews again and meet with the group to discuss their progress. It will also be an opportunity to celebrate the successes they may have.

It is important to note that the case example that is used describes the situation as if the HR professional assessed and implemented the intervention. Although that is the way this case proceeds, it may not be the wisest way to assess, implement, and evaluate the assignment. Sometimes the HR professional does not have the competencies and/or credibility to facilitate the assignment. An external service provider with skills in assessment, design, communications, facilitation, and evaluation may be needed. At other times the HR professional will not have the time to conduct the processes single-handedly. As a result, they often develop relationships with external resources that work with them and the client to perform the assignment. However, even if the HR professional uses external consulting assistance, the HR professional would be wise to at least participate in the off-site session with this team to further his or her alliance with John and to show support for the team.

Even with the most effective consulting intervention, something can go wrong. Often, the HR professional will not even know what happened. The following are ten tips to enhance the likelihood of organizational consulting success.

Ten Tips to Enhance Organizational Consulting Success

1. Find a "shadow consultant" internally or externally to talk through the assignments behind the scenes.

2. Build a network of external consultants to call upon as the need arises.

3. Be diligent in writing proposal letters and review them regularly before meeting with clients.

4. Know the pressure points for the client and tread carefully.

5. Be very well prepared for clients at all times.

6. Suffer fools gladly—they have more influence than you may think.

7. Always meet commitments and time lines.

8. Have a unique database but share it willingly.

9. Choose your timing and manage your impulse control.

10. Use organizational consulting experiences as an opportunity to learn and share learning.

A Final Note on Organizational Value-Add Processes

The organizational value-add processes of technology, learning and organizational consulting do not cover all the possible organizational ways that HR professionals can add value to their clients. However, HR will be expected to develop excellence and deliver effectively in these three very important areas. If they do this, the clients will have received enhanced value to enable their businesses to perform effectively and efficiently.

These three areas will also be essential foundation pieces for the HR business transformation processes described in the next four chapters. Each of these processes will require excellent technology platforms, will benefit from a life-long learning work environment, and will be based on an assumption that the HR professional is competent in organizational consulting. In addition, as HR professionals are able to manage the organizational processes described in this chapter, HR will develop the credibility necessary to expand to more strategic areas of value creation for the company.

Summary

- The organizational value-add work that is done by HR has broad impact on the entire workforce.

- HR can enable the overall organization to deliver value to the business through its organizational work—in technology, learning, and organizational consulting.

- Many companies used the problem of re-coding their information technology architecture to be Year 2000 compatible as an opportunity to abandon the old technology and invest in a new and more flexible system. Benefits of the introduction of new technology are:
  - Employee access and modifying the central database
  - Enhancing core people process
  - Compensation and bonuses
  - HR financial management and reporting
  - Aligning HR systems with other databases in the company

- Some of the creative ways HR will be able to add value to employees through technological services are as follows:
  - As employee career agents
  - As packagers of content
  - As vendor relations representatives
  - As builders of virtual communities

- If technology fulfills the promise of its potential, it is likely that HR technology will be elevated to a business transformation strategic process within three to five years' time. When that occurs, HR will have another important reason to be discussing issues at the executive table with the senior executive team.

- Seven principles emerge for companies wanting to transform the "core" training and development to create an "added value" continuous learning environment:

  1. The primary purpose of training is to teach people how to self-learn and not to teach content.

  2. Managers are accountable for creating an ongoing learning environment.

  3. All employees are accountable for their own learning.

4. All employees are able to teach as well as learn.

5. Learning occurs "just-in-time" when and how it is needed

6. Continuous feedback techniques are used to measure the effectiveness of ongoing learning

7 The entire organization shares what has been learned.

- HR professionals are expected to work with internal clients in three different consulting interventions: organizational consulting, technical counsel, and by being "walking-talking" consultants.

- The organizational consulting process can be divided into four processes: Understand the Issue, Assess and Recommend, Design and Implement, Evaluate and Continually Improve.

PART THREE

Strategic
Business
Processes

Business Transformation: An Overview

HR professionals are recognizing that to thrive in today's business environment they must develop a new role, one that focuses on the company's strategic direction and develops new ways to help transform the business. The challenge is to find the right way to proceed.

Part One of this book established that HR should focus on 1) delivering value to the external customer and 2) abandoning specific work in order to concentrate on the new strategic business process outcomes. By shedding some of the traditional "core" responsibilities, HR will be free to focus on strategic business processes that contribute significantly to the company's competitive advantage. Part Two described the people and organizational processes that HR needs to execute in order to support the ongoing work of the company.

Part Three explores in detail some emerging HR roles that can provide the strategic advantage the company needs to succeed. These roles are in areas that are uniquely suited to Human Resources. Two major benefits will occur when HR shifts its emphasis to these new roles: (1) HR's opportunity to help the company achieve competitive advantage is increased and (2) HR can enhance its value to the customer.

Each of the four strategic business processes described in Part Three contributes to business transformation. The strategic business processes reduce or remove risks that may limit the company from implementing its strategy. It also creates the opportunities that need to be realized to fulfill the strategy. Executives understand risk reduction and the loss associated with missed opportunities. They also appreciate that as the company changes these risks and opportunities need to be addressed professionally.

Business Transformation Risks and Opportunities

Figure 6.1 depicts what may occur when executives commit to a company vision and strategic direction. In the creative process required to produce a comprehensive vision, the executives are encouraged to apply certain assumptions that may not be true but will be helpful to the process. Of the many assumptions they make, several relate specifically to people and organizations.

After the executives identify a company vision, HR must devote its efforts to reducing the risks and capitalizing on the opportunities associated with the people and organizational assumptions. It is these risks and opportunities that are elevated to a strategic business process level for HR. They are also the risks and opportunities that capture the attention of executives because they mitigate some assumptions they made in the creation of the company vision.

Figure 6.1 shows four of the major people and organizational process assumptions senior executives often make (either explicitly or implicitly) as they define the company's vision of its preferred future.

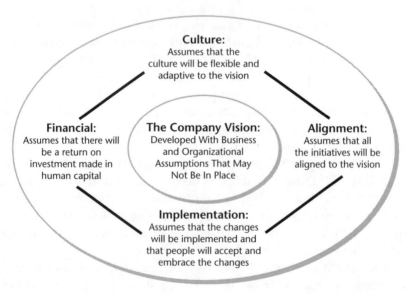

Figure 6.1: The Vision Assumes That Business Transformation Will Occur

The next four chapters explore four strategic business process outcomes that provide opportunities for business transformation. By reducing the risks and capitalizing on the opportunities associated with these four process outcomes, HR enables the business vision to become a reality. Other strategic risks and assumptions may exist that are both related to the HR area and other areas within the company. However, these four provide great value to the company and capture the attention of executives. They are also directly related to the contribution that HR professionals are able to offer. The four strategic business process outcomes are:

1. *Cultivate a Flexible Culture (Chapter 7):* The need for a flexible culture is most evident during dramatic transitions such as when companies downsize, merge, acquire other companies, and grow. During times like these, companies must be ready to implement changes with speed and consistency. This strategic business process outcome was identified in the growth curve discussion (Chapter One) as essential in Phase Two when a company attempts to avoid the trappings of success, and in Phase Three when the company seeks to revitalize. Executives often assume that the culture is robust and will flex to the challenge of the vision. In most companies though, that is a false assumption. HR can apply its expertise to cultivate the work environment so that the culture will be flexible to the company vision and its strategic direction.

2. *Champion Strategic Alignment (Chapter 8):* Strategic alignment is essential to insure that all initiatives throughout the business and organization support the company's strategic direction and provide value to the external customer. Executives assume that strategic alignment will take place when they create a vision and that the executive team will be able to insure this occurs. However, in many cases, this is not what happens. HR has access to all the people and the leadership to champion alignment of initiatives throughout the company. Of course, HR also aligns its own practices and initiatives with the company's strategic direction.

3. *Implement Change and Transition (Chapter 9):* Executives often assume that if they "will" a change to occur, then it will happen. Unfortunately, many executives have learned too late that there are limits to their power to make things happen. Many executives now look to HR to become a catalyst and an influencer to insure that the required changes actually occur. Implementation of change requires people to accept and deliver a new direction. HR has the capability to influence and enable the transition of people and the organization to embrace and implement the new changes.

4. ***Insure a Return on Investment in Human Capital (Chapter 10):***
Human Resources initiatives are often a concern of executives
because of the associated costs. Many executives would love to see
the cost of human capital reduced as much as possible. However,
the dramatic cost cutting of human capital in the first half of the
1990s has depleted companies and left a legacy of mistrust and
overworked employees. The time is ripe for a change in the assumption concerning human capital. This shift implies viewing human
capital as an investment that can appreciate in value and provide a
meaningful return on investment. HR can influence this shift by
doing the following:

- – Determine the return on investment in human capital by providing
labor costs and productivity analyses.

- – Contribute to the annual business planning process and the
development of the company strategy.

- – Apply HR's expertise to insure that the investment in human capital
is spent wisely.

Core People and Organizational Processes Can Become Strategic

In addition to the four potential business transformations described in
the next four chapters, on occasion, some of the core people processes
and/or the organizational processes can become strategic for the company. For example, many high-tech companies are viewing the resource
base of software engineers as a strategic issue. The competition for these
people is intense. In one company, the HR vice president has recognized
the need to delay some efforts in culture building to re-focus efforts on
recruitment of this scarce resource. She has realized that the company
needs people with special skills, which will require her to focus all of her
efforts on achieving those ends. Her remaining resources are focused on
retention of these employees once they join the company. Cultivating
a flexible culture will have to wait until the resource crisis is over.

In a discussion with this vice president, it became evident that
because the core people process was elevated to a strategic level, every
effort in that company is being devoted to changing that situation. She
anticipates that the need for the software engineers will be addressed
eventually through the education system, through internal training within companies, and through the development of external service providers

who fill the resource gap until the resources are available at a reasonable supply. After the supply of software engineers becomes more normal, the requirement to resource and retain people with these competencies will return to its traditional place as a core people process that is not strategic.

For other companies, the technology investment may become strategic and not simply an organizational value-add process. The cost associated with the new technology may be very high, but it also may be essential to enable the company to implement new ways for employees to work with customers and to work with their colleagues. However, once the implementation is completed to a certain threshold, the technology initiative will once again revert to its place as an organizational value-add process.

Choosing the Priority Business Transformation

Although the four strategic business processes are of great value to companies, most HR leaders choose one or two areas in which they will excel because it is very difficult for them to be excellent in all areas. They identify the most urgent assumptions that need to be addressed and then focus the business transformation on those areas. For example, some companies have very flexible cultures already. They operate in a fluid environment in which people are willing to embrace new changes. However, as they move quickly to the next challenge, they may not be aligning their activities with others in the company. They waste effort by re-creating the work that was done elsewhere. If HR is alert to the possibility of this situation occurring, they can apply the appropriate business transformation process, which in this case would be alignment.

In other companies, executives are truly not worried about the cost of labor and the associated return on investment. These companies often have very high margins, which are built into their cost structure. For example, many pharmaceutical companies that research and develop new patent drugs are less concerned about the cost of labor. As the patent holder of specific drugs, they can charge high rates to recover their research investment. Cost of labor is a small part of that overall infrastructure. On the other hand, generic pharmaceutical firms that compete intensely for market share for their drugs operate with low margins and push volume as the way to generate shareholder value. Executives in these companies may view the investment in human capital as very strategic and of great importance to the profitability of the company. However, they may not be as concerned with culture, alignment, or implementing change.

HR needs to choose the business transformation that is of special importance to the company. All other strategic business processes can be put aside or developed to a level of proficiency (rather than excellence) until it becomes evident that other business processes are required in order to maintain the company's competitive advantage.

Match the Choice of Business Transformation to the Competitive Context

At any phase of development on the growth curve (described in Chapter One), the company looks at its relative position against its competition. There are four positions that companies can have. They can be *ahead* of the pack, *competitive* with other companies, attempting to *catch-up* to the competition, or in a *survival* mode. In each competitive context, the resistance to invest in HR-related strategic business processes will vary and so will the choice by HR of the strategic business process on which to focus. The following describes some areas of resistance in each competitive context and the potential strategies that HR may choose for that situation.

- *Ahead of the competition:* Sometimes executives are not as concerned about HR-related business transformation when they are far ahead of the competition. They do not feel the urgency to pay attention to people and organizational issues. In these cases, HR may be successful by focusing on cultivating a flexible culture. If the company is successful and has expendable funds, they may be more open to re-investing in developing a more flexible culture. The return on investment can be very high especially for the Phase Two growth company because it will help them stay ahead of the competition and remain successful.

- *Competitive with the competition:* In some situations, the executives are so focused on external competitiveness that they only concentrate on how the business can stay with the competition or get ahead of it. The people and organizational aspects are internal issues that do not receive executive attention. Attempts by HR to deliver strategic value will often be dependent on the HR vice president's ability to communicate a competitive business orientation. If the VP does not have a focus on competitiveness, the resistance to HR playing a role in strategic business processes may be high. In these cases, HR's greatest success may be in focusing on the alignment of all initiatives to a common direction. In highly competitive environments, all efforts must be focused on a common goal and the same end state. Alignment will help achieve that focus.

- *Catch-up with the competition:* For each company that is ahead of the competition there are multiple companies trying to catch-up to the leader in the industry. For the executives in the "catch-up" companies, strategy is expanded from providing "competitive advantage" to achieving "competitive parity" with the leader. The challenge to "catch-up" can be all consuming. The executives are fearful of the abyss that awaits them if they fall too far behind. Some of them are concerned about their own careers if the company's performance can be attributed to their leadership. These compelling issues may cause the executives to underestimate the strategic contribution that HR can make. They may not recognize that HR will be able to focus on implementing change and transition quickly and repeatedly. The company needs the changes to occur. HR can help make that happen to enable the company to have a better chance of catching-up to the competition.

- *Struggling for survival:* At any phase of the growth curve, a company can enter into a struggle for survival. The company may not find the growth formula in start-up Phase One, they may be faced with new forms of technology that replace their growth formula in Phase Two, or they can be a mature Phase Three company that needs to transform in order to survive. As the company struggles to survive, many executives do not think about HR-related business transformations. They only focus on survival and the protection of the company. In these cases, HR can concentrate on the bottom line and determine the return on investment in human capital. Companies in this survival mode will need to justify every dollar spent, and a return will be necessary for it to continue. Also, as the company will have to transform in order to survive, information on the return on investment in human capital will be one guide to help it make the wisest strategic business decisions.

In each of these competitive positions, HR leaders need to identify the company's major strategic issues. They then focus their business transformation efforts on the single most pressing issue that will enable the strategy to occur. As long as the business transformation strategy moves the company ahead, there will likely be support for it. However, if the business transformation pushes the company too far ahead of itself, then there may be resistance to those kinds of efforts.

For example, in a manufacturing company that was in a "catch-up" competitive position, the Vice President of HR was very committed to transforming his training department into a learning organization. He positioned the learning organization as a distinct business advantage that the company should pursue. He was able to influence the company executives that his direction was the correct one.

However, as the new initiative was introduced, the reaction from the workforce was negative. The timing of the announcement was apparently off. Managers expressed concern about the lack of resources to implement the current business strategy. They were also concerned about improving the technology in the plant, enhancing quality, and delivering better results. They believed there were more important needs than a long range investment in the creation of a learning organization.

Although this strategy is appropriate in some work environments, it apparently did not fit this one. The strategy was perceived as too far ahead of what was needed. Eventually the approach was pursued in a much more low-key fashion and other more fundamental activities were undertaken similar to what the managers requested.

In some cases the competitive position creates a situation in which the executives do not know what strategy to employ. In these cases, HR leaders can focus attention on helping the executives develop the strategy. They often have access to strategy consultants who can facilitate such a process. They can influence the executives to spend time on developing the strategy so they can align around a common direction to gain or re-gain a better competitive position relative to the competition.

When HR develops excellence in one or more of the strategic business process outcomes and is able to use this capability to help the company meet strategic goals, it can become a vital cog in the delivery of the strategy for the company. HR then has a chance to finally win its coveted seat at the executive table and to have its opinions heard and valued. Without the delivery of at least one of these business transformations that remove risks and/or create opportunities, HR will be correctly perceived as a support function that is necessary but not strategic.

HR Professionals Must Be Strategic Partners to Deliver Business Transformation

Strategic partnerships have been discussed before in this book. In Chapter Two, the role of a strategic partner was explained as an essential role for HR professionals when they work with executives as an HR business within a business. For business transformation to occur, HR professionals must also operate at a strategic partnership level for several reasons. These include:

- Strategic partners are part of the formulation of strategy. This role will help the HR leader and the executives choose the most appropriate strategic business process on which to focus.

- Strategic partners have the relationships to secure commitment from their executive colleagues as the business transformation proceeds. A high level of executive commitment to the strategic business processes is important to their achievement.

- Strategic partners have ongoing access and relationships with executive team members. This access and relationship will enable them to notice early warning signals of when the strategic business process is veering off course. They can make adjustments to the business transformation sooner and increase the likelihood of its successful implementation.

The organizational consulting interventions described in Chapter Five differ somewhat from the strategic partner relationship. Essentially, being a strategic partner is an advanced level of a consulting relationship. All strategic partners need to have strong competency in consulting; however, most HR professionals who are engaged in consulting are not working as strategic partners. Some distinctions include the following:

- The strategic partner is invited into conversations with their partner clients even before there is a problem. They are part of the senior management strategic planning and thinking meetings. On the other hand, most HR professionals, when they act as consultants, are invited in when there is a problem of some kind after the strategy has been set.

- The focus of strategic partner conversations is on how to give the business relative advantage against the competition or at least to achieve competitive parity. These conversations often extend beyond the people and organizational process domain typically reserved for HR professionals. The HR professional, on the other hand, often focuses on the organizational value-add that they provide as it relates to people and organizational process interventions and solutions.

- The strategic partner relationship is characterized by a situation in which the client wants to see and support the HR professional as much as the HR professional wants to see and support them. They are partners in the true sense of the word. As consultants, HR professionals often want to see and support the client more than the client wants to see and support them.

As strategic partners, HR professionals need to be integrated with the company's strategy. They need to have the cognitive capability to think strategically with executives and have the desire to operate at that level. They also need to think first about the company and the customer and only afterwards consider the implications for the way that HR can deliver value to the company and the customer. They must be focusing their efforts on the external customer just as the rest of their executives must be thinking about the customer as well.

With the right HR strategic leader and HR team in place, and with an astute understanding of the right strategic business process on which to choose to focus, HR can elevate itself to the strategic position it will deserve. HR will not be asking to be part of the executive as a favor, but instead it will be welcomed as an important part of the executive team.

Two Contrasting Examples of HR's Potential Role in Business Transformation

To illustrate how important HR can be to a company's success when it is involved in business transformation, this section will contrast two companies. (These examples will be referred to several times in Part Three of this book.) In the first example, the need for HR's participation in business transformation is not appreciated, and HR is absent from the change process. By contrast, the second example describes what happens when HR is valued as a vital part of the change process resulting in HR professionals helping the business transform to one that is adaptable enough to adjust to change. The examples describe two companies in the throes of mergers.

Example #1: A multi-national financial services company aggressively pursues acquisitions of related financial institutions. The due diligence process for this particular acquisition is very detailed.

However, the senior executive does not include HR in this process and does not explore culture variables, leadership issues, and the cost of labor of the company to be acquired. After the acquisition, the senior executive concentrates on the next purchase rather than on the integration of the two companies. He sets up a mid-level management team headed by a senior manager, who champions the takeover. The team encounters intense resistance from both the purchasing company and the acquired company.

One reason that the acquisition is not completely successful is that the cultures of the two companies clash repeatedly over their different approaches to people. The acquiring company is very results-oriented and not sensitive to employee needs. The purchased company is very people-focused. The culture clash was not anticipated and is not dealt with effectively, which reduces the overall benefits from the merger.

The benefits of the acquisition look good on paper but do not come to fruition. Eventually, after most of the senior executives of the acquired company are laid off and portions of the acquired company are sold, the remaining sectors are reorganized into the existing company. The customers, shareholders, and employees voice their displeasure with the way the company handled the merger. The leaders, in the privacy of their boardroom, deem the acquisition to have been unsuccessful.

Example # 2: Another company is also expanding through acquisitions. HR has been participating in designing, creating, and implementing a flexible culture. This culture must be able to introduce changes in the company and absorb other cultures and business environments immediately and with minimal disruption. This will allow the company to acquire other companies with confidence and to show the benefits quickly.

This company is now in the process of acquiring a major competitor. The executive team driving the purchase recognizes a major risk in the acquisition. The company may not be able to retain the benefits of both the newly acquired competitor and the original company. The president forms a cross-functional, senior-level, due-diligence team. Included on the team is the HR vice president, who is held accountable for three recommendations, 1) an audit of the cost of labor, 2) a characterization of the leadership style, and 3) a description of the culture and values of the company to be acquired.

The cost of labor analysis identifies that the company to be acquired has a lower labor cost than their own company. This analysis leads to the recommendation that some of the work can be moved from the purchasing company to the company to be acquired because the work can be done at a better return on investment. They also identify that the two companies have differences in leadership style and culture.

In a strategy meeting with the president, the HR vice president describes the implications of the culture and leadership differences between the two companies. He explains that the ticket to failure is to ignore the culture issue and let the culture evolve without any direction to merge or not to merge. He suggests three alternative approaches to address the culture clashes with the new company (referred to as "Newco"). These are:

1. *Design the "Newco" organization so that the two cultures do not merge:* This approach can be effective for acquisitions of distinct territories, products, or sevices. In this approach, they avoid the potential of a culture clash, and they maintain two independent businesses perhaps with merged organizational support functions. They recognize that this approach removes the possibility of integrating the best practices of the two companies and will limit the benefits they can reap from the acquisition.

2. *Take-over the acquired company and dictate the new way that they will be operating:* This approach can be effective when the acquisition is for reasons other than the purchase of the people asset. Although this approach is quick and clear, it may alienate many in the acquired company. It does have the advantage of avoiding the endless debates about whose policy to choose on sensitive matters such as compensation and benefits. It also reflects the reality for most acquired companies when an acquisition takes place.

3. *Integrate the best practices of the two companies:* In this scenario, the "Newco" attempts to leverage the people asset and integrate the best practices of the two companies. This approach has the greatest potential to help people adapt, appreciate diversity, be ready to absorb other new cultures, enhance shareholder value, and give greater return on investment. However, it may take more time than a clear take-over and has a higher failure rate. Also, the integration approach will lose credibility quickly if the selection of the best practices is all one-sided to the benefit of the acquiring company. People will become discouraged and feel deceived that the "integration" approach was really a ruse to lull employees of the acquired company into a false sense of security, while the acquiring company actually proceeded with a take-over in the disguise of an integration. If that is the acquiring company's plan, it would be smarter to simply declare that it will be a take-over and deal with the implications for the people immediately.

A key factor in integrating the two companies successfully is to realize that two fixed cultures do not easily converge into a third culture. Each company's resistance to giving up its former culture may become a matter of pride, and the resistance can create overwhelming "noise" in the system. The preferable approach is to respect the diversity of both cultures and make them more flexible so that the employees in the two companies become more accepting of each other. This approach will increase the probability that the work environment will embrace change and absorb new innovations with greater ease and speed.

The purchasing company's president acknowledges that a primary reason for the acquisition is to acquire the people asset of the competitor. As a result of the consultation with the HR vice president, he decides and then publicly announces that although his company acquired the competitor, it will approach the merger as an integration of the best practices of both companies. He also says he will give as much emphasis to the integration of the two companies as he gave to the decision to purchase the acquired company. He sets up an integration process that is based on the following:

- *Formation of an executive steering committee:* The steering committee consists of the senior executives of both the purchasing and the acquired companies. They define the strategic objectives of the newly integrated company. The president is the executive sponsor for the integration. He establishes a three-month timeline in which to complete the integration analysis and to form Newco. The executives make no organizational changes for the two companies during a three-month transition period. After the transition period, the president of the purchasing company selects the executives and the senior managers of the new company.

- *Creation of an integration project team:* The executives form an integration project team consisting of the 30 most talented people from both companies. They select the project leader who will have an important leadership role in Newco. The team is given two key accountabilities: 1) to recommend the best practices from each company that will form the basis of Newco, and 2) to identify the "quick hits" they can implement that will give almost immediate return on investment for the integrated Newco.

  The selection of the 30 key resources for the integration project team is led by the HR vice president and is done very carefully and quickly. Fifteen people from each company are selected. These people are guaranteed a role in Newco, and they are released from the responsibilities of their regular jobs for the three-month transition. The 30 key resources who are selected are both honored (because of the task force's strategic importance) and relieved (because of the increased job security) to be selected for the integration project team. During their planning time, the 30 employees are divided into task forces in which they design the work and the process outcomes to make the integrated company successful.

- *Constant communications to keep employees of both companies informed about the integration:* Multiple communication vehicles are used to reach employees of both the purchasing and acquired companies. Voice mail communications to all employees occur every week at the same time whether or not there is something major to communicate. Town hall meetings, in which any question can be asked and answered, occur every two weeks. The regularity of communication helps stabilize the turbulent environment. It also demonstrates a willingness to keep people informed directly and to listen attentively to employee questions and concerns in a time of change.

One responsibility of the integration project leader and the project team is to focus on the organizational and people process outcomes of Newco. The task force is aware of a concern that the two cultures may not integrate and that even if they do it may take too long for the investment to be worthwhile. They decide to reduce the risk and increase the likelihood that the integration will be successful by placing a strong emphasis on developing shared values and designing the rewards system to support the integration of the two companies.

Through joint planning and decision making, the executive steering committee, the integration project team and the HR professionals help cultivate a flexible culture and an aligned leadership. Their collaborative approach helps them survive the selection process of the new executive team (even though some executives from both companies do not retain their positions in the new integrated company). The performance of the HR professionals is deemed to be a critical factor in the success of the integrated company.

The Next Four Chapters

The next four chapters clarify four of the choices for business transformation on which leaders can focus. The HR leadership and their colleagues on the executive team determine the best strategic business process or processes to choose. However, in most companies at least one or two strategic business processes will enable the company to succeed and are within HR's competency areas. If there is an openness to proceed with the strategic business process, then the HR leadership will have the opportunity to provide strategic value and help the business gain competitive advantage.

Summary

- HR professionals are recognizing that to thrive in today's business environment, they must develop a new role, one that focuses on the company's strategic direction and develops new ways to help transform the business. The challenge is to find the right way to proceed.

- In the creative process required to produce a comprehensive vision, the executives are encouraged to apply certain assumptions that may not be true but will be helpful to the process. Of the many assumptions they make, several relate specifically to people and organizations.

- The need for a flexible culture is most evident during dramatic transitions such as when companies downsize, merge, acquire other companies, and grow.

- Strategic alignment is essential to insure that all initiatives throughout the business and organization support the company's strategic direction and provides value to the external customer. Executives determine that this assumption will take place when they create a vision and that the executive team will be able to insure that this occurs. However, in many cases, this is not what happens.

- Executives often assume that if they "will" a change to occur, then it will happen. Unfortunately, many executives have found out too late that there are limits to their power to make things happen. Many executives now look to HR to become a catalyst and an influencer to insure that the required changes actually occur.

- The time is ripe for a change in the assumption concerning human capital. This shift implies viewing human capital as an investment that can appreciate in value and provide a meaningful return on investment.

- In addition to the four potential business transformations described in the next four chapters, on occasion, some of the core people processes and/or the organizational processes can become strategic for the company.

- Although the four strategic business processes are of great value to companies, most HR leaders have chosen one or two areas in which they will excel. It appears that it is very difficult to be excellent in all areas within HR.

- HR needs to choose the business transformation process that is of special importance to the company. All other strategic business processes can be put aside or developed to a level of proficiency (rather than excellence) until it becomes evident that it requires further attention to provide the company with its competitive advantage.

- As HR considers which business transformation strategy they will focus on, they need to remember the developmental level of the company. As long as the business transformation moves the company ahead, there will likely be support for it. If the business transformation pushes the company too far ahead of itself, then there may be resistance to those kinds of efforts.

- The HR professionals must operate at a strategic partnership level when they focus on business transformation.

- The next four chapters clarify four of the choices for business transformation on which leaders can focus. The HR leaders, along with their colleagues on the executive, determine the best strategic business process to choose.

CHAPTER SEVEN

ೞ

Cultivate a
Flexible Culture

In today's business environment, it is essential for companies to be able to change direction quickly to meet market demands. Without this capability a company will eventually go the way of the Irish Elk. A flexible culture increases the company's chances of being able to change effectively, quickly, and repeatedly.

The term "flexible culture" is actually an oxymoron. "Culture" is usually associated with what unites people. Being "flexible" implies that the environment has the ability to be adaptable and that people are receptive to change. A flexible culture combines both a unified set of values with a state of readiness for employees to respond to and implement changes.

The image of "cultivating" reflects the care and attention that is needed to bring a flexible culture to life. It takes special handling by the company leadership and the Human Resources professionals to grow and develop the culture so that the context for this kind of business transformation will emerge.

How to Cultivate a Flexible Culture

This chapter will explain how HR professionals can cultivate a flexible culture to bring the desired work environment to fruition. The four primary ways involved in cultivating a flexible culture are the following:

1. *Shared Values:* One effective way to cultivate a flexible culture is to co-create and live shared values with employees. Values identify what is important and what is cared about in the company. The values need to be brought to life so that all employees, from the executives to the front-line workers, can internalize the values and operate and behave with values as their guideposts.

2. *Leadership Dialogue:* The leaders need to be able to dialogue about a flexible culture and explore the meaning of the work. They instill the purpose of work so that employees can make independent and empowered decisions with an understanding of the implications of their decisions.

3. *Organizational Elasticity:* Organizational elasticity refers to an organizational design that can grow or shrink based on the needs of the business. An organization that is elastic is able to stretch and contract like a rubber band. When the rubber band is stretched, the shape changes; however, when the tension is removed, it reverts back to its original form. Company leaders need to foster an elastic organizational design that creates the climate in which employees will be alert and responsive and adapt to the business challenges as they arise.

4. *Rewards and Recognition:* The rewards and recognition in the company need to support and be aligned with the flexible culture. They must be designed to motivate employees to embrace the flexible culture and the desired way of operating.

Create and Live the Shared Values

In most companies the executives develop the values—frequently at off-site meetings and without any participation by employees. Later, when they announce the values to the employees, the executives are often greatly disappointed because the employees are not dumbfounded by the brilliance of the values selected. Employees often say the values resemble those of almost every company they have seen.

Companies can choose another way for developing values—one that will result in employees taking ownership of the values. For example, consider an approach by an executive team that is working to create their company's vision, mission, and values. They find they are able to articulate the vision (of their preferred future) and their mission (the work they do on an ongoing basis in the process of achieving the vision). However, as they reason together about identifying the values, one of the executives asks, "How can we tell employees how to feel?" The values (meaning what needs to be important to each and every employee at work as they strive toward the vision) are a source of controversy among them.

This senior executive team is determined to identify values in a different way so that the workforce will embrace them. They realize that vision and mission can be developed "top-down" but that values must be developed with the participation of all the people who will be asked to live by them. It's not enough for people to "believe it when they see it." A better statement would be, "You'll see it when I believe it." In other words, only after the employees "intrinsically" take ownership and believe in the values and behaviors they choose will the executives begin to see the employees exhibit those values and behaviors at work regularly.

Employee Participation in the Development of Shared Values

Continuing our example, the senior executive team commits to developing meaningful shared values and behavior that they believe will provide competitive advantage. They recognize that the values, in and of themselves, are not that important. The distinguishing variable is the internalization of the values. Basic values that everyone internalizes provide more competitive advantage than inventive values that no one does.

The executive team starts with the premise that those who will share the values must be the ones to develop them. They decide to test the premise on themselves by first identifying the values and behaviors to which they can commit. To do this, they discuss the commitments they will make to each other. They approach the task by asking, "What company values do you want that are consistent with your own personal values?" (Figure 7.1 illustrates the overlap between company and personal values.)

Company-driven values that overlap with personal values are easier to live by. The values the team chooses gravitate to issues of integrity, openness, honesty, achieving full potential, and personal and work-life balance. The team also discusses values that tend to be more to the company's benefit such as customer focus, innovation, teamwork, and simplicity.

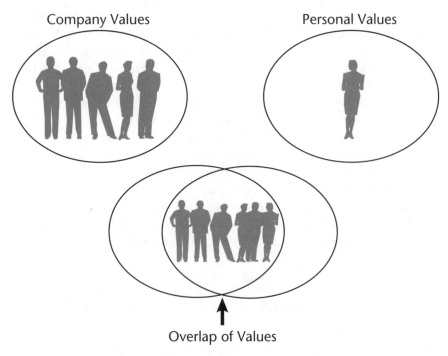

Overlap of Values

Figure 7.1: Identify the Overlap of Values

They choose a short list of values to which they all feel they can commit. They believe they will have no difficulty being accountable for these values because they live them all the time anyway. They write the values on a flip chart and then celebrate by signing the chart. They decide to laminate the chart, and it hangs on the president's office wall in its handwritten form. The chart is brought to executive strategy meetings as a symbol of the commitments they made to each other. It is also used as part of the orientation process for any person who joins the executive team at a later time.

The executive team decides not to unveil the commitments they made to each other with the typical fanfare and hoopla. They do not hide it, but they do not flaunt it either. Instead, they realize that they feel so good about the values they developed that they want all employees to feel the same level of commitment and ownership as well. They decide to proceed with the development of shared values with the entire company.

Developing shared values with thousands of people is easier said than done. The senior executive team decides to introduce the idea at a middle managers' forum where the company vision and mission are discussed. Using a values card-sorting exercise, the middle managers identify the top priority values they feel the company should have that are also consistent with their personal values.

But values without behaviors are no more useful than slogans without action plans. The middle managers are asked to articulate the behaviors they think will bring the priority values to life. They can easily identify the "do" list—the positive behaviors, but these behaviors sound like the dream of the perfectly behaving individual. The conversation is far more intriguing when they start exploring the "don't" list—the negative behaviors.

They decide to define what they really want from the "don't" list, which they call the "yellow line," or the line below which people begin to yell. The behaviors below the yellow line are those that are just beyond the tolerable level. The participants explore the "yellow line" of the "don't" list with intensity. Some of the comments include the following:

- "If we value respect for every individual, does that mean we do not come late for meetings anymore?"
- "Does excellence in everything mean we don't sacrifice quality for timeliness?"
- "Do openness and honesty suggest we don't spread rumors anymore or say anything outside a meeting that we wouldn't say during the meeting?"

The feelings are deep, and the dialogue starts to create shared meaning. Through the vehicle of the "yellow line," the employees surface their concerns about the way work is done and how they want to live the values.

By the end of the discussion, the middle managers agree on their priority values and a short "do" and "don't" list for each value. They take ownership of their decision and recommend that all employees in the company do the exercise. They recognize that clear boundaries on behavior for each value are helpful. Rather than constraining behavior, the boundaries free people to express their individuality because they know they are behaving in the arena of acceptability. The boundaries of behaviour also allow people to adapt more easily as changes are introduced, and it fosters an environment in which a flexible culture is possible.

After the front-line employees participate in similar sessions on values and behaviors, a multi-level, cross-functional team merges the results of each of the sessions to propose a list of values and behaviors for the entire company. When the list is complete, an "all-employees" annual meeting is held. There, the multi-level, cross-functional team unveils the list to all employees, and the acceptance is widespread. The employees commit to making the values come alive in their day-to-day work. They eventually find that the values and behaviors help people when they transfer to other areas. Their adjustment is faster because of the assumptions about how they will behave based on the employees' shared values. The common values and behaviors are also helpful as the minimum criteria for effective decision-making.

If people are told what to feel, they are often resistant and reject all that is said even if they are willing to accept part of what is proposed. A better and more relevant method is to ask people how they feel rather than tell them how to feel. Of course, if you are transforming a company from an old to a new set of values, then asking all employees to articulate their values may produce the old set that is not useful for the new business. In these cases, the leadership defines the values and finds ways to help employees internalize them. However, top-down development of values is done only if there is no other participatory way to proceed.

Consider this example of "top-down" values development in an internal information technology function. The group was transforming to become an information technology business within a business. They decided to launch the new internal service business through an explanation of the new values that would drive their business. They were convinced that these values were essential to the achievement of their business vision.

The old implicit values were entitlement, technical expertise, stability, discipline, and internal customer satisfaction. The new values they developed focused on a belief in the importance of the "value of creating value." They emphasized delivering value to the external customer, the shareholder (the company), and the employees. Their values were inspired leadership, proactive innovation, external customer focus, teamwork, and shared success.

They used the new set of values to dialogue about the differences between the old and new ways of working. They designed interactive sessions to orient employees to the new values and to define the behavioral "do's" and "don'ts" to bring the values to life. The workshop exercises created a frame of reference that allowed employees to decide if they wanted to go on this journey with the information technology function as it transformed into an internal I/T business within a business.

The HR Role in Creating and Living Shared Values and Behaviors

HR's role in developing shared company values and behaviors is significant in these ways:

- *Facilitates the development of the shared company values and behaviors with managers and employees:* HR re-designs the rewards and recognition efforts to reinforce the values and behaviors. For example, HR professionals can include the values in the performance partnership between management and employees, in performance reviews, and in employee surveys. Also, they can identify team behavioral commitments based on the values.

- *Commits to reflect the values and behaviors in each HR initiative that is introduced:* The core people and organizational processes are performed according to the standards of the shared values and behaviors. For example, when an employee is being terminated and one of the company values is to treat others with respect, the company should do everything possible to help that individual find another position. HR insures that the values and behaviors are exhibited whether HR professionals do the work themselves, whether others in the company do it, or whether an external service provider does it.

- *Models the way to exhibit the shared values and behaviors in everything they do within the HR organization:* This includes modeling respect for multiple ways of working; treasuring the diversity of people, their approaches and directions; and encouraging flexibility in organizational reporting lines and structures. The HR leaders also refer to the values when they announce new initiatives and changes.

Develop Leaders Who Inspire Shared Meaning in the Work

One executive leader is fond of saying that "leadership is like a bottle of milk—the cream always rises to the top." He believes the cream leads his business to success. The problem today is that everyone is drinking skim milk, and the cream has been associated with coronary heart disease. A different kind of healthy leadership is needed to create a flexible culture and lead companies to success in the new business environment. This section begins with an exploration of leadership and management. It then explores how the approach to leadership will require leaders to cultivate a flexible culture through their conversations and dialogues with employees.

Leadership and Management

The terms "leadership" and "management" have been studied and analyzed in many professional works. Dr. Jagdish Sheth of Emory University distinguishes in his lectures[1] between management and leadership using financial symbols. He says management relates to dividends and leadership to stocks. "Dividends get their value," he says, "from their past performance. Only after the company performance is known do they redistribute the earnings as dividends." In a similar way, management gets its value from past performance. If the department performs well, the manager and the team are able to reap the benefits from the dividends. "On the other hand, stocks get their value," he says, "from the anticipation of the future. Once the stock performs, the anticipated growth of the stock is realized and its value goes down." In a similar way, leadership gets its value from the anticipation of a preferred future. Leaders are able to create the hopes, the dreams, and the vision of the preferred future.

Most people with direct reports spend a great deal of time managing today's performance and very little time leading people to the preferred future. Although they can benefit from increasing the time they spend focusing on the future rather than the current performance, both are important. The debate has become somewhat dysfunctional. The issue is not an "either-or" question of whether one should be a manager or a leader. It's an "and-also" question of the proportion of time the person should spend as a manager versus as a leader, which depends on the nature of the work expectations and the strategic challenges. People with direct reports need to have both management and leadership skills in their repertoire.

Leaders create the environment in which people can be flexible so that they are willing to invest in the future as if they are buying stock in the enterprise. Leaders focus their team on the preferred future and the end-state they want to reach and help them achieve a meaningful understanding of this future. They also foster a work environment and culture that allows people to be flexible to the changes to the processes by which the end-state will be reached. When leaders are able to do this, employees are more confident that the independent decisions they make will be aligned with the end-state they identified.

In order to achieve a meaningful understanding of the preferred future, leaders need to relentlessly inspire the forces of change and cultivate a flexible culture by:

---

[1] Dr. Jagdish Sheth. Comments during lectures in the Telecommunications Executive Development Program. Toronto, Ontario. 1997.

- Becoming excellent at conversations that help people understand and internalize the new vision, mission, and values.

- Looking at the preferred future and having ongoing conversations with their teams to insure that their understanding is shared.

- Respecting differences of opinion and drawing out the wisdom that each person can contribute.

- Debriefing decisions and changes to learn from past experience and to continuously improve.

Leaders Have Conversations that Inspire Shared Meaning

"I never wanted to manage people in the first place," an excellent scientist says, "but it pays more, so how can I turn it down?" This individual has been promoted because the company hopes he will be able to make his six direct reports as good as he is. Also, it is the only way the company can give him a financial incentive that will encourage him to stay rather than join a competitor.

It does not work out as planned. The scientist manager is handling even more complex work than previously and spends almost no time with his employees. The employees respect his brilliance, but they feel neglected and need more supervision. They want to have a chance to talk to him on an ongoing basis and to learn from him, but the manager doesn't spend time with them. Employees comment that the company took a great scientist and promoted him to become a terrible manager.

People are promoted in companies for many reasons. Many have achieved their positions based on the ability to problem solve, assign tasks, and make decisions. Unfortunately, the reasons often have little to do with the person's ability to lead others to an anticipated future and guide employees to discover shared meaning in the proposed direction.

Victor Frankl, the author of the book, *Man's Search for Meaning* (1964)[2], discusses the need for people to discover meaning in their lives in order to survive. He observes that when people lose faith in their own future, they let themselves decline and become subject to mental and physical decay.

In a similar sense, leaders are accountable for helping people discover meaning in their work. Leaders need to have conversations to insure that all parties understand the deeper meaning of what they are trying to accomplish. Then the leaders will feel more secure that

---

[2] Viktor E. Frankl. *Man's Search For Meaning*, Beacon Press, 1959.

decisions employees or service providers make will be consistent with what they would have done themselves. In these conversations leaders must do the following:

- Make an initial offer of information, a dilemma, or a proposed direction.
- Identify possibilities that are inclusive of other people.
- Look for assumptions to unearth new ideas and inspire shared meaning in their teams.
- Dialogue with people—share ideas, listen to their ideas, and ensure that each party really hears the other.
- Summarize the shared understanding of the implications of the information. Consider how it can help when responding to dilemmas and achieving the proposed direction.

Dialogue as a New Leadership Core Competency

A joke is told describing the difference between monologue and dialogue. Simply put, monologue is one person talking to him or herself, and dialogue is two people talking to themselves. Sometimes this is true. But real leaders know how to lead dialogues that are meaningful conversations between two people who are listening to and communicating with each other at a deep level.

Martin Buber, in his book, *I and Thou* (1970)[3], describes dialogue as an "I-Thou" relationship in which the "I" and the "Thou (you)" transform each other through the conversation. They have a conversation for possibilities that is wide open. In the I-Thou relationship, I understand you deeply, and you understand me deeply. As a result I fully appreciate what you are saying, and you fully appreciate what I am saying. We emerge with a new understanding and a new way of doing things. Each person's self-dignity is enhanced through this kind of dialogue.

Buber also describes a second kind of relationship referred to as an "I-It" relationship. In this relationship, "I" uses the "It" as an object through which to get something done. Many people use conversations to achieve an end result on which they can immediately render a judgment to determine what should happen next. They achieve their results through I-It relationships and not through I-Thou relationships.

---

[3] Martin Buber, *I and Thou*, Charles Scribner's Sons, New York, translated by Walter Kaufmann, 1970.

The I-Thou relationship is the essence of what dialogue is meant to be. Through this kind of dialogue, leaders have non-judgmental conversations with employees that do the following:

- Articulate that which is almost subliminal and make the implicit explicit.
- Mutually share their interests (attitudes and concerns) and their intent.
- Emerge with a common understanding of the meaning of the situation.

In environments in which people operate globally and manage remote work forces, it is sometimes very difficult to inspire shared meaning. The same is the case when leaders have to work with external service providers and outsourced firms. However, the most challenging situations to dialogue are often within and between teams that are not working well together. For example, consider a situation in which the leader is unable to break down the communication impasse among team members who are working on a strategic initiative. The team members are relating in an I-It manner. They are in the habit of shooting down a speaker before he or she has had the opportunity to complete his or her thoughts. They are operating in a dysfunctional manner—not communicating *with* each other but *at* each other.

The team members have almost given up hope that they can succeed on this strategic initiative. The leader asks the team members who are having so much difficulty communicating if they are willing to risk a different kind of conversation based on dialogue. They accept the opportunity to talk to each other in a different way. He then asks: "Are you willing to be blindfolded while you have a conversation about how you will function as a team on this strategic initiative?" (He uses a technique of a blindfolded conversation to shock the team members into engaging in meaningful dialogue.) After some explaining and influencing, they agree and then sit in a circle in the center of the room, blindfolded. The leader asks them to begin to talk to each other about how they can work together as a team on the strategic initiative.

A wondrous event occurs. As they sit there blindfolded and not able to see each other, they have more of a desire to listen. They wait for the other person to finish speaking before they give their opinion. They really hear what the other person says and reflect back what they heard. Even though the other people can not see them, they lean forward to hear what is said and make hand movements to emphasize points. For the first time, team members are really talking with each other about how they will implement the strategic initiative. Finally, there is some hope.

After 30 minutes of dialogue, the leader asks them to remove their blindfolds. The effect is astonishing. They sit there silently, and, when they open their eyes to see each other, their faces have changed. There is a calm that overtakes them. They look at each other and say they want to resume talking and exploring how their work links them together rather than how it divides them and how they can design and implement this strategic initiative effectively. They want to continue the dialogue with their eyes open.

After an hour of intense dialogue, the team members ask the leader to comment on what he saw and heard. He speaks of the intensity and focus of the team members and expresses pleasure that they are finally talking to each other. The team members remain silent as they hear the feedback. They recognize that they first started to become a team while they began engaging in a dialogue. Up until that point, they were a band of renegades fighting for turf. In the darkness created by their blindfolds, they realized that the only way they would succeed individually was first to learn how to dialogue with each other and succeed together.

They decide to document the characteristics of dialogue that they incorporated into their conversation. They create the following list:

- Listen to each other rather than think about what is the next thing you want to say.
- Suspend judgment and explore differences to achieve understanding.
- Make the ideas and beliefs that you feel are implicit, explicit. You may be surprised that what you feel is obvious is not so obvious for everybody else.
- Surface the underlying assumptions, issues, and concerns that are causing the miscommunication.
- Say what is in your hearts and not only what is in your heads.
- Discover a way to work together, and then move forward together.

Surfacing underlying assumptions in a non-judgmental way is not therapy but rather a professional understanding and communication. It is similar to a due-diligence process on the thoughts and feelings of each person. The thoughts and feelings need to be fully understood so that each person truly understands what the other one believes. Dialogue enhances the chances of mutual understanding and shared meaning.

Many applications of dialogue in the work environment are far less dramatic than the example cited in which people were deficient in dialogue skills and were blindfolded in order to have a meaningful conversation. In one situation, a high-tech company engaged in dialogue to identify "meaningful shared goals" as a method to develop a flexible culture to help them implement changes quickly. They aligned all systems, processes and rewards to support the shared goals. They also expanded the latitude for employees to act independently as long as they were acting in support of the "meaningful shared goals." As new projects were introduced, the leadership held dialogue sessions about how the new projects supported the shared goals. Employees were able to shift priorities quickly to focus on new initiatives. As a result they were able to deliver excellent performance as their business continually evolved.

Leaders can use dialogue in the following situations:

- *When they are struggling with ambiguous issues and unclear directions:* Trust is built through the shared struggle with ambiguity, which often results in new directions.

- *When they take ownership of people and organizational responsibilities* such as creating an environment that welcomes new people, integrates them, and derives benefit from the new diversity.

- *When they need to enhance their ability to mentor and coach employees* in their conversations.

- *When they engage in performance development discussions with their employees or teams and when they receive feedback on their own performance:* For example, when leaders receive 360° feedback from their employees and others on their performance, they debrief the feedback by using dialogue discussions. Leaders create shared meaning through dialogue, and they gain a better appreciation of the underlying issues that need to be changed for them to be more effective in their role.

When leaders engage in dialogue, especially about their own performance, employees respond in predictable ways. Initially, they are surprised that the leader is willing to be open about the feedback he or she received. After the dialogue, the employees invariably say that they respect the leader for his/her courage to engage in this kind of conversation. They suggest that the process enhanced their respect for the leader, and they felt that the respect was reciprocated in the dialogue. Of course, the true test will be if the leader actually modifies his or her behavior as a result of the feedback and dialogue. If the leader does, the trust will be enhanced among the team members, and the flexible culture in that work unit will begin to be cultivated.

HR professionals foster an environment that is enriched through dialogue, so that a more flexible culture will emerge from these conversations. Their approaches can include:

- *Champion this approach to leadership:* This leadership approach includes an expectation to dialogue and share meaning on an ongoing basis in the work environment.

- *Coach leaders on how to dialogue:* They coach leaders on how to take *apparent* consensus and deepen it through dialogue so that people will understand differences and reach more meaningful resolutions to dilemmas.

- *Teach employees how to participate in dialogue:* Leaders will have difficulty facilitating dialogue if the employees do not know how to participate. With this capability, employees are better able to self-manage their contribution to the team discussions and develop their skills as leaders and followers.

- *Facilitate dialogue on sensitive issues that require shared meaning:* HR professionals facilitate dialogue on sensitive issues. For example, in one company the HR professionals facilitated the dialogue on issues such as diversity in the workplace and the cultural differences between two parts of the company that recently merged.

Foster Organizational Elasticity

It has become clear to many leaders that the organization's structure can be the barrier that inhibits the ability of the workforce to adapt to changes. For many years, organizational structure has been thought to be constant. The structure has been perceived as a method of keeping order, of "crowd control," of delegating and evaluating work. Changes to the structure are often traumatic and almost always are experienced as stressful. In these environments, people say, "We will be flexible— just don't ask us to change." As long as the unit is left intact, people can work together and get the job done; but once the unit is broken up, people take too long to re-form the group.

Many executives have realized that they need to transform; however, their inflexible infrastructure stifles change. They attempt to foster an organization that has greater flexibility to absorb change as the demands on the business change. Many begin by introducing flexibility in various aspects of the organization. As discussed earlier in this chapter, shared values and a leadership that helps build shared meaning can contribute to cultivating a more flexible culture. However, the work environment represented by the organizational design itself also needs to evolve and become more "elastic" for that culture to be sustained.

This chapter defined *organizational elasticity*[4] as an organizational design that can grow or shrink based upon the needs of the business. The organization requires that kind of elasticity to cultivate a flexible culture. It needs to expand or contract flexibly when the business need arises. It also needs to be able to revert back to its original structure when the tension is released. A high school "homeroom class" is a useful analogy for organizational elasticity. Students attend many classes but also have a homeroom to which they belong. Similarly, employees work in many places and with other people as the demands of the work change but regularly return to the safety and comfort of their "homeroom" or primary work unit.

This section explores the impact of organizational elasticity on the following:

• How work is done and by whom.
• The commitment to foster innovation by all employees.
• The use of virtual teams to enhance flexibility in the workplace.

How Work Is Done and by Whom

With organizational elasticity, leaders are able to respond quickly and effectively to this question, "What work needs to be done and how can we insure it is done within the fastest time, at the highest quality, and at the lowest cost?" Today's organizational design that will enable the best time, quality, and cost may need to change tomorrow; therefore, its methods of operation need to be more flexible.

For example, one company was committed to changing its distribution system; however, its infrastructure was inflexible. The competition—start-up companies that did not have a distribution legacy with which they had to contend—was able to introduce advanced distribution technology easily and quickly. The challenge to the company was intense. Some executives believed they were unable to compete because of their inflexibility and rigid distribution system. They realized they

---

[4] The term "organizational elasticity" was proposed by Malcolm Bernstein of Geller, Shedletsky & Weiss, 1998.

needed to take action immediately and that rebuilding their distribution system would take too long. They decided to outsource distribution for a two-year period with the intention of learning from the outsourced service provider how distribution should be done. Their plan was to bring the distribution function back into the company within two years.

During the two years, they were able to keep customers satisfied with the outsourced distribution services. To prepare for the re-absorption of distribution into the company, they made sweeping changes, building a technology-driven distribution process that was state-of-the-art. They were able to shrink and expand their own distribution organization to make it a strategic asset for the company.

The characteristics of how work is done in an elastic organization are the following:

- *Keep most of the strategic work in the company:* The company keeps strategically important work within the company. They insure that the employees who are major contributors to the strategic direction see the company as their employer of choice.

- *Develop preferred supplier relationships for specialized strategic work:* The new team in companies consists of full-time employees and ex-officio external preferred suppliers who assist the company on strategic work. When the strategic external resources are asked to be part of the team, the team expands and they are treated as team members. They must be very familiar with the company's strategic developments and be committed to an intense strategic supplier relationship that will be called upon when the need arises. They add value to the team when their competencies are needed and leave the team when they are no longer needed. The company then either develops the skills internally and "re-insources" (as in the above example) or it maintains the external supplier relationship for situations in which that strategic value is needed.

- *Use external vendors for some non-strategic work:* Having relationships with external vendors who are willing to have flexible contracts is very helpful to companies. It allows them to shrink and grow their workforce by altering their reliance on external service providers when they are not adding value. Of course, sometimes companies keep a portion of the non-strategic work in house if it is more efficient to do so or if it will result in better internal client services.

- *Form time-limited, multi-disciplinary teams:* Companies that have flexible cultures often form multi-disciplinary teams that work on strategic initiatives for a period of time and then split up to return to their daily work. The temporary nature of the teams creates the opportunity for individuals who can add the most value to an initiative to join the multi-disciplinary team when their skills are needed. These multi-disciplinary teams often have either "sunset clauses" that identify when they will conclude their responsibility or decision points to determine whether they will continue on the team. (This way of working will be described later in this section in an exploration of how virtual teams contribute to organizational elasticity.)

- *Support resilience of employees to work in an elastic organization:* The previous sections on how to create and live the values and how to build leadership that inspires shared meaning will help employees have the resilience to adapt more regularly. In the best-case scenarios, employees adjust easily to new people on their teams, enjoy working in new contexts and on new challenges, and welcome and even crave change. The employees commit to innovation and breakthroughs and are open to sharing information about effective and ineffective practices. When employees are more resilient, the organization has a better chance of being elastic, and the culture is more flexible to the changes that are introduced.

The Commitment to Foster Innovation by All Employees

Organizational elasticity implies that employees are committed to create a work environment in which innovations and breakthroughs are encouraged and welcomed. If employees are thinking about innovation, they are more likely to accept innovative organizational designs and a flexible culture.

As one leader said, "Nothing is more expensive than an opportunity missed." The elastic organization craves opportunities and innovations that appear in several forms. These include:

- *The breakthrough idea:* A "breakthrough" is a new idea that radically transforms the way products, processes, systems, or work are conceptualized and done. Breakthroughs appear to occur "creatio ex-nihilo," as a creation out of nothing. In reality, however, breakthroughs most often arise from accidents. Wise employees know that nothing ever happens by accident that can not be done intentionally later. Anybody can *see* an accidental success occur. It is the responsibility of all employees to *identify* and *study* the accidental successes to discover why they work and to *develop* a breakthrough approach that allows people to have the same accidental success on purpose.

Many companies seem unable to discover multiple break-throughs and that eventually leads to their demise. A focus on breakthroughs encourages employees to think about the next work transformation as they continue their day-to-day responsibilities.

Figure 7.2 depicts the growth curve representation of a break-through. Notice the curve in the figure. It is the exact same slope as the Phase Three slope shown in the Chapter One growth curve. It illustrates the transformation required in Phase Three to break through the mature phase to a new growth phase rather than to degenerate into organizational disintegration. The same is evident for every breakthrough.

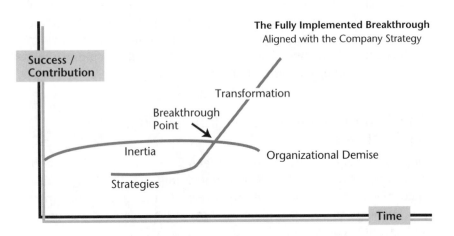

Figure 7.2: The Breakthrough Curve

Here is an analogy to bring the breakthrough image to life: A company that designs and manufactures submarines and rockets has invited the Defense Department to a special presentation of its newest submarine. On the day of the event, the submarine is under water. The department has been invited to view this event without knowing what innovative changes have been applied to the sub. When the submarine is ready, instead of the conventional surfacing, it suddenly bursts out of the ocean and into the sky transformed into a rocket. The moment the breakthrough is evident is when the submarine emerges from the waters and is airborne.

The process of creating breakthroughs starts with the new idea that is submerged. The actual breakthrough occurs at the point the idea surfaces and the new direction is visible. Eventually, if the breakthrough is implemented effectively, it becomes a competitive advantage for the company and a new standard in the industry of how business is done.

- *Evolving existing ideas:* Most innovations are really not new. They are reformulations of a variety of ideas that appear innovative when they are combined in a new form. The ability to transform existing ideas is a basic characteristic of organizational elasticity. It is a tool of continuous improvement and product, process, and systems development.

- *Matching solutions to problems in unique ways:* It is the responsibility of all employees to be innovative and to discover underlying problems and the best solutions to apply to them. People need to think about the root causes of problems and determine the best ways to resolve them. In a flexible culture with an elastic organizational design, the ability to match solutions to problems is a vital skill.

The Use of Virtual Teams to Enhance Flexibility in the Workplace

Traditional teams are characterized by all members reporting to one person, who is the single manager for the team. The membership on the traditional team is constant, with the team members working in a common location and frequently having opportunities to meet face to face. Team members often have clear and documented responsibilities for themselves, their team, and their departments. The manager has "position power" to determine who does what and to evaluate performance. This power is mainly derived from the manager's position in the hierarchy given to him or her by someone other than the team members (usually the person to whom the team manager reports).

Many attempts have been made to create alternate team models to enhance organizational elasticity. The approaches can be described as either 1) creating flexibility in the leadership of the team or 2) creating flexibility in the membership and location of the team.

- *Creating flexibility in the leadership of the team:* The first approach has been explored under many different names and has most of the characteristics of the traditional team except that it is leaderless. An autonomous work team is similar to the traditional team in that it has constant members, a common work location and relatively clear responsibilities for the team itself, the team members and their department. However, the autonomous work team differs in its approach to team leadership, the assignment of work and, in some cases, the evaluation of performance, which is often done by the team members with each other. This approach to teams increases the flexibility of the workplace and can foster organizational elasticity. It is sometimes unsuccessful with teams that are not able to work well with a shared leadership approach and teams that are unable to handle crises well without a leader to give them direction.

• *Creating flexibility in the membership and location of the team:* The second approach is a rather recent model, which has been enabled through technology. It introduces flexibility in team membership with a clearly defined leader of the team. The teams operate as "virtual teams," which consist of team members who are often in remote locations and do not share a common physical space. They often "belong" to home departments other than the virtual team's. Team membership can change frequently based on the needs of the virtual team at that time, although some members stay with the team on a constant basis. Their communications are facilitated by technology through voice and data transmissions. The leader has more position power than in autonomous work teams but often less than in traditional teams. Virtual team leaders rely heavily on their influence skills because of their remote access to employees.

It appears that virtual teams have great potential to enhance organizational elasticity. They enhance the culture's flexibility to get the work done with the best people who can participate in that part of the work. There are opportunities to leverage internal expertise by putting people on a virtual team temporarily as that input is required. Virtual teams have great potential to maximize the utilization of the employees' intellectual capital no matter where they are in the world and to re-use ideas once they are developed for multiple virtual teams.

Virtual teams appear also to have some positive implications for employee retention. Employees are usually exposed to many virtual teams, which expands their knowledge base and provides them with personal development opportunities. This exposure allows employees to have more opportunities for career development since they may not have to move to a specific location in order to receive a promotion. Virtual teams are also often characterized by fewer political agendas, personality conflicts, and bureaucracy among the team members.

As with all good ideas, virtual teams have challenges that can be overcome by HR professionals if they are given proper attention. These include:

- *Selection of members who want to be part of the virtual team:* Selection on the virtual teams is sometimes based on convenience or coercion. People on the teams can be unmotivated, mistrusting, burdened, and have many excuses for non-participation. Virtual teams require very high levels of employee commitment to be successful since the employees must motivate themselves in their remote locations. HR professionals insure that members of virtual teams are motivated and want to be part of the team.

- *Acknowledgment that virtual teamwork is real work:* In certain situations, employees do not consider work on the virtual teams to be part of the real expectations of work. They often treat the work on virtual teams as overtime work. Speed of delivery can then slow down to non-delivery as people place virtual teamwork at the bottom of their priority list. HR professionals insure that work on a virtual team is part of the employee's work expectations and not viewed as extra-curricular activities.

- *Communications:* Inadequate communications among virtual team members and with the virtual team leader can occur. Communications are very important for virtual teams. Through the use of technology, teams can insure that communications occur regularly. In addition, virtual teams do need to meet face to face every so often to build their relationships with the people on their team.

- *Rewards and recognition:* The rewards and recognition are sometimes not aligned with the virtual team approach. It is essential to establish clear deliverables for the team so that all can focus on the same end point. The virtual team must develop clear accountabilities for itself and the members, specify the metrics for the accountabilities, and evaluate the performance of both the team and each member of the team.

Even with the list of challenges, virtual teams do appear to be an approach that will contribute to organizational elasticity. They have the capability to expand and remove team members without the trauma of re-organizations. The external customers often benefit as well when virtual teams are assigned to customer issues because they receive the best service by employees who are highly committed and motivated.

HR Removes Barriers to Organizational Elasticity

To reduce the risk to a flexible culture, HR professionals need to be very conscious of the many barriers to implementing organizational elasticity. HR professionals must hold back the forces that want to bind organizational structure and reduce elasticity. Some of the most prominent barriers include the following:

- *Leaders who are more committed to hierarchy than flexibility:* Leaders must be mature enough to recognize that they will be more successful if they operate flexibly rather than with an approach that is based on a rigid hierarchical control. For example, if leaders want all communications to proceed through channels, then the organization and the culture will likely be rigid. By giving away control, the leaders create the context for more flexibility. They enable employees to work in the best interests of the customer. Leaders in flexible cultures that foster organizational elasticity are regularly meeting with employees in "skip-level" meetings (one level of the hierarchy speaking to employees two or more levels below them). Communication and shared meaning do not depend on hierarchy to be effective. Leaders need to encourage this kind of openness at all levels or organizational elasticity will not occur.

- *Rigid definitions of jobs:* Job descriptions can create more structure than may be necessary and may limit elasticity. Some organizations have been moving away from specific job descriptions to allow people to work in different ways and in different contexts. In Chapter Three we described the "tie goes to the runner" decision rule. This rule applies to job descriptions (as with all matters that create rigidity in the organizational system). If the reasons to do job descriptions are equal to the reasons to avoid doing them, then "the tie goes to *not* doing job descriptions" so that the organization is more elastic and adaptable to change.

- *Poor union and management relationships:* In unionized environments, removing job descriptions can be a source of difficult negotiations. A different kind of collaborative relationship with the union will be necessary to create the organizational elasticity. The methodology for doing this includes following the principles and practices outlined in my book, *Beyond the Walls of Conflict: Mutual Gains Negotiations for Unions and Management.* (Weiss, 1996)[5].

- *Employee insecurity about their careers:* Employees who are afraid of losing their personal market value for work in the company or elsewhere are rarely committed to organizational change. Employees need honest conversations about the direction of the company and their future. If their future is tenuous, employees need companies to commit to educating them so that they remain employable even if they may go to work for another company. The deal is that the employee delivers value to the company, and the company insures that the employee remains employable whether in this company or elsewhere.

HR Fosters Organizational Elasticity

Human Resources professionals play an important role in fostering a fluid and responsive organization by doing the following:

- Insuring that the organizational design is based on achieving strategic benefits rather than building structure for its own sake.

- Taking a minimalist approach to structure and using it as a vehicle only if it helps.

- Rejecting a rigid system and fighting the rigidity just as white blood cells attack bacteria.

- Cultivating a culture that repeatedly reinforces the message that innovative breakthroughs are essential for the company's growth and transformation and part of every employee's responsibility.

- Reinforcing innovation, creativity, and breakthrough thinking in all developmental learning experiences. For example, in one company HR conducts seminars that deliver actual dollar return on investment through the breakthrough benefits the leaders generate during the program.

- Using virtual teams where appropriate to enhance organizational elasticity and the flexible culture.

---

[5] David Weiss, *Beyond The Walls Of Conflict*, Irwin Professional Publishing, Chicago, 1996.

Insure Rewards and Recognition Support the Flexible Culture

People tend to perform as they are rewarded and recognized to perform, and therefore the rewards and recognition efforts must be aligned to drive desired behaviors. It is no surprise that the rewards and recognition efforts need to support the creation of a flexible culture in order to increase the probability that it will occur. Also, there need to be some expected outcomes for a flexible culture. For example:

- The ability to absorb new companies and product lines rapidly so that the benefits from these investments will be realized as soon as possible.
- A reduction in lead-time to introduce new business strategies and accept new organizational designs.
- The ability to form and dismantle multi-disciplinary teams with fluidity and excellent results.
- Quick and easy access by managers and employees to information resulting in effective changes and the maximum re-use of business practices.

Removing Rewards that Motivate People in an Undesirable Direction

Chapter Three described the motivators that drive people to behave in ways that are not in the interest of the company. HR professionals need to remove the "noise" that distracts the managers and employees from supporting a flexible culture, which may include:

- Having cross-functional groups competing rather than collaborating with each other.
- Recognizing individual performance only and not team performance.
- Keeping the internal resources separate from the external service providers, which breeds mistrust between them and results in relationships not being built.
- Promoting people who do not behave in a manner consistent with the values.
- Requiring excessive reporting and tracking that distracts employees from focusing on the customer.

Creating Rewards and Recognition to Promote a Flexible Culture

In addition, the HR professionals need to encourage the line managers to build in rewards and recognition systems that motivate people to be flexible in the workplace. HR's rewards and recognition efforts also need to support this direction. Some methods include:

- Giving bonuses or recognizing people for participating in multi-disciplinary task forces.
- Acknowledging extra special efforts that are beyond the expectations of the normal work.
- Recognizing honest efforts at innovation when they are successful and when they are not.
- Using values to test the integrity of decisions and actions taken on behalf of the company.
- Changing the employee survey to include questions about core values, including questions about their importance, their relevance to the individuals, and to what extent the values are practical in each business.
- Using web-based technology to conduct quarterly culture check-ups to assess the extent to which the culture is evolving in the desired direction.

Building Rewards into Executive Compensation that Promote a Flexible Culture

Perhaps one of the more powerful ways to cultivate a flexible culture is by targeting the executive team's behavior. As described earlier, executives must lead the way and identify their own values and behaviors and operate accordingly. They can also build in rewards for themselves to drive their behavior to support a flexible culture.

Some executive teams have done this through identifying mutual accountabilities to which all the executives commit that will help the team succeed in their mandate. When executives focus on mutual rather than individual accountabilities, they have more freedom to be flexible to do what needs to be done for the company rather than just for their individual functions.

Another benefit of mutual accountabilities is that the executives are motivated and recognize the need to help each other succeed. This is consistent with what most successful executives have learned as they progressed in their careers. They realize that they may have strengths, but they have weaknesses as well. The challenge to the successful executive is to learn how to minimize their weaknesses. Some use elaborate methods of covering up their weaknesses such as hiring people with specific talents and designing unusual methods to avoid exposing their weaknesses. When executives work together as a team, they support each other by minimizing their weaknesses and determining how to capitalize on each other's strengths.

For example, consider how a company can address both the executives' individual and mutual accountabilities. The executive team decides that when they work as a team they do not wear their functional "hats." They agree that approximately 20 percent of the time (approximately one day a week) they operate like a board of directors. They all own every decision whether it relates to their functional responsibility or not. The other 80 percent of the time they are functional leaders responsible for the specific mandate they have been given.

To reinforce this desired behavior, the senior executive team decides that their bonuses will be tied to the mutual accountabilities. They identify 20 percent of their objectives as mutual accountabilities and 80 percent as individual. Each mutual accountability is also repeated as an individual objective for an executive. The senior executive has the primary accountability to lead or sponsor the successful implementation of his or her individual objective, but, because it is a mutual accountability as well, it is of interest to all the executives. The shared values, behaviors, and mutual accountabilities create an intensity for the executive as a team. It makes their executive leadership more focused and inspiring to all members, and their openness to a flexible culture is enhanced.

Human Resources Enables the Flexible Culture

This chapter has explored how Human Resources can transform the business by cultivating and creating the context for a flexible culture. HR focuses its attention on enabling the leadership and the work environment to be more adaptive to deliver the company strategy and to add value to the customer.

However, it may be difficult for HR to obtain the credibility to cultivate a flexible culture. The old maxim that "You can never be a prophet in your own city," may apply to HR if it does not have a flexible culture in its own area. If HR professionals cultivate their own flexible culture, they won't hear statements from others such as, "How can you say we should be more flexible if your own organization is so rigid?" The HR team must be willing to live by what it attempts to enable others to do—to model the flexible culture.

Ways HR Can Model the Flexible Culture

1. Live the company values and behaviors so that it can be an example to the rest of the company.
2. Have leadership that creates shared meaning in its work environment, using dialogue as a form of conversation with clients and with each other.
3. Have a structure that reflects organizational elasticity. Continually model innovation and the development of breakthroughs.
4. Recognize that resistance to innovation is much lower when there is an ongoing willingness to abandon old ideas. If people feel that innovation is just adding on to a full workload, they may be resistant to thinking in fresh, new ways.
5. Build a work force that is resilient to the ever-changing and dynamic work environment.
6. Remove "noise" within the HR organization as well as within client organizations that distracts HR professionals from delivering strategic value.
7. Have the internal rewards and recognition systems that motivate the desired behaviors within HR and other client organizations.
8. Use the HR organization to test out new strategies for creating a flexible culture. HR then becomes a microcosm of the company. Identify the problems as ideas are piloted. Then modify them so that when they are implemented in the company they have a higher likelihood of succeeding.

Enabling the flexible culture is not an easy task, but it is essential for the company as it transforms. Human Resources can enable this business transformation to occur by creating small successes and letting the results rather than promises sell the importance of the flexible culture. HR can also model how this kind of work environment is planned, organized and delivered within its own HR area.

Summary

- In today's business environment, it is essential for companies to be able to change direction quickly to meet market demands. A flexible culture increases the company's chances of being able to change effectively, quickly, and repeatedly.

- The four primary ways of cultivating a flexible culture include the creation of shared values, having leaders that can dialogue with employees to create shared meaning in the work environment, the development of an organizational design that is "elastic," and to reward and recognize efforts that support the flexible culture.

- *Shared Values:* A foundation of the flexible culture is its shared values and behaviors. HR's role in creating shared company values and behaviors is significant in these ways:

  - Facilitates the development of the shared values and behaviors with managers and employees.

  - Re-designs the rewards and recognition efforts to reinforce the values and behaviors.

  - Commits to reflect the values and behaviors in each HR initiative.

  - Models within the HR organization the way to exhibit the shared values and behaviors in everything they do.

- *Leadership Dialogues:* Leaders are accountable for helping people discover meaning in their work. Leaders need to have conversations to insure that all parties understand the deeper meaning of what they are trying to accomplish. Then the leaders will feel more secure that decisions employees or service providers make will be consistent with what they would have done themselves.

- *Organizational Elasticity:* It has become clear to many leaders that the organization's structure can be the barrier that inhibits the ability of the work force to adapt to changes. There is a need for organizational elasticity so that the organizational design can grow or shrink based on the needs of the business. Organizational elasticity implies that employees are committed to create a work environment in which innovations and breakthroughs are encouraged and welcomed. The opportunities and innovations appear in several forms. These include the breakthrough idea, evolving existing ideas, and matching solutions to problems in unique ways. To reduce the risk to a flexible culture, HR needs to focus its attention on many of the barriers to implementing organizational elasticity. Some of the most prominent barriers include the following:

– leaders who are more committed to hierarchy than flexibility

– rigid definitions of jobs

– poor union and management relationships

– employee insecurity about their careers

• *Rewards and Recognition:* People tend to perform as they are rewarded and recognized to perform. It is no surprise then that the rewards and recognition efforts need to support the creation of a flexible culture in order to increase the probability that it will occur. The HR professionals need to encourage the line managers to build in internal rewards and recognition systems that motivate people to be flexible in the workplace. The rewards and recognition efforts that HR develops for its organization need to also support this direction.

• Human Resources is accountable for creating the context for a flexible culture. HR can also be the model of how this kind of environment can be planned, organized, and delivered.

CHAPTER EIGHT

෨෨

Champion
Strategic Alignment

One interesting way to begin exploring this strategic business process outcome is by considering the concept of alignment in microbiology. It will provide a helpful analogy to strategic alignment in the business environment.

In microbiology, alignment is not complementary but instead creates a higher level of functioning. For example, consider a person who is expected to take two antibiotic drugs simultaneously. Three kinds of reactions can occur:

1. *A neutral or "indifferent" reaction:* The two antibiotics taken in their normal dosages deliver no greater value than the more active drug taken by itself.

2. *A negative or "antagonistic" reaction:* The effect of one antibiotic is reduced by the presence of another, or it produces a toxic reaction.

3. *A positive aligned or "synergistic" reaction:* The two antibiotics produce a better outcome when they are combined than the singular effects of either drug alone. This can mean that the dosage required of each drug can be reduced when the two drugs are combined. In addition, the alignment may produce a need for fewer antibiotics to deliver an even better outcome.

In business settings, strategic alignment produces the same higher level of functioning as a positive alignment of two antibiotics. In other words, the alignment of two or more initiatives results in less effort and better outcomes. When alignment does not occur, the process can be antagonistic with people working at cross-purposes and generating a toxic reaction. If no connection is made between the two initiatives, the result may not be antagonism, but there may also be no incremental gain. When alignment does occur, it will produce greater benefit than when the two initiatives are undertaken independently.

Now consider a typical company that has multiple variables interacting all the time. Various businesses, divisions, functions, products, and people interact with each other to meet their own individual interests. Without attention to strategic alignment, the company can anticipate some antagonistic responses. Inertia and unaligned action can lead to a toxic reaction. HR professionals are in a unique position to champion strategic alignment. In this chapter we'll explore how this alignment can be achieved.

An Example of Strategic Alignment

The following example describes a situation in which strategic alignment is needed. A team of ten senior executives holds a session to establish the company's future direction. In preparation for the meeting, the division leaders develop vision statements. The executives do not share their reports nor align their objectives with any of the other executives prior to this meeting.

The president and executives meet in the boardroom. As the leaders give their presentations, it is obvious they are making their presentations to the president only. It appears that the president's opinion is the only one that is important. Each executive has developed a vision statement and presents detailed plans of how to make his or her vision a reality. After the first three presentations by Development, Operations, and Marketing, the president speaks out, "We sound like three different companies. Did you talk to each other before developing your presentations?" The silence in the room is deafening. Those executives who have not yet presented are doing mental somersaults to align their reports with at least one of the previous presentations.

The president continues, "Don't you understand why you each lead a division? We have one vision for the company. The company divisions must make that one vision a reality. Your charge as division leaders is to demonstrate supervision and to do your part to implement the company vision." The executives have heard the president expound on this 'vision-division-supervision' idea before but have never considered it more than a cute play on words. "From now on we only have one vision for the company; all other visions are eliminated," the president says to a hushed room.

The HR vice president, who has been trying to get the other executives to collaborate and align their plans, looks around the room at his colleagues, who are obviously disturbed and fearful. The president is agitated, his face red with frustration and anger. The room remains silent for several minutes while no one moves or, as it appears, even breathes.

The HR vice president breaks the silence. "I think we should adjourn the meeting for a week. We have work to do on our plans." Some of the executives are relieved; others are surprised by the HR leader's directness. Everyone waits for the president to speak as he twirls his Mont Blanc pen between his fingers. "Take two weeks," he says, "and make sure your presentations build the company, not your divisions." The meeting is adjourned.

The president leaves the boardroom. The rest of the executives sit stunned. "I knew we shouldn't have had this meeting so close to Christmas," says one person. "I don't know how I'm going to tell my staff that I didn't get a chance to present today," says another. The Marketing VP says, "I don't think you heard him. He is saying that we have to work together and build one company plan. What we have now is not good enough, and I think he is right."

The HR vice president has been waiting for this moment to champion strategic alignment. The sense of urgency for the executives to work together and align their strategies has arrived. He offers to help. "Maybe we can work together to see where the gaps and overlaps are in our presentations," he says. "We can meet to discuss our ideas and see how they align to a common company vision." After a moment of hesitation, the Marketing VP agrees, and one by one the others decide it is a good idea.

The astute HR vice president is one of the few leaders who has the trust of others. He recognizes that all the leaders are operating in good faith but are heading in different directions. Their individual visions, values and strategies are not aligned. He is also aware of a great deal of unresolved conflict among the executives, which leads them to set up their own businesses to the exclusion of others, leading to a company that is splintered. The result is that when customers speak to different divisions, they complain that they are dealing with more than one company.

The HR vice president decides to mediate some of the executive disputes. To get the maximum value from his efforts, he starts with one of the more complex interpersonal conflicts. To the company's benefit, he is able to facilitate a resolution to the problem. The two disputing executives resolve some basic problems while agreeing to disagree on some matters. Once they begin to resolve their differences, they are ready to dialogue about how they will align their divisions. Other divisions immediately take note of the change in the leaders' relationship and begin to talk to each other.

After extensive work, the leaders meet with the president two weeks later. They affirm the importance of one company vision and one set of values. They describe the alignment process in which each division identifies its own preferred future and how it contributes to fulfilling the vision. Then they each present how their division implements their strategic initiatives as part of the entire company. At the conclusion of the meeting, they agree (in this example) that the outcome of the alignment will be measured by the reduction of lead-time and time to market in the implementation of the company's overall strategy.

HR professionals can facilitate executive alignment to the vision through their comprehensive knowledge base, which includes:

- Information about what the company's divisions are doing, and an understanding about how to provide knowledge to other leaders.

- A network of resources and ideas that could be channeled in the best interest of the company's external customer.

- Understanding of work processes that have been used in the past to help divisions identify ways to improve quality and economies of scale.

- Comprehension of the company vision, organizational structure, and leadership.

HR professionals can use their knowledge of the company and the customer along with their personal credibility, timing, and influence skills to champion strategic alignment. The HR executive in the example contributed to business transformation by helping the company executives produce a better outcome together then they were able to accomplish independently.

The Five Areas of Strategic Alignment

Figure 8.1 shows the five areas that HR professionals assess to determine whether the company is strategically aligned. The discussion in this chapter will focus on the alignment of teams that are working on strategic initiatives.

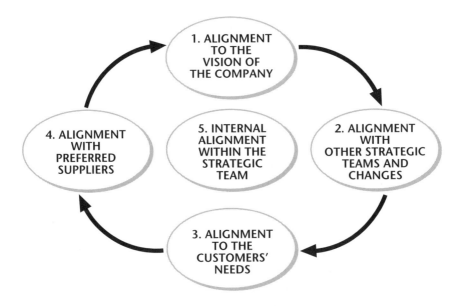

Figure 8.1: The Five Areas of Strategic Alignment

The figure illustrates the five areas of strategic alignment. In the center is the team that needs to be aligned to specific major areas as well as to be internally aligned. The company vision, other strategic teams, customers, and suppliers form the circle of influence to which the team needs to align. Of course, there may be other areas to which the strategic team may need to align, but the five areas are the most prominent areas to consider. Next, this chapter looks at each of these areas.

1. Alignment to the Vision of the Company

This area of alignment involves insuring that each team (as well as individuals) operates in alignment with the company vision and strategic direction. When I think of visions that generated the impetus to create a new reality, several come to mind. Most of them are on a societal level in which new energy is channeled to a preferred future. An often-cited example of a vision with focus and power is that of U.S. President John F. Kennedy, who envisioned putting a person on the moon by the end of the 1960s. As we all know, this vision was achieved in 1969. The vision had power that created action, investment, and creativity to deliver results that were, quite literally, out of this world.

On that maiden voyage to the moon, the control center (NASA) decided the mission would follow a very exact course and planned the voyage with incredible precision. But even as precise as they were, the spaceship was off course a tremendous amount of the time as it flew to the moon and back. Research to discover just how often it was off course yielded some surprising results. It was on course only 3 percent of the time. Imagine—97 percent of the time off course! The vision was very specific, but NASA had to realign their direction constantly. Once the vision was set for the course to take, NASA's job was to align, align, align.[1]

Even in the best of scenarios, the vision is not enough to get a company to the preferred future. The commitment to strategic alignment is a vital part of achieving a vision. Also required is a culture that is flexible, enabling all employees to take initiative and the actions necessary to align people, teams, and systems to proceed towards the vision.

Companies must align initiatives to the strategies that will deliver their vision. If the initiatives do not align, they are good candidates for antagonism or for abandonment. In the integration example cited at the end of Chapter Six, the executives developed a vision that the merger would be an integration of the best practices in each company. All executive initiatives had to align to the strategies developed to achieve that vision. If for some reason an initiative did not align, it was discarded. As a result of this alignment, the company had a more successful integration.

Executives Have A Vital Role In Fostering Alignment To The Vision

Executives must foster alignment, challenging activities that do not align. They must create shared meaning through dialogue and reflect alignment in everything they do and in conversations they have. Some of the ways they can do this are as follows:

---

[1] The 3 percent statistic that they were on course on the maiden voyage to the moon as well as the description of what occurred in NASA at that time was confirmed as correct by Roger D. Launius, Ph.D., the NASA Chief Historian of the NASA History Office, Code ZH, Washington, DC, 20546, on August 4, 1998.

- *Articulate the vision:* Executives inspire a shared vision of what the future could be and how their divisions fit into the overall vision. The executives need to apply the basic wisdom of speaking in the language of the listeners, which is too often ignored by leaders. It enhances their ability to be inspirational and to align with their employees.

- *Merge strategic initiatives under "umbrella" strategies:* The leaders need to know how to merge many strategic initiatives under several clearly defined "umbrella" strategies. Consider the company that has 45 strategic initiatives. People complain that the work is not focused and that, therefore, there are few good results. The leader establishes five umbrella strategies with nine initiatives each. He finds he can more clearly communicate the message of the key strategies the company plans to deliver and, therefore, help employees focus their attention on the bigger picture.

- *Use high-profile events to reinforce what is important:* Leaders use high-profile events to reinforce the vision and values, thereby helping to create alignment. These high-profile actions can occur in a brief instant that sends a message to the workforce that the vision is shaping the executives' decision-making. For example, employees watch very closely who is hired, promoted, and fired. They watch with whom the company decides to do business and with whom the company decides to build strategic alliances. If these high-profile events are aligned with the vision, employees become even more committed to the articulated direction. When the high-profile events are inconsistent with the vision, employees often reinterpret the vision as another slogan that has limited importance for the senior executives and for themselves.

- *Have high expectations and provide clear feedback:* Leaders often have high-performance expectations for employees and the company. They also provide clear feedback to re-align individuals and teams to the desired outcomes. This often enhances employee development and affects the goals they accept for themselves.

- *Be role models:* To be effective role models, leaders must be perceived as forward-looking, inspiring, honest, and competent. They must align their values and behaviors with those that are important for the company to achieve its vision. Leaders who are role models can have a positive effect on the employees' motivation and performance levels.

An Example of Aligning Key Resources to the Vision

One company decided to experiment with alignment by involving key resources who were not executives in developing the company strategy. The executive leader recognized that these key resources have a great influence on the potential for alignment in the company. The process they followed was very innovative. The key resources observed the presentations that were made to the executives in preparation for the strategic planning process. They were then asked to independently analyze the data presented and recommend a strategic direction for the company. At the next executive strategy session, the key resources presented their ideas, which were very useful for the executives as they considered the strategy for the next few years.

In addition to the direct benefit to strategy development, the process yielded positive secondary benefits. For example, the key resources were usually involved in their area only, but as a result of the analysis of the company's strategic direction, they developed an interest in the company as a whole instead of focusing on just their areas. They also were able to understand the company-wide challenges better and how they related to their business areas. In addition, the key resources came to appreciate the company's strategy and vision to a far greater extent. They became ambassadors for aligning their colleagues' and employees' activities to the vision.

HR Champions Alignment to the Vision of the Company

A company's president is the only person with official responsibility for aligning all strategies. He or she is the one executive who is part of only one team in the company—the executive cabinet. All other executive team members have the additional responsibility of leading divisional teams. The president has to bring all these strong people together and form them into one team that is focused and aligned. Only the exceptional president has the leadership skills to make this happen. In most companies, the risk that this alignment will not occur is high, whether the culture is flexible or rigid.

Human Resource professionals are well suited to help the president ensure strategic alignment to a common direction throughout the company. Because HR professionals add value to all internal clients, they have a broad view of the company. In addition, they often have an advanced level of interpersonal excellence and trustworthiness to facilitate alignment.

HR can take a leadership position in facilitating alignment to the vision. Some of the ways this can happen include:

- *Insure that the strategic initiatives align with the vision:* HR can champion the alignment of strategic initiatives with the company's vision by following the processes for alignment and abandonment described in this chapter and Chapter Three.

- *Insure the vision cascades to divisional business plans:* Executive leaders can share the responsibility to insure that the vision extends to divisional business plans. However, interpersonal issues and personal interests may create difficulties among them. HR leaders often have the executives' trust and the competency to mediate these disputes before they grow out of proportion, enabling them to align their business plans.

- *Influence leaders to collaborate on projects:* HR can increase focus and better collaboration in many ways including creating cross-functional leadership teams to work on projects and encouraging executives to sponsor at least one project outside their own areas.

- *Align the vision to the performance of front-line employees and teams:* The real test of the vision is the extent to which the front-line supervisors and employees live the vision each day. They need to incorporate the vision into their work, their teams, and their individual performance objectives. HR has numerous skills and tools to help managers align vision and work, including effective performance management systems, strategic feedback surveys to measure alignment, rewards and recognition programs, and learning and development initiatives. Specifically, the performance management approach should focus all performance objectives for teams and individuals on both meeting the needs of key stakeholders and aligning the metrics to those of the company as a whole.

2. Alignment with Other Strategic Teams and Changes within the Company

Aligning the parts within a company is necessary just as aligning the wheels of a car is necessary. Without alignment, the car vibrates, causing wear and tear on the tires. If the situation is really serious, the car may be subject to a potentially dangerous blow out.

Cross-team alignment is often an overlooked area and a source of antagonism in many companies. Without alignment, people and systems may be at odds, "vibrating" unnecessarily and distracting employees from attending to the important issues. Employees may spend more time struggling with the confusion and "noise" created by the lack of alignment than doing the work required to achieve the strategic direction.

A company will need to achieve alignment among strategic initiatives even if it does not choose to create a flexible culture. Executives may be too busy to recognize the need to create alignment with other divisions' ideas and plans. Their workday pressures are immense. Often, they do not know what is happening in the company as a whole. For some, the business section of the newspapers is a faster way to get information about their company than through their own internal network.

The inter-team alignment is vital to success. This section explores ways to achieve this alignment through:

- Aligning teams with other strategic teams.
- Aligning with internal best practices.
- Aligning to reduce duplication.
- Aligning behavior during the "hand-off" between teams.

Align Strategic Teams with Other Strategic Teams

Many companies suffer from the problem of strategic teams working in isolation. Shared learning that occurs between project leaders who are implementing significant change is limited. They do not talk to each other about what they are doing and how they can collaborate or engage in post-implementation reviews to learn from the strengths and weaknesses of the process. In the cases when they do post-project reviews, they do not communicate with the other project leaders. As a result, others do not benefit from the experience of another group that went through a similar process.

Consider a scenario that describes how strategic teams can benefit from alignment with each other. In this example, a health services company has introduced cross-functional teams to implement its strategic initiatives. HR decides to insure alignment of the strategic teams and holds a meeting with the company's 15 project leaders.

As a result of their communication in the meeting, two of the project leaders have an eye-opening experience. One tells of designing a strategic capability to improve health outcomes in the company's areas of specialization. The other relates how she is designing a process to build relationships with the company's customers—the community health centers in the local neighborhoods. After they describe their projects, the two leaders look at each other in surprise. "We should be talking to each other more," says the customer relationships project leader. "I never thought of it, but in my approach to our customers, I should be using the strategy that we will improve health outcomes."

The project leaders are surprised that this is the first time the customer relationship group is considering leveraging the work of the health outcomes group to their benefit. "We are all too busy to find out what each other is doing," the customer relationships project leader says. "We are wasting time building everything from scratch when we can work together and get it done faster with better quality and better results." They decide they have to meet on a regular basis to keep each other informed about how their projects are developing, to seek feedback from each other, and to ensure they are aligned to the company's strategic direction.

Align with Internal Best Practices

The internal best practices in the company is another area of alignment that is often overlooked. Often a company realizes they have a best practice only when an outsider points it out to them. HR can look for the practices the company does extremely well and use them as internal best practices that all other areas of the company can emulate.

For example, it became evident in one company that while it was a leader in service to its external customers, it was inadequate in its internal employee satisfaction and services. This company had attempted to benchmark other companies' employee services but did not find a model that fit their unique culture. Finally, they realized that the best process existed in their company—their own external customer service. They conducted a study of this service that included how the company establishes customer expectations, how they market and deliver new services, and how they evaluate services for ongoing customer feedback.

The company decided to apply their external customer service processes to their internal employee services and satisfaction. This was accepted widely and was a great success. After some careful analysis, the company realized that the acceptance was due to the following factors:

- *Familiarity with the systems:* Many employees were aware of the systems used with external customers. Therefore, it was easier for them to accept the processes when they were introduced internally.

- *Appreciation of employee needs:* Employees complained that they felt like second-class citizens to the external customers. Once the company gave the employees what they requested, employee satisfaction started to improve.

- *Cost savings through re-use of systems:* The company was able to realize cost savings through the re-use of systems that already worked with the external customer.

- *Alignment created:* Alignment was created between internal employee services and the processes used for conducting business externally.

Align to Reduce Duplication

In a company in which people feel they are always "re-creating the wheel," aligning strategic initiatives helps avoid duplication of effort. Many initiatives often overlap with one another. When a company misses alignment opportunities and duplicates efforts, it can incur major costs, loss of time, and waste.

For example, in one company two teams each built a triage process that defined the priorities between multiple tasks. The teams did not communicate with one another and, therefore, duplicated efforts. Eventually, the company had to merge the two processes because the systems needed to be in common. Unfortunately, because the systems were antagonistic, the merger produced inefficiencies. As a result the company had to dismantle one of the triage systems to build a new one. The new effort to create efficiency to sidestep the antagonism was extremely costly and an unnecessary waste of time and money.

Align Behavior during the "Hand-Off" Between Teams

In many cases, even if a particular team's work is effective, the hand-off from that team to another may be done poorly. The image of a hand-off is taken from relay teams. Most professional runners are outstanding; but what makes a relay team exceptional is the gracefulness with which a team member hands the baton to the next runner. If the team members transfer the baton without losing speed or quality, they have a chance of performing excellently. If they slow down or lose their rhythm when they hand off the baton, they are likely to lose the race.

The relay race image applies to companies as well. Many hand-offs occur in companies between teams that are responsible for different parts of a process. For example, there are hand-offs between distribution, warehousing, and sales. If any one of these hand-offs slows down the process, all the parts will slow down. Another example is a company that has shift workers that struggle to insure a smooth transition between shifts. As the engineering principle suggests, a process will move as quickly as its slowest part. The hand-off is a very important activity that can slow down the process and create company inefficiencies.

When a process involves hand-offs between work teams, great benefits can be achieved if the hand-offs are aligned. If they are not, it may create antagonism, which can have negative implications.

HR Champions Alignment among Strategic Teams

HR professionals are often in a unique position to be a catalyst for change and to work with all the strategic teams. In addition, they are able to work with all the functional groups in the company. HR professionals can see the disconnects among the strategic teams as well as the functional groups and can help them work together more effectively. They champion this kind of strategic alignment by doing the following:

- Facilitating discussions amongst project leaders to open lines of communication about their initiatives and how their work can benefit from the work of others.

- Leveraging internal best practices that already exist and are known to them through their internal database that tracks what is being done in the company.

- Creating opportunities for alignment across geographical areas and business units to reduce duplication and achieve economies of scale that would otherwise not be realized. For example, a company's divisions located in different parts of the country or the world should use the same principles for developing systems to avoid duplications.

- Focusing on alignment to integrate new businesses with the current business and to align strategy company-wide where appropriate.

- Operating as a model of cross-functional team effectiveness to insure cross-team collaboration of others.

3. Alignment to the Customer's Needs

Chapter Two established that all departments in a company need to focus on the external customer. When this occurs, the customer becomes the connection point for everyone in the company. In essence, the customer becomes the axis that creates the internal balance and focus for all company strategies and initiatives.

The focus on alignment to customers' needs also affects the potential for the company's customer share. The external customer should be the focal point for all teams and activities in the company. The more the company aligns with the customer, the more likely the customer will invest in the company. The company's trust *in* the customer begets trust *from* the customer, establishing a relationship that is difficult for a competitor to break.

The wise company carefully nurtures the customers with whom it needs to build strategic relationships. These relationships often benefit the company because of the amount of revenue that can be generated as well as the number and quality of referrals to other customers. The customer benefits by receiving more personalized service and opportunities for more customized products.

One company created "think-tank" sessions with their strategic customers. They held sessions with a mix of strategic customers and senior executives to discuss the company's future direction and to seek input from the customers on the directions the company was considering. They also shared information about how the customers used the company's products and services. The customer "think-tanks" generated a great deal of interest because customers learned what other customers were doing. In addition, the interactions helped customers build their personal network.

When a company aligns with a customer, the points of contact between the customer and the company increase as well. In the past, the primary contacts were sales and purchasing. Recently, companies have recognized the strategic value of service as another important point of contact to build the relationship and identify additional areas of customer need. Other areas can build relationships with their counterparts in the customers' organization. For example, the company's HR department can build professional relationships with HR professionals in the customer's organization.

The company gives good service to non-strategic customers as well, although it does not make the same investment in alignment. For example, companies may not provide the same level of personal relationships to non-strategic customers. Often, companies use technology to mass-customize services to non-strategic customers so that they experience individualized attention through company clubs, awarding prizes such as credits for future purchases and service enhancements.

HR Champions Alignment to the Customers' Needs

HR can help the company establish strategic customer relationships by:

- *Expanding the visibility of strategic customers in the company:* HR can bring customers into various company meetings such as training programs in which customers can be guest speakers or even participants in strategy sessions. For example, in a financial services organization, the treasury department invites customers' CFOs to participate in their strategy sessions. The customer helps develop a treasury strategy that is in full alignment with the customers' needs.

- *Developing ways to help leaders focus on the needs of the customer:* In one situation an inventive HR leader has found a way to increase leaders' awareness of customer needs during their management planning sessions. He brings a baseball cap labeled "customer" to the meetings. One person wears the cap and plays the part of the customer. This individual's assignment is to think about the customer's needs and articulate those needs as the managers develop new ideas and plans. It is a simple device and one that illustrates to the managers the need to listen to the voice of the customer in every meeting.

- *Building a common focus on the external customer:* HR can help all areas of the company focus on the external customers and align their work to their needs.

4. Alignment with Preferred Suppliers

The supplier is often overlooked as an important stakeholder to which each team must align in order to reap the benefits from a positive supplier relationship. While many companies can see the benefit of enhancing their alignment with customers, they do not readily see the advantage of aligning with their suppliers. Some companies are opposed to aligning with suppliers because they perceive them as entities that don't contribute revenue to the company but instead take it from them. For example, some companies delay payment to suppliers, believing the traditional business school logic that longer payable timelines are beneficial to the company because they function as interest-free loans. They take little note of what this does to alignment between the company and the supplier.

Consider the different values and approaches to suppliers between two departments in the following company. The company's purchasing department is passionately committed to cutting costs. They are known as aggressive negotiators and are always able to squeeze an extra few percentage points from a supplier. Suppliers tend to avoid negotiating with this company because they are always in a competitive position, and the company's negotiating style often reduces their margins. The purchasing department manager has received bonuses each of the past three years for cutting costs.

The company's sales planners prioritize the sales department's needs and tell the buyers what to purchase. Because the planners believe that preferred suppliers will be very responsive to their needs, they are interested in reducing the number of suppliers and developing preferred supplier relationships. They see a number of benefits to be achieved through this relationship. For example, preferred suppliers can retain inventory and manage the automatic replenishment of stock for the company, share information about new product developments, and act as consultants to the company's customers on complicated service problems.

In addition, from the planners' vantage point, integrity is an issue. If a company wants to be a customer's preferred supplier, why would they not be willing to align with their preferred supplier when they are the customer? If companies talk out of both sides of their mouth on this issue, they are not going to be credible to their customers or with their own employees.

The sales planning and purchasing departments do not align with one other. They each assume they can achieve their objectives without the other party's involvement. However, their differing objectives result in frustrating results for each. Every time the sales planners approach a supplier with ideas, the supplier responds with mixed enthusiasm. When the planners do reach a contractual preferred relationship with a supplier, the purchasers are discouraged because they cannot reduce prices to former levels.

This kind of disconnect between a company and its suppliers is extremely common in large organizations. HR often knows that the lack of alignment exists but does not feel empowered to intervene. What gives HR this authority is the accountability for facilitating strategic alignment, which includes mediating disputes to the company's best strategic interest.

Some companies have implemented a formal process of assessing suppliers. The selected preferred suppliers have a special status with the company, which yields benefits such as less competition for selling their products, a retainer relationship with the company, and often annual sales commitments.

The company benefits from the preferred supplier relationships as well. Some of the benefits preferred suppliers can bring to the company include:

- Being more responsive to the company.
- Retaining the company's inventory and managing the automatic stock replenishment.
- Furnishing information about new technologies and product development.
- Being consultants to their customers on complicated service problems.
- Saving the company money on costly tendering processes.
- Increasing the accuracy of the company's forecasts.

HR Champions Alignment with Preferred Suppliers

HR can champion alignment with strategic suppliers by encouraging the company to identify where preferred supplier relationships will be helpful. In addition, they can assist in the process of selecting, developing the relationship, and managing the performance of suppliers.

Here is an example of how HR can help a company develop excellence in managing preferred supplier relationships. For example, consider a company that decides to outsource the role of sales representative to a preferred supplier. The challenge to HR is to insure that internal and external sales representatives deliver the same quality service to customers. To do this, HR introduces a quality control system and manages it to insure this level of quality occurs. Some of the aspects of this system include:

- Specifications to insure that the external service provider hires quality people and trains them to deliver high-quality customer relationships and sales.
- Building alignment with the preferred supplier to shape the supplier's values and behaviors.
- Conducting joint training programs to insure that the supplier represents the company in the best way possible.
- Excellent vendor management skills and computer systems that provide the data about vendor performance. The competencies HR professionals develop in managing their own preferred suppliers will enable them to help other departments in this process as well.

5. Internal Alignment within the Strategic Team

Chapter Seven described different kinds of teams, including traditional, autonomous, and virtual teams. Each strategic team, regardless of how it is set up, needs to be aligned within itself as well as with the company's direction. The challenge may be greatest for virtual teams that are not in the same location and whose membership may change more frequently. This section describes how team building can be used to facilitate internal alignment for all kinds of teams. Afterwards, it explores some examples that describe why teams are unaligned and the kinds of interventions that will help the team regain alignment to a common objective.

Internal Alignment through Effective Team Building

Team building is a very common activity that has achieved great popularity in the business environment. Unfortunately, team building varies in its effectiveness to achieve the envisioned results. In some cases, it is unclear why the team building is taking place and what the team needs to do to enhance its overall performance.

Although team building for "its own sake" is a nice perk, it too often does not add value to the company's strategic direction. HR has an important role to play in helping strategic teams diagnose their issues and develop a process to align their direction with the company. HR professionals act as a catalyst to enable the manager to lead the team. HR professionals help the manager and the team get "unstuck." If they are at an impasse at some juncture and believe the solution is team building, HR has the ability to help them discover the reason for the barrier and to start them moving again. Once the team is making progress, HR steps aside for the manager to be the leader.

The following anecdote illustrates internal team alignment and shows that when team building is done for its own sake and not to achieve a higher purpose (such as alignment), it often does not yield meaningful results: "We shouldn't do team building just for the sake of team building," an HR professional says to her manager. She explains that team building is actually an opportunity for alignment within the team and should focus on the barrier that is blocking the team from working together. The "team-ness" then can be a secondary gain as the underlying problem is resolved.

The HR professional learned her lessons from experience. She recalls the manager who told her, "We need some team building." He put together an experiential session that focused on building team cohesion and relationships. After the session, the team members appeared to like each other more, but they still did not work well as a team and, therefore, their effectiveness was not improved. She discovered that team building can be a waste of time if it does not focus on how the team needs to develop to become a better team.

HR suggests that no group of people should call themselves a team unless they have defined mutual accountabilities upon which all the members are measured and which help the team align to the company's strategic imperatives. She also shares four questions with the manager that will help the participants identify their focus for team building.

1. Why do you want to do team building?
2. What is the problem that led you to believe that team building was necessary?
3. What would your group look like if they functioned at their optimum level?
4. What are the mutual accountabilities (if any) that make this group a team?

She explains that the answers shape the way she proceeds with a facilitation process. Almost no team-building session is the same. Each session meets the needs of the team to help it respond more effectively to an area in which it is showing some weakness or an opportunity area.

Examples of Mis-Aligned Teams and Potential Interventions

Here are some other examples of specific barriers to internal team alignment. These examples may help HR professionals diagnose the kinds of problems that typically occur for teams. The examples also include illustrations of different kinds of team interventions to achieve performance enhancement and better alignment within the team.

- *No direction:* In answer to the question, What is the problem that led you to believe that team building was necessary? A project leader says his team has no direction. "We do not seem to know what we are working on from day to day. People are just putting in time. Some are not even working all the time—they have just quit and stayed." The HR professional realizes that the desired outcome for this team is to find an inspiring team purpose. She arranges a workshop that involves everyone in the development of the preferred future for the strategic team in a fun and interactive manner.

As a result of knowing its purpose, the strategic team has an additional benefit—it becomes more of an aligned team.

- *No alignment to the company's direction:* A project leader asks an HR professional for a team-building workshop. The HR professional asks him why he needs it. The project leader relates that his team is "too much of a team." He says, "They do everything together and are inseparable. Rather than focusing on the company's direction, they seem to concentrate only on team objectives and interests. It's a team gone wild." After some further discussions, the HR professional realizes that the team is unaligned to the company's strategic direction and as a result the group's work and interests are counterproductive. The HR professional's objective is to channel the team's energy to align with the company direction. To achieve that result, they proceed with the following:

  – Some senior executives are brought into a planning session.

  – The team is included in a dialogue session about the company strategy.

  – The team and the executives define a shared end state that helps the company achieve its goals.

  – The leaders solicit the team's help in leading the project to help the company implement its strategy.

- *Lack of clear accountabilities:* A project leader describes a complex virtual team environment that does not work cohesively. The virtual team is a dispersed team that communicates by telephone or e-mail and does not have any shared space. This strategic team needs to reach an understanding of its accountabilities and to trust that people will follow through on their responsibilities even though they do not work in the same location. They decide that even though they are a virtual team, it does not mean that they never physically see each other. They agree to meet for a two-day session to agree upon the expected deliverables for the team, to develop a clearer definition of accountabilities, and to define how they can align their activities better as a virtual team.

- *Demoralized team:* A company introduces a strategic initiative to enable all employees to take responsibility for the quality of their products. The initiative involves allowing any employee to place a sticker on a truck if he or she believes it is carrying contaminated goods or products of an unsatisfactory quality.

A new warehouse supervisor describes a demoralized group of workers and an event that provoked this situation: When the supervisor was a packer in the warehouse, he saw a product leaving the warehouse in a defective state, took initiative and placed the sticker on the truck. The truck was not allowed to move or leave the site. Bedlam broke out. The warehouse supervisor shouted that the shipment had to leave to meet the customers' timelines and that the product was safe. However, after an investigation, it was found that the product was unsafe and the young packer was right. The supervisor was released and no explanation was given to the workers. Senior management then decided to appoint the young packer as the new warehouse supervisor.

To help the demoralized team, the HR professional arranges a team-building process that focuses on both the quality of work and the importance of taking initiative. Also included in the session is a new supervisor orientation process that helps the supervisor take leadership and begin to rebuild the group into a team.

- *Limited value to customers:* A project leader describes a strategic team that is not focusing on delivering value to customers. The members of the team are not handling the complexity of the assignment. Their customers are more sophisticated than they are and do not see the strategic team as providing value. The team needs to insure that there is a proper fit between the capability of the members of the team and the complexity of the work. Also, because the complexity of work does not stay stagnant but continues to evolve, the team members must be able to adjust to the customer's changing needs. The team leader meets with team members to determine who should be deployed to meet the needs of specific customers. The initial work is to redesign the allocation of work to create a better match between the customer's needs and the team members' ability to meet those needs. The team members also engage in a team process to define mutual expectations.

- *Team leader is ineffective as a leader:* On occasion, the source of the problem for a team is its leader. Sometimes it can be due to the competence of the leader. In that case, specific training or coaching would be appropriate. The training or coaching should be designed to ensure that the leader can apply a coherent approach to a strategic initiative. It should also help the leader develop a common language with other team leaders and team members in order to align work effectively. At other times there is a mismatch between the requirements of the strategic initiative on which the team is working and the capabilities of the team leader. This mismatch sometimes happens as projects proceed to new phases of their development. In these cases, the team leader chosen to lead at the beginning of an initiative may not be as well suited to lead at this point in the project. Just as the company may need to change leaders at different growth phases, the same applies to team leaders. The company needs to have the flexibility and maturity to deploy people to the stage of an initiative that best suits their capability to contribute value.

The HR professional contributes value to alignment as strategic teams form, work together, and are dismantled. HR's responsibility is to insure that the strategic team understands the external customer's needs and then to identify the appropriate intervention to help them align effectively with each other as they strive to deliver value to the customer.

HR Champions Internal Alignment of the Strategic Team

The HR professional champions the internal alignment of strategic teams by doing the following:

- *Facilitate team building to help the team deliver its strategic imperatives:* In many companies HR professionals have experience providing team-building experiences for groups of employees. They often identify the need and then deliver the session themselves or involve a preferred supplier who works closely with them to deliver the session.

- *Consult with the team leaders:* HR professionals guide team leaders to use multiple approaches to motivate team members and to align to the company direction. They help team leaders to create a climate in which team members will take personal ownership to drive the initiative to completion. The HR professionals also encourage the team leaders to go the extra mile to help people adjust to changes so that they can participate effectively in the initiative.

- *Support and reinforce team accomplishments:* HR professionals lead by example, follow through on promises (being careful not to over promise), and encourage others to follow through as well.

They reward and recognize the accomplishments of those involved in the initiative. They also insure that the team has defined mutual accountabilities and that each individual has specific account-abilities.

How to Fail at Strategic Alignment

A common reason companies are not successful with strategic initiatives is that they do not pay attention to strategic alignment as a major issue and keep it uppermost in their minds. Some other reasons exist for failure such as:

- *Employees assume the company initiatives are aligned because senior executives developed them:* This assumption is not always true. In many organizations the senior executives are not working in alignment with one another and, therefore, their initiatives are not linked. Executives need to dialogue about tough alignment questions.

- *Not focusing on alignment to the external customer:* HR and other departments need to think of the external customer's interests in all their work. If all employees focus on the same customer value, the alignment potential has a greater chance of being realized.

- *Assume the power of the design will create compliance:* Too many people believe that if an initiative's design is aligned to the strategic direction it will automatically create alignment in the group. Unfortunately, this is not always the case in the actual implementation.

- *Assume people are self-motivated to align activities:* It is the responsibility of leaders of a strategic initiative to communicate the importance of strategic alignment to employees and to keep it on the agenda. They must believe in the direction and model it, especially in times of crisis. They must communicate consistent messages and deliver them on time as promised (or explain in detail why the messages are late). They also should not be surprised when people resist. People often deny and resist change. Leaders help them by normalizing the change adaptation process. It is also important to properly reward and recognize the behaviors that will focus people on the company's desired direction. Rewards and recognition should promote alignment and cross-functionality.

HR Measures 360° Alignment

Alignment should have clearly defined and measurable objectives. An excellent tool for measurement is the 360° survey. The term, "360° survey," refers to aligning the entire 360 degrees in the *circle of influence* that is important to an individual or a team to deliver value to a business. The use of the 360° survey tool and the results from it help shape behaviors and alignment.

HR professionals have already taken accountability for conducting 360° surveys of individuals in some companies. The 360° survey usually seeks feedback from the manager of an employee, the employee's direct reports (if any), and their peers. The manager is often effective at assessing results but not as effective at assessing the process by which the results are achieved. Direct reports can assess the process by which results are achieved but have less knowledge of the extent to which the actual results are achieved. Peers seem to have knowledge of both the results achieved and the process by which the results are achieved. The conclusion is that all parties should be consulted in a 360° survey feedback process, and the peers often can provide the most astute feedback. When the customers and suppliers are added, the full 360° circle of influence is complete.

HR can extend that role to include assessing the 360° alignment of strategic teams as well. HR can apply some of the lessons they have learned from individual 360° surveys and apply those lessons to the measurement of the 360° alignment of strategic teams.

For example, many HR professionals have realized that the data from the 360° surveys is not an end itself. Rather, it is a start, a place to begin a dialogue conversation about some feedback on the individual or team. In addition, there are some methods to tailor 360° surveys to be useful as a measure of 360° alignment of strategic teams. For example:

- Identify which of the stakeholders will respond to the 360° alignment survey. Insure confidentiality for the respondent throughout the process. Do whatever it takes to help people answer the survey honestly rather than what they believe the person wants to hear.

- Tailor the items on the survey to the issues of specific importance to the stakeholders.

- Use web-based technology to provide access to respondents in the easiest way possible.

- Give the team the chance to review the data from the 360° survey on them and suggest their own interpretations and recommendations and to align their work more effectively.

- Provide coaching for individuals and teams so that they know how to interpret the data feedback and can understand its implications for behavior change.

- Teach the teams and individuals the best way to give feedback to the stakeholders who respond to the 360° alignment survey.

Human Resources Models Strategic Alignment

Human Resources must stand up to the test of alignment within its own function in order to be a viable champion of strategic alignment for the company. HR can start with aligning its own initiatives to the company strategic direction. As HR achieves a reasonable level of credibility in its internal alignment, then it can take on the greater business transformation role of aligning the entire company.

HR strategic initiatives must focus on the company vision, be aligned with other HR and company initiatives, and align with customers' needs and preferred suppliers. HR professionals must also work together as a team that defines its mutual accountabilities and internally aligns to a common direction.

HR can model the way of strategic alignment by doing the following:

- Have one point of contact with clients so that they are clear about whom to contact within HR for specific services.

- Insure HR initiatives are internally aligned so that managers are not burdened with unnecessary requests.

- Demonstrate a commitment in HR to sharing information so that all HR professionals can contribute to aligning activities in their department and in the company.

- Create a flexible culture within HR so that HR professionals will have the adaptability to meet the changing needs of the company.

- Align its work with others in the company who participate in HR-related work but under different titles (for example, change agents, communication specialists, managers).

A successful internal alignment within HR gives HR the credibility it needs to help other departments align to the company's strategic direction. HR's successful alignment has a ripple effect to other departments that will encourage them to focus on alignment as well.

Summary

- Alignment needs to take place from the executive level to individual performance objectives, across the company and to the customers and suppliers and within teams.

- Executives must champion alignment, challenging activities that do not align. Some of the ways they can do this are: articulate the vision, merge strategic initiatives under umbrella strategies, use high profile events to reinforce what is important, have high expectations and confidence, and be role models.

- HR can take a leadership position in facilitating this alignment by
  - Insuring that the strategic initiatives align with the vision.
  - Influencing leaders to collaborate on projects to help them focus on the vision.
  - Insuring the vision cascades to divisional business plans.
  - Aligning the vision to the performance of front-line employees and teams.

- One overlooked source of information is the internal best practices in the company. HR can position itself as an essential contributor to continuous improvement by helping the organization align and gain maximum advantage from internal best practices.

- The focus on alignment with customers also affects the potential for the company's customer share. The more the company aligns with the customer, the more likely the customer will invest in the company. When a company aligns with a customer, the points of contact between the customer and the company increase. The wise company carefully nurtures the customers with whom it needs to build these kinds of strategic relationships.

- HR can help the company establish strategic customer relationships by:
  - expanding the visibility of strategic customers in the company by bringing customers into various company meetings,
  - developing ways to help leaders focus on the needs of the customer, and
  - creating "think-tanks" with strategic customers.

- In addition to identifying strategic customers, companies should identify strategic suppliers. The selected strategic suppliers have a special status with the company, which yields benefits such as

  - Less competition for selling their products.

  - A retainer relationship with the company.

  - Annual sales commitments.

  - Being more responsive to the company.

  - Retaining the company's inventory and managing automatic stock replenishment.

  - Furnishing information about new technologies and product development.

  - Being consultants to their customers on complicated service problems.

  - Saving the company money on costly tendering processes.

  - Increasing the accuracy of the company's forecasts.

- Human Resources can help a company develop excellence in managing preferred supplier relationships. To do this, HR needs excellent vendor management skills and computer systems that provide the data about vendor performance. The competencies HR professionals develop in managing their own preferred suppliers will enable them to help other departments in this process as well.

- Specific barriers to team alignment include: no direction, no alignment to the company direction, lack of cohesiveness, demoralization, limited value to customers, and ineffective leaders. Many companies also suffer from the problem of teams working in isolation.

- The most common reason that companies are not successful with strategic alignment initiatives is that they do not pay attention to alignment as a major issue and keep it uppermost in their minds. Other reasons include:

  - Employees assume the company initiatives are aligned because senior executives developed them.

  - Not focusing strategic alignment on the external customer.

- Assume the power of the design will create compliance.

- Not measuring and not rewarding alignment.

• Alignment needs to have clearly defined and measurable objectives. An excellent tool for measurement is the 360° survey, which measures the alignment of major stakeholders surrounding an individual and/or a team. The use of the tool and the results from it help shape behaviors and alignment.

• Human Resources must stand up to the test of alignment within its own function in order to be a viable champion of alignment. A successful internal alignment within HR gives HR the credibility it needs to help other departments align to the company's strategic direction.

Implement Change and Transition

While some companies are fortunate to have leaders who are able to focus on change implementation and the human transition elements associated with change, others are not. HR professionals can have a significant influence in companies by guiding leaders in these two areas.

Consider an example of a company that is having difficulty with the implementation of change. The executives introduce a strategic initiative and assign it to junior managers to implement the change. The executives then proceed to plan the next major initiative. Several months after delegating the initiative to junior managers, the executives find that little change is accomplished. The line managers perceive the strategic initiative as another example of how the company loses focus as it tries to implement change. At an executive meeting, the HR vice president suggests that the managers and employees need a strong message to convince them that the company is committed to carrying good ideas to implementation. The executive team agrees.

The company's president takes the initiative, and, in her annual employee address, begins her remarks with a surprising opening comment, "Our vision is only as good as what it makes us do today." Later she explains, "This year we will not have new change initiatives. We are overloaded with good initiatives that still need to be achieved." She then proceeds to articulate what becomes known in the company as the "Year of the Tissue Paper Strategy." "I can fit a tissue paper between our strategy and our competition's," she says. "We all read the same books, listen to the same gurus, target the same markets. The only difference between the winners and the losers is who will *implement* the strategy successfully." The president backs up her words with action. She and the executive team make certain that the company focuses on implementing the chosen initiatives successfully.

Leaders must select the changes that are in alignment with their strategic direction. At the same time, they must insure that the changes actually occur. HR professionals assist the leaders by taking a far greater role in advocating and facilitating the effective implementation of change and transition. This includes the following:

- *Ensuring that the selected changes are implemented:* Some companies suffer from a lack of focus on the implementation of the changes they would like to make. Often, the leadership sees the *identification* of the change as the primary focus and does not place equal emphasis on making the change happen. Within these companies, the leadership often loses credibility as they announce new changes. People begin to disbelieve them. The changes may be the right thing to do, but they lose momentum if the leadership does not attend to implementing the changes successfully. HR professionals can advocate and facilitate change implementation by using the process described in this chapter.

- *Giving attention to the human transition elements in change:* In some cases, leaders implement changes but do not give equal attention to the human transition elements in the change process that help people understand and commit to the change. In other cases, external changes are imposed that require the leadership and employees to adjust quickly to the new reality. These are situations in which HR professionals can have great impact. They can facilitate human transition factors that help people adjust, accept, and participate in change.

Change and Transition

To implement change successfully, a balance must be achieved between achieving excellence in the process and focusing on the outcomes that are expected from the process. My preferred term is *implement change and transition* to focus the process on its primary purpose, which is to make the change occur and to have people commit to it willingly.

Change and transition represent distinctly different parts of the Implementing Change and Transition Process:

- **Change** refers to the *business* elements required when planning and implementing change. The business elements include understanding competitive forces, identifying the objectives of the change, developing a detailed implementation plan, and making the change happen.

- **Transition** refers to the *human* elements that are important in change. The human elements include selecting the right change leaders; involving key stakeholders; communicating, training, and helping people adjust; and ensuring that the learnings from the change are shared.

When leaders do not give attention to both the implementation and the human transition elements in the change, it is less likely that the company will implement the change successfully. HR can play an important role in enabling business transformation to occur through an effective balance of the two.

The Process of Implementing Change and Transition

Many leading organizational thinkers have developed models of how change can be defined and implemented. Most of the processes (called by various names, such as organizational change and change management) have common features. Almost all have ideas that are worth exploring.

Companies should select one primary change process from which all change initiatives can vary. Too many approaches and models confuse employees and can become a barrier to successful implementation. Figure 9.1 shows the "Implementing Change And Transition Process." It is based on best practices' research in this area.[1]

The eight elements in the process provide the structure for this chapter and define HR's role to help the change occur successfully. Four of the elements (1, 3, 5, and 7) are the *business* aspects of the process of implementing change and transition. The business elements are:

- Understand competitive forces and customer value.

- Identify the preferred future and the urgency for the change.

---

[1] The Implementing Change and Transition model was developed by Janet Burt and David Weiss based, in part, on the best practices research conducted by Janet Burt of the firm of Geller, Shedletsky & Weiss, 1998.

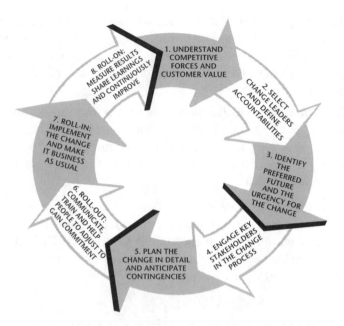

Figure 9.1: The Implementing Change And Transition Process

- Plan the change in detail and anticipate contingencies.
- Roll-in: Implement the change and make it business as usual.

The other four elements (2, 4, 6, and 8) are the *human transition* aspects of implementing change. Often, the transition elements require the change leaders to influence and educate people so that they will be open to the changes that will occur and commit to them. With the human transition elements, HR has an especially important role. The human transition elements are:

- Select change leaders and define accountabilities.
- Engage key stakeholders in the change process.
- Roll-out: communicate, train and help people adjust.
- Roll-on: measure results, share learnings and continuously improve.

HR professionals can use the Implementing Change and Transition Process and modify it to fit their specific context and work environment. It is often easier for professionals to modify a proposed approach than to develop a new process from scratch. The Implementing Change and Transition Process and the comments in this chapter should be used in a similar manner. The process is a guide and not a restrictive set of rules about how to implement change. In addition, the reader can explore the book *Human Resource Champions* (Ulrich, 1997)[2] in which a "pilot's checklist" is described for the effective implementation of change. Those ideas are also very helpful for HR professionals as they proceed to work as change agents.

Some additional characteristics of the Implementing Change and Transition Process shown in Figure 9.1 include the following:

- *The approach can be expanded, shrunk or re-ordered:* Although the model is presented in a continuous format, the context will shape the actual model of change that will be used. The context defines the process and not the reverse. In some cases, the context will require specific elements to be added. In others, some elements will be removed. In yet others, the order of the elements will be changed. The Implementing Change and Transition Process is useful as a starting point to help begin the conversation about how the change can proceed to implementation. It is meant to be a stimulus and not the definitive answer.

- *Build in formal approval checkpoints for more complex changes:* At the conclusion of three elements in the Implementing Change and Transition Process (shown in Figure 9.1 with thicker lines) there are major checkpoints at which executives assess and decide whether the project should be terminated or should proceed. These are at the completion of:

  - Element #3: Identify the Preferred Future and the Urgency for the Change

  - Element #5: Plan the Change in Detail and Anticipate Contingencies

  - Element #8: Roll-On, Measure Results, Share Learnings, and Continuously Improve

    At various stages these checkpoints function as controls to ensure that the company analyzes and measures the change implementation carefully. The controls are not meant to slow down the process; rather, they are intended to increase the probability that the company will implement the change effectively. If the controls slow down the process and get in the way of implementing the change, the company should reassess the controls to determine if they are a barrier to implementation.

---

[2] David Ulrich, *Human Resource Champions*, Harvard Business School Press, 1997.

- *The process assumes you are the originator of the change:* The Implementing Change and Transition Process assumes that the leaders are the creators of the change. However, in some cases, the company and its leaders are not the originators of the change but instead are stakeholders in someone else's change (as described in Element 4 of this process). Wherever possible, the stakeholders need to focus on enhancing their partnership role with those who are introducing the change in order to be involved in the process as early as possible. In addition, the stakeholders may want to focus specifically on Elements 4, 6, and 8 of the Implementing Change and Transition Process.

The HR professional should be an advocate and an active facilitator for the implementation of change and transition from the beginning to the end of the process. This chapter explores each of the elements and HR's role in this process.

Element #1: Understand Competitive Forces and Customer Value

Leaders are responsible for selecting the appropriate changes for their companies to implement. Two key criteria in making this kind of selection are to understand how the change will affect the company's 1) competitive advantage and 2) customer value. *Competitive forces* can be anywhere and can be identified even in situations in which the competition is not obvious. For example, customers can become the competition by deciding to build their own capabilities if service providers are unable to meet their needs. *Customer value* refers to providing the customer with the value they desire. Within a company, the constant focus should be on the work that is of greatest value to the customer.

Many company leaders have realized that they need to identify how they can gain relative advantage against their competitors and at the same time enhance the value they deliver to customers. Without understanding competitive forces and customer value, company leaders will find that the change they select will lose focus and lack the urgency required for people to commit to the change.

Executives must also aggressively reject changes they have selected that are not working. An example of a company that chose an inadequate change action is a pharmaceutical company that decided to open a health clinic for the public. They believed this action would change the public's opinion that pharmaceutical companies sold drugs only to generate revenue. The company leaders gave a great deal of attention and thought to the strategic initiative. They acknowledged that they were taking a risk that the strategy would not work, but they also recognized an even greater risk—that if the company was too deep into the implementation, they would not have the courage to terminate the project.

The clinic was successful as a clinic, and it was running effectively in servicing its patients. However, it was ineffective in contributing to the company's strategic position as a pharmaceutical firm that had a focus on more than just selling drugs. The executives decided to discontinue the initiative one year after it began because they realized it was not meeting their original strategic objectives. Ending the project was the right solution because the strategy did not provide the anticipated competitive advantage and customer value.

Most companies have professionals who are devoted to understanding competitive forces and customer value. While HR's role in this element is often limited, understanding the competition and customer value in the selection of change initiatives has some definite benefits for HR:

- *It helps HR professionals to create their own strategy and change their own function from the "outside-in" rather than from the "inside-out":* This means that as HR professionals develop their people and organizational strategy, they will define the strategy by the external competitive forces and the customer value rather than by the internal desire to make change.

- *It changes the way HR professionals work with their internal clients:* As a result they will be more responsive to competitive pressures, enabling them to partner with clients more effectively and deliver value to external customers.

Element #2: Select Change Leaders and Define Accountabilities

HR professionals are involved in identifying the criteria for selecting the change leaders and the change team members and recruiting them. In addition, they may assist in selecting the executive sponsor(s) who has the overall responsibility for the team's work.

The Change Leader's Role

The change leader is very important to the success of any strategic initiative. Some of the change leader's specific responsibilities include:

- *Develop and execute the change plans*: Change leaders develop, execute, and measure implementation plans in alignment with the company's overall strategy. At review meetings they recommend whether the change process should proceed or whether it should be terminated. Other aspects of this responsibility include:
  - Identifying linkages with other initiatives.
  - Gathering ideas and feedback, and incorporating them into their plans.
  - Testing out the viability of the initiative.
  - Measuring the progress of the change at regular intervals.
  - Demonstrating flexibility and adapting to the context as it changes their plans.

- *Build an effective change team:* Change leaders help the change team do the following:
  - See the entire project and not just the specific areas over which the team will have responsibility.
  - Insure alignment of team activities with the company vision and other strategic initiatives.
  - Understand the Implementing Change and Transition Process.
  - Facilitate the team to reach effective decisions.
  - Build a climate in which members of the team can communicate with openness and candor.
  - Share what they have learned and what has not worked as they reflect on the possibilities of this change initiative.

- *Make things happen:* Change leaders must be able to make things happen and to push the project ahead. Some of the capabilities required to do this include:
  - Being attentive to the process and giving equal weight to the deliverables.
  - Having the personal drive and commitment to ensure that action will be taken on the decisions made by the change team.
  - Knowing how to use data to adjust the process as they proceed with the implementation of change and transition.

– Understanding how to modify their plans as the situation changes so that the initiative proceeds towards the end state they define.

Assisting the change leaders is an important role for HR professionals. Some of the ways they can contribute include the following:

- Identify the criteria for selecting and then recruiting the change leaders for a particular change process.
- Coach the change leaders throughout the process. Contribute their knowledge of internal and external best practices about how change teams can function most effectively.
- Facilitate discussion among change leaders of different initiatives so they can share information and align their activities to the company's vision.
- Step in or find the resource that can help the change team become "unstuck" if they are unable to proceed. Help the change team start moving again.
- Guide the change leaders to follow the implementing change and transition process through training, coaching, mentoring and measuring how the change project is proceeding. They can also remind change leaders to involve people in change, as the popular phrase suggests that "People do not mind change; they mind being changed."

The Change Team's Role

The change team members are people who can add value to the change initiative and who are committed to the idea the change represents. When change team members are assigned to a team but have no interest in that process, the results are often of lower quality.

HR must help the change team members stay focused and motivated. Many of the ideas suggested about virtual teams (Chapter Seven) and team alignment (Chapter Eight) will be helpful here. Virtual teams enhance the flexibility of change leaders to choose team members who are best suited for the initiative and who can add the most value when needed. Two other specific roles for the change team are worthy of reinforcing:

- *Make the change initiative part of the team members' jobs:* Many projects fail because the change team members are told that the project work is an "add on" to their normal day jobs. Usually, excessive workload demands mean that the project will not work as effectively because people will not give it the time it deserves even if they want to be committed to it. The HR professional can advocate for the allocation of work time to a change project so that people experience work on the change team as part of their regular jobs.

- **Ensure that throughout the implementing change process some continuity of change team members exists:** At times, turnovers of change team members occur. To ensure that the implementation accurately reflects the original end state that has been envisioned, some change team members should stay with the project from beginning to end.

The Role of the Executive Sponsor

Executive sponsors help ensure that senior-level attention to the change occurs through their access and influence on the executive team. They also help change leaders understand the pressing issues that the senior executives are concerned about.

Executive sponsors work with the change leaders in a variety of ways, including the following:

- Define the change leader's specific accountabilities and the change initiative's expected deliverables.
- Identify cross-functional links between this change and others in the company.
- Liaise with the rest of the executives about the change. Provide the executives with the necessary updates and discuss the progress of the change and the anticipated impact on the company.
- Coach the change leader on an as-required basis.
- Periodically measure and approve the progress of the change initiative at check points.

HR professionals can help executive sponsors fulfill their role in the following ways:

- **Guide the executive sponsor:** HR professionals should avoid taking over the project. Instead they guide executive sponsors in their role of holding change leaders accountable for change initiatives and giving them the space to make decisions.

- *Coach the executive sponsor if the change leader is not delivering according to expectations:* When a change leader's performance is not adequate, the HR professional can help the sponsor define whether the change leader is making bad judgments. For example, the change leader may be making an inappropriate selection of individuals to assume specific roles in the process. HR professionals must be skilled in coaching so that they can guide executive sponsors to make their own coaching role a constructive rather than a destructive process.

Executive Sponsors Interim Gate Reviews

Periodic executive reviews are common in product development situations and insure that product development is done on time and with high quality. Unfortunately, companies do not always give the same care to other complex changes. Much can be learned from product development review processes. One review process that is useful is called a "gate review." Gate reviews have specific milestones that must be reached within a certain time span. At each milestone, the change leader presents the results achieved to the executive team or sponsor. If the milestones have been reached, the executive team or sponsor either gives approval to proceed, requires further work, or recommends abandoning the project.

Conducting gate reviews may be unnecessary for fairly simple changes that have lower implementation risk. However, for more complex changes, gate reviews are very helpful and have some important benefits, which include:

- The change team and leader receive clear feedback on their progress because of the clarity of the decision in a gate review. Typically, the decision is a "go" or "no-go" decision. Sometimes the decision is to proceed with further analysis, but the expectation is that short timelines will be given if further research is required.

- The executives' expectation is to give top priority to the gate review so that they will not slow down the change team's progress. In one company, the executives guaranteed a 24-hour turnaround for a decision after a planned gate review meeting. This ensured that the gate review process did not slow down the momentum of implementing the change.

- Executives are not involved in the change projects in between gate reviews unless requested otherwise by the change leader. This creates a great deal of ownership by the change leader. It enables him or her to make independent decisions on a daily basis without intervention by the executives. It also saves time for the executives if they are involved only at critical junctures.

The gate review process must be kept as simple as possible. In most cases, three gates are sufficient. In product development environments, the gates are referred to by numbers such as Gate 0, Gate 1, and Gate 2. Each higher number gate reflects a phase of implementation that often involves more people, is more costly, and requires greater intervention in the actual business system and the way work is done on a daily basis.

The three gates (or check points) can be described as follows:

Gate 0 – Adopt the Concept: The Gate 0 review is held at the conclusion of Element #3 – Identify the Preferred Future and the Urgency for the Change. The executives adopt the concept and either give approval for the project to proceed or reject it. In most cases, executives have a great deal of involvement in the process of reaching Gate 0. The concept has a better chance of being compelling if it is based on competitive forces and customer value. The concept must also have an articulated preferred future, with a sense of urgency to proceed and defined metrics to measure success.

Gate 1 – Define and Approve Plans for the Change: The Gate 1 review is held at the conclusion of Element #5 – Plan the Change in Detail and Anticipate Contingencies. Once the concept is adopted, the change team needs to define clearly how the change will be introduced and how the anticipated results will be achieved. Gate 1 is the point at which the executives can approve the change implementation to proceed. In complex change initiatives, companies often reduce the risk that the implementation will be poor by piloting the changes and/or creating simulations to test the change. The testing may also identify "quick hits" that can be initiated immediately and show benefit from the change even before full implementation. The Gate 1 executive review approval means that the executives are willing to expend additional money on this change, to intervene within the actual work environment, and to involve many more people to make the change happen.

Gate 2 – Implement Change: The Gate 2 review is held at the conclusion of Element #8-Roll-On: – Measure Results, Share Learnings, and Continuously Improve. Many companies often ignore this gate review.

They assume that once they clearly define the change, it will be implemented according to its plan. Executives sometimes become uninterested at this point and begin focusing on the next concept to adopt. When companies decide that Gate 2 is part of their process, it compels the executives to think about the change until the conclusion of implementation.

When companies use gate reviews to anchor the change process, a number of distinct benefits emerge including:

- The project has more precise definition, allowing for clearer follow-up measurements to determine the return on investment from the change.

- The care in the development of the change increases the likelihood that the change will become part of the company's ongoing way of doing business. The change is no longer viewed as a project; it becomes the new way for the company to do business.

- The change initiative will have a greater probability of providing relative advantage against the competition or at least competitive parity because it is carefully chosen and implemented.

HR professionals help the change leaders, teams, and executive sponsors focus on the gate reviews and deliver on their expectations. They need to advocate for the change process, helping make the changes occur by focusing on the organizational and people elements. When HR professionals contribute this kind of value, they become part of the company's strategic thinking and are able to partner with the business leaders.

Element #3: Identify the Preferred Future and the Urgency for the Change

The first two elements of the process focus on understanding competitive forces and customer value and selecting the change leaders and team. In this element, the change team defines the compelling reasons for the change. They do this by identifying what they believe is the change's preferred future and why it is urgent for this change to occur. HR professionals also need to determine the anticipated outcome of this change process. They then can begin to plan the changes that will be needed in the organization and identify how to assist people to embrace the envisioned changes.

The compelling reason for the change can be explained as a formula with three variables. The three variables involved are:

Compelling change = f (preferred future, urgency, first steps)

This section looks at each of the three variables that contribute to creating a compelling change.

- *Define the preferred future:* The term "preferred future" identifies the end state for a *specific* change initiative. The word "vision" is often used instead, but I have avoided it because if the term were used to indicate the end states for *various* change initiatives, the company would have multiple visions, which would often create mis-alignment.

  The preferred future must be compelling to the team members and motivate people who are not on the team. When the preferred future is defined clearly, the change team can sense it, smell it, taste it, and see it clearly so that they know what they will have when the change is fully implemented. This level of clarity also helps the executive sponsor understand the change and will increase the likelihood that the concept will be adopted. One organization attempted to show the preferred future symbolically. They built a 4' x 6' landscape depicting the preferred future with each part of the change symbolically represented by a different plant in the landscape. The landscape model was helpful to people who read about the preferred future but didn't understand it. It also became a showpiece or banner for this particular change throughout the implementation that helped create the focus necessary to make the change occur.

- *Identify the sense of urgency:* Change will not occur if people do not experience a sense of urgency for the change. The more imminent the urgency, the more intense the desire to achieve the preferred future. If the change does not have urgency, motivating people to make the change occur will be a greater challenge. Under no circumstances should the urgency be fabricated and unreal. That kind of manipulation creates a loss of integrity in the process of implementing specific changes and in the role of leadership within the company.

- *Identify the first steps:* At this stage of the process, only the first steps need to be clarified. The details of the entire plan cannot be known until further research is undertaken. The term, "first steps" includes the following:

- What will be the initial actions in the initiative?
- The metrics to assess progress and how the data will be collected and used.
- The overall work plan that will be taken to launch the change.

Some change leaders are relieved that they have only the first steps to define. When this process is not followed companies often spend too much time upfront on the whole plan. It can cause major delays in the process of implementing change, and it is often unnecessary in this element.

Some implications of this equation are important to consider. For a change to pass Gate 0 – Adopt the Concept, all three variables must be present. The table below describes the consequences if any one of those three variables is missing.

CONSEQUENCES OF MISSING ONE OF THE VARIABLES FROM COMPELLING CHANGE EQUATION

Scenario	Consequence
The change initiative specifies the urgency and the first step but not the preferred future.	People have a desire to act without knowing where the company is going. They may go down the wrong path and make wrong decisions.
The change initiative specifies a preferred future and the first step but does not clarify the sense of urgency.	People may not be motivated to take action.
The change initiative has a clearly defined preferred future and an urgency to proceed but does not have a clear first step.	People may be frustrated because they won't know what to do first although they will feel the desire to act and to begin the process of changing.

The HR professional has some important roles to play in the identification of the preferred future, the urgency for the change, and the first step. In addition, HR contributes to the interim gate reviews for more complex changes. The HR roles include the following:

- *Facilitator:* In many cases, the development of a compelling change concept requires excellent facilitation. HR professionals need to be good facilitators or have access to people with the skills.

- *Leader of an organizational change diagnosis:* Occasionally, HR professionals will be asked to conduct organizational consulting interventions (described in Chapter 5). To assess what the change team is missing, HR professionals may find the change equation is helpful. They can explore whether the preferred future is clearly defined, the extent to which the urgency to proceed has been demonstrated, and whether the first step has been developed. The missing areas are usually the places in which the intervention will be most appropriate.

- *Communicator of ideas on best practices:* HR's role in aligning changes can be very helpful to the team as they attempt to define their first step in the preferred future for this particular change. HR professionals can contribute ideas on the company's internal best practices regarding changes that have been planned and implemented.

- *Coach the change leaders:* HR helps the change leaders and their teams prepare for the Gate 0 – Adopt the Concept review. For this review the change leaders define what they will present, and the HR professional coaches them to help reduce the risk that a good idea will be rejected because it was presented poorly.

Element #4: Engage Key Stakeholders and Identify Their Interests

A common error in the process of implementing change is that companies involve key stakeholders at a very late stage in the process. Actually, companies should solicit their opinions in Element #4 immediately after the change concept is adopted. HR should identify the key stakeholders, understand their interests, and involve them in the process of defining the change. Doing this will help increase the likelihood that the stakeholders will understand the urgency, the preferred future, accept the change, and that it will be implemented successfully.

Some of the stakeholders who are often involved in a large change include the boards of directors, senior executives, and senior managers. These groups may be involved even earlier (often in Element #3) because they are the major decision-makers and designers of the change. However, other stakeholders, including employee representatives, selected managers and employees, some divisional leaders, leaders of subsidiaries, customers and suppliers, may first become involved during Element #4.

HR professionals can help identify the stakeholders who should participate early in the process by building relationships to identify the stakeholders' interests. For example, a major utility was engaged in the process of redesigning the way it was doing business. They were aware that their future direction would have great implications for the nature of work as well as for the workforce. The company had a very strong union leadership that was a major stakeholder in this change and decided to invite two of the union leaders to be on the planning team from the beginning and throughout the planning phase. The union representatives became active participants in determining how the company would redefine itself, create an organizational structure, and downsize its workforce. The company downsized the workforce considerably with the union's participation. Many safeguards were introduced to enhance the dignity of individuals in this dramatic change, and union participation was an important success factor.

HR professionals can also harness managers' and employees' opinions by using electronic surveys, focus groups and informal employee relations contacts to anticipate the interests of these groups. In a similar manner, key customers and suppliers can give their ideas about the change process. HR can support the purchasing, sales, and marketing groups as they collect this information that will shape how the change will be defined.

HR also identifies other stakeholders who may be "accidental losers" as a result of the change. These are individuals or groups of people who may lose something through the change even though they are not meant to be the ones who are directly affected. For example, if a company decides to change the nature of how work is done through a multi-skilling process, there may be some negative effects for individuals who are specialists in specific areas. These specialists are often essential to the company's success. The specialists may feel threatened or devalued because other individuals will be doing parts of their work, and at the same time, these specialists may do other work of perhaps lesser value. The specialists may need particular attention at an early stage of change. HR professionals can involve them in the design of the multi-skilling process so that they know what others can do and what should be reserved for the specialists. If the specialists are not involved, the company may risk losing people who may be essential to its success.

Stakeholders have underlying interests that may help shape the way change proceeds. HR professionals can help change leaders have conversations with stakeholders that will surface these interests. Five distinct benefits emerge when the conversations focus on interests:[3]

1. *Misunderstandings are clarified:* Open discussions with stakeholders about interests often reveal mistaken assumptions about their concerns. Once assumptions and interests are clarified, meaningful solutions can be identified and can be incorporated within the change process.

2. *The problems are re-defined:* Discussions of stakeholder interests can often reveal that stakeholders' important issues are not the ones they are discussing. For example, in one discussion of interests, the change leaders learned that the stakeholders' real concern was that the problems might escalate before the change leaders made a decision. The change was not the problem for stakeholders; it was the process by which the change leaders would deal with problems.

3. *Both the company's and the stakeholders' interests are met more adequately:* Not all stakeholders' interests will be satisfied. However, stakeholders cannot be satisfied if they feel they have lost. A successful result of discussions with stakeholders is that they believe their interests were adequately met even if the change leader's interests have been met as well. Change leaders pay close attention to those interests that are particularly important to stakeholders and may find that they can offer to meet some of these interests at a minimal cost to the change effort. In some cases, stakeholders' interests that are inconsistent with the plans for change must be met as well.

4. *The parties find solutions with less "waste":* If change leaders know the stakeholders' *real* interests, they have a better chance of not spending energy on *perceived* interests. Interests are clues of how to adjust the change plan. The attention to interests helps change leaders fit the change plans to the stakeholders' interests without wasting effort on unnecessary ideas.

5. *The change leader slows down and builds relationships:* One of the biggest problems in implementing change successfully is the change leader's lack of impulse control. People are too quick to jump to what they want, and they do not spend enough time listening to what the stakeholders need. Change leaders need to learn

---

[3] The five benefits are based on an article by the author, David Weiss, "What's So Interesting About Interest," in *Labour Alert*, Carswell, 1997.

how to slow down at times. They are forced to do this as they listen and dialogue about the stakeholders' concerns, motivations, and interests.

In many change initiatives, the discussions with the stakeholders can be essential in understanding the urgency and in leading to acceptance of the change. There is no downside to a discussion of interests with stakeholders. The change leader loses nothing by the conversation. The HR professional should guide the change leaders to slow down, listen carefully, build the relationship and the issues based on interests. Once change leaders understand stakeholders' interests, they can begin to plan the change in detail.

Element #5: Plan the Change in Detail and Anticipate Contingencies

This element focuses on defining how the change will be implemented and developing the necessary contingency plans in the event the implementation does not proceed as envisioned. The end result of this element is a presentation to the executive sponsor for the Gate 1 review. Upon approval, the company is expected to invest more money to implement the change, allocate more resources to make it occur, and start changing how things are done.

Many change leaders are skilled at developing project and contingency plans to implement a change. In addition, companies often have experts outside the HR function who can facilitate the business process reengineering to define how the change should proceed in detail. HR professionals can add some value to this element by providing consultation on the extent to which gap analyses should be done, identifying methods by which pilots and simulations should be conducted, and by promoting the implementation of "quick hits."

Determine the Extent to Which Research and Gap Analyses Are Required

Change leaders are expected to collect the necessary data and measure progress to make recommendations about how the change should proceed. They should also understand that not all changes require extensive research or a detailed gap analysis. Gap analyses are often the most expensive and extensive part of a plan to implement change. Sometimes, gap analyses can be extremely helpful. In other cases though, they can distract the change leader from proceeding in the direction of the preferred future.

The change leader should have the wisdom to know whether the preferred future will compel him or her to do a detailed gap analysis or whether a less formalized analysis of current reality will be acceptable. Here are two examples in which the change leader should question whether to conduct a gap analysis:

- When the change that is envisioned requires a radical change from current reality, understanding the current reality and gap analysis will be less important.

- When a gap analysis can result in people becoming over-committed to defining the current reality. In those cases, it may block the creative process and exhaust the change team from focusing on developing the plans to implement the change.

Pilot Test the Change Plan

For more complex change projects, it may be useful to engage in simulations or pilot studies to pre-test the changes before they are fully implemented. Pilots also increase the change team's confidence because they can point out with more certainty (at the Gate 1 review) that this change will likely produce the positive results they anticipate.

The assumption is that a pilot study can be generalized to the real work environment, but this is not always the case. HR professionals should be aware of the traps that can occur in pilot projects, such as:

- *The pilot team is focused on the pilot and not the eventual implementation:* Sometimes the pilot project team can become so immersed in the success of the pilot that they find it difficult to raise their awareness to the more important issues of the broader implementation. The most important purpose of a pilot is to learn how the pilot results can be generalized to the full implementation. Debriefing the pilot project at the end is not sufficient. The pilot team needs to reflect on how to generalize what they are learning throughout the time they work on the pilot project.

- *Pilots often have team members who are more motivated than the workforce:* The pilot project members frequently build intense relationships and have high commitment to making the pilot successful. Often, when a pilot is generalized to the larger work environment, the work force does not have the same motivation and acceptance of the change. Specific strategies to motivate the entire workforce will be needed.

- *A pilot often does not have a scale for increased volume*: The nature of pilot projects is that they may not be designed to generalize to a broader audience.

In some situations, a simulation of the change can achieve the same result as a pilot. A simulation is a "walk through" of how the change will actually work in a simulated environment. Often a large training room is used to model how the change would proceed. Each of the steps of the change is talked through from beginning to end. Contingencies are anticipated and adjustments are made to the process. In contrast, pilot projects implement the change in a specific area within the company. If a simulation can test the change adequately, it is preferred because it disrupts the business flow less than a pilot does. Simulations can often be completed more quickly than pilots, and more aspects of the change can be controlled in the simulated environment. If you are not sure whether to do a simulation or a pilot, the "tie" goes to a simulation.

To avoid some of the pitfalls, HR professionals coach change leaders as they implement pilots and simulations and help them involve key stakeholders who will be affected by the change.

Identify "Quick Hits" in the Change

In addition, as a result of the simulation and/or the pilot study and the analysis of how to implement the change, HR can identify specific quick hits that can be implemented immediately. These are easy-to-do, high performance changes that can be done for minimal cost. Quick hits are valuable for a variety of reasons:

- If they can be done quickly and generate an immediate benefit, quick hits may avoid an elaborate implementation process and save time and cost.
- Quick hits have the benefit of helping executives understand that the change will actually work. A pilot study and analysis are theoretical for many senior executives. A "quick hit" benefit will demonstrate that something can occur that will be beneficial to the company.

- They provide some ongoing motivation and momentum for the change team as they work on the initiative.

- Employees who will be affected by the change often are motivated by quick hits. They begin to believe that things will really change and perhaps they will change for the better.

While quick hits can motivate senior executives and the workforce, they can sometimes be so attractive to executives that they may want the entire change project to be implemented as one big quick hit. HR professionals should be able to advise change leaders about how to restrain the executives from this response. They also guide them to implement quick hits in the most effective way to maximize the acceptance of these changes and to use the quick hits as part of their communication strategy.

Determine the Leadership Requirements and Organizational Design

As change leaders and teams plan the change implementation, they are expected to explain the leadership requirements and the approach to the employees. However, sometimes leadership and people issues are not their areas of expertise. HR, with its expertise in this area, should contribute to this role.

HR professionals also help change leaders clearly define the organizational design, roles, and accountabilities. They coach the change leader on how to motivate people to explore and accept new directions and changes. Their professional knowledge can help remove people-related barriers and reduce resistance, ensuring that employees understand and increasing the likelihood that they will participate in implementing the change. HR professionals can contribute to the communications approach that will be implemented after the Gate 1 review. They can also help prepare the necessary training programs for all the constituents as described in the next element of the Implementing Change and Transition Process.

Decide Whether the Project Will Proceed or Be Terminated

Element #5 culminates with the presentation at the Gate 1 review. At that meeting, the executives will determine whether the change will proceed or be terminated. Astute change leaders confront this question so that they can make a recommendation at the review meeting based on precise measures and a thorough analysis of the situation.

Change leaders need to know when a change initiative is not proceeding well and, if it is not, recommend that it be abandoned or adapted. HR professionals can support change leaders in this role because they sometimes have information about other changes in the company that may impact the change being considered. They may also identify early warning signals about potential human resistance to the change and can identify if the changes are not working well.

Element #6: Roll-Out—Communicate, Train and Help People adjust to Gain Commitment to the Change

For many changes, Gate 1 approval (after completion of Element #5) is a major accomplishment. The change team receives the permission, and approval to proceed to implementation. They often have a great desire to start implementing immediately. However, many good changes fail because people skip the transition Element #6. This element focuses on excellence in communication, training, and helping people adjust. HR professionals often have a particularly good understanding of this transition element and can contribute a great deal of value to the change leaders as they attempt to make change happen successfully.

Excellence in Communications

Throughout the Implementing Change and Transition Process, communication is essential. However, it becomes particularly important at this element of the process. It is important to communicate regularly, clearly, and simply in a variety of ways. Most change leaders believe that if they explain the change to the workforce once, they will understand it and be willing to implement it. Unfortunately, this is not the case in most situations. People need to hear about the change several times in different ways for them to really absorb what the change will be and to understand the implications for their own work.

Effective communication during change implementations often includes the following characteristics:

- *Multiple communication media are chosen to influence people to accept the change:* Companies use different media (e.g., written, spoken, electronic, experiential, educational) to raise the profile of the change. People with high credibility who will support the change can be selected to speak on behalf of the positive aspects and potential risks of what will occur. Companies can find the areas (departments, people) where the greatest resistance to change will be and help those areas respond to the change effectively.

- *A specific time and a medium are identified for regular communication:* When people know that communication will take place regularly, at a specific time and through a specific medium, they can adjust to the changes more effectively. Communication is important at those times even if not many new developments have occurred.

- *Every action is linked to the desired preferred future of the change:* This is another mechanism to help everyone understand why the change is being implemented. It also reinforces anticipated results. However, when actions occur that contradict the communications, people tend to believe the actions, and the credibility of the initiative suffers.

- *Successes are identified and celebrated as they occur:* The positive aspects of successes motivate people to more readily accept the change.

- *Manage expectations of the speed and quality with which the change will be implemented:* It is a tremendous demotivator if change leaders promise more than they can deliver. They must be open and honest about the progress of the change initiative and the speed of implementation.

In the process of implementing change, HR professionals can help enhance communications. At a minimum, they can remind the change leaders of the importance of communications. They can also assist the change leaders by guiding them to recognize the characteristics of successful communication.

Focused Training and Development to Prepare People for the Change

When companies introduce change, they often find a need for training and development that will help employees be willing, ready, and able to accept the new ideas and put them to use. The premise is that enough time should be given to individuals to learn new things, to practice, to make mistakes, to receive coaching, and to gain confidence in the new way of working. People often perform less effectively immediately after a change is introduced. If they are expected to perform perfectly, they can become very resistant to the change, and the likelihood of implementation occurring effectively will be reduced.

HR professionals can help people assess their ability to succeed at the new behaviors required. People will need the opportunity to think about whether they have the competencies for the new kind of work. An understanding of the anticipated competencies will help people assess their own potential to perform this work. In addition, a variety of training and development initiatives can help employees accept and adapt to change:

- *Orientation sessions:* All managers and employees need to understand what the change means and become committed to making it happen. In the process of orienting people, it is often helpful to "service the hierarchy." This means that people at higher levels within the company often feel it is helpful if they understand what the change will be prior to the people who report to them. This allows them to answer questions and be part of the change implementation. In situations in which people at higher levels are skipped, they may be so upset that they were not informed first that they sabotage the project because they feel ignored.

- *Basic skills training:* Employees will need basic skills training to know how to function within the changed environment. The company should recognize that people need to learn about the changes and understand how to access ongoing information as the change continually evolves.

- *More detailed training and coaching for the people who will be most affected by the change*: If the changes are in a specific area— for example, to certain services within internal service functions— the professionals in that area will need more intensive training and coaching to know how to respond to questions and implement the changes effectively. In addition, the people who are affected by the change will need to understand how they can access the new way of working and how it will change the way they work on an ongoing basis.

While the training should be done before people are asked to perform the new skills, people should also have opportunities to revisit the training after they begin working. Often, after people have the experiences of doing the new work, they have questions, which would not have been anticipated when they were learning about the changes. Revisiting the material and sharing the questions and learnings after working in the change environment for a period of time is a good way to reinforce and fine tune the implementation of the new way of working.

Finally, HR professionals can consider conducting team-building activities both before and while the change is introduced. The focus on the change is an excellent way to help the team create the environment in which they can help each other work differently. Employees can also develop their team effectiveness as they plan to make the changes occur in the workplace.

Help People Adjust

Most changes, even if they are implemented effectively, require people to adjust. People sometimes have difficulty changing no matter how good the change is. In fact, quite ironically, sometimes the people who are most vocal about the need for change are the most resistant when that change is actually introduced.

A conscious effort needs to be made to help people adjust to a change. Some leaders assume people have a personal responsibility to adjust to new situations. However, in planning for change, wise leaders know they can create the conditions in which it is easier for people to adjust. If they do it properly, they can also reduce the number of people who will be resistant. HR professionals often have the capability to give that kind of guidance to ensure that people adjust effectively.

For example, one company introduced a re-organization in its Customer Service department. The employees in the department took pride in the way they serviced the customer. However, with advances in technology, the company realized they could provide even better service. They decided to merge three different Customer Service departments that were servicing three different product lines. The new structure required all of the Customer Service professionals to service all of the customers. The change leaders believed that rather than having to go to three locations for customer service issues, customers would be happier to go to one location. The idea was well conceived and made sense. However, the employees were not happy about the new direction. After some investigation, three reasons for their discontent became apparent:

1. Some did not understand why the change was occurring.

2. Others were unclear about the implications for how they would have to do their work.

3. Others were worried about the speed of introduction.

The pattern that emerged from the above example is consistent with what occurs in many other situations. Because HR professionals often understand the need for people to adjust effectively as well as see the underlying stresses that may have contributed to the problem, they can provide the guidance to help overcome these stresses.

The major areas of stress that typically occur in the process of change are due to the following[4]:

- *The novelty and unpredictability of the situation:* For some employees, the novelty and unpredictability of the change can cause a great deal of stress. If they have never experienced the change before or have no knowledge about the issue, they may not know how to respond to the change.

- *Ambiguity and uncertainty*: Ambiguity is a major stress for most people in general situations and especially during times of change. Often, the creators of the change are the only people who know the purpose of the change and its implications. Others who are affected by the change function are in a wait-and-see position. The ambiguity of the situation or the presence of conflicting information creates unnecessary stress. Typically, in the absence of clear information, people make up information. The rumor mill starts to work overtime, and people paint the ambiguous change in the most negative way. The rumors escalate to the point that people panic about the changes without real information on which they can base their reactions.

- *Imminence and duration:* Changes that are going to occur immediately or that will last for an extended period often cause high levels of stress. Some leaders, in a spirit of candor, say things like, "If you believe things are tough now, wait until next year when things will be even tougher." Although they do not know if this is really true, they feel they are preparing people for the changes in the future. However, this statement actually backfires. The people hearing this

---

[4] Many of the concepts in the section on "Helping People Adjust" are based on Nora Gold, *Motivation: The Crucial But Unexplored Component In Social Work Practice*. Social Work, 35 (1), 49–56, 1990.

feel that their stress will last for a much longer time and that increases their anxiety and resistance to accept the change.

- *Personal issues associated with timing in life:* When a person's stress associated with change in the organization is based on personal difficulties, an organization can do little to handle it directly. However, these stresses cannot be discounted and some support should be provided. Employees may have personal problems, sick family members, difficulty in relationships, etc., and these extenuating circumstances add to their stress and make it more difficult for them to accept change at work.

It is a change leader's responsibility to help people adjust, and HR professionals should be skilled at guiding and coaching the change leader in this role. The HR professional can also intervene where appropriate so that the adjustment process occurs effectively. Some strategies that can be used to overcome the four areas of stress include:

- *Provide information:* It is essential to provide information and to communicate readily. As described earlier in this section, people need to know what is happening. The times for communication should occur on a regular basis. Just knowing what will occur, even if it is not good news, eliminates some of the stress. As one leader once said, "The misery of not knowing is much worse than the misery of knowing what will occur."

- *Create a climate for acceptance of social support:* Social support is perhaps the most effective way to reduce stress during change. People need to talk with others about the change. If someone is resistant, the challenge is to absorb the resistance by hearing it and not labeling it as bad. People need to understand that resistance is part of the normal process of change, especially when the change is of a difficult nature. The social support helps people explore options and consider how the change may actually work to their benefit.

- *Develop understanding:* Many people do not truly understand why the change is occurring. The change may not make sense to them. They need to understand the longer-range picture of the preferred future so that they can put it into context. People often create erroneous interpretations of an initiative if they do not understand and talk about what the change will achieve and how it affects their work.

- *Direct action:* Wise leaders know that in the process of change they must give people something meaningful to do so that they can be active as the change is being implemented. In one organization that was undergoing restructuring, the employees were asked to meet to discuss the new ideas and the implication they had for how they would do their work. Because they were given something meaningful to do, their anxiety about the change was reduced, and they were helped to take some ownership of the new way of working.

HR professionals can also help change leaders be aware of the many changes people in the company are facing. Change leaders may think only of the change they are trying to implement and not consider the multitude of changes that employees or managers are being asked to accept at the same time. The overload can cause problems and resistance, which HR professionals may be aware of because of their involvement in the alignment of strategy. HR professionals can help to establish more realistic time frames and to stagger the changes so that they are implemented at times when they have the greatest likelihood of being accepted.

Element #7: Roll-In—Implement the Change and Make It Business As Usual

The primary objective of a change is to implement it so that it is not considered a change anymore—to move it from the status of a change to business as usual. The implemented initiative is successful when it is the way work is done and is not perceived to be an initiative anymore.

The roll-in element of implementing change is often more successful if it is done with certain principles in mind. These include:

- *Simplify the approach to fit the needs:* The implementation approach should be done in the simplest possible manner. The HR professional can help the change leader scale back the approach so that it achieves its objectives in the quickest and simplest way. It is important not to make the implementation process more complicated than it needs to be.

- *Expedite the approach as quickly as possible:* The launch of the new way of working should be done as fully and as quickly as possible. In this way, people will experience change at once rather than in a slow change over time. If it is clearly packaged and the roll-out is done well, people will be more likely to respond to it positively.

If a change takes too long to implement, it may be ignored. As one leader said "If I have an idea and nothing is done in one week, we can forget about it ever being done." It's better to get it done and not let it die through a slow implementation.

- *Be tolerant of the need to modify the design:* Anticipate that in the process of implementaion, changes will occur. As with all plans, develop them clearly but be prepared to modify them once they are tested in real situations. It will be important to build the expectation that adjustments and modifications will occur to make sure that the change is correct. The context will shape reality. Allow it to do that so that your design will be most effective and the change will be implemented successfully.

Human Resource professionals contribute value to this element in a variety of ways including:

- *Define roles, accountabilities, and interdependencies:* HR professionals should be able to define roles in the broader sense to allow for maximum flexibility within the culture. They can contribute to making the organizational design "elastic" so that it can expand and contract based upon the needs. This kind of organizational elasticity is defined in Chapter 7 of this book.

- *Redefine the processes (such as performance measurement systems) to reflect the change in environment:* HR often has accountability for the people-related processes. Processes, such as the performance management system and its measurement may need to be modified. HR works closely with the change leaders to alter the processes and systems as necessary and to determine how performance feedback will be given to support the change on a regular basis.

- *Provide support for people development:* As change is implemented, HR professionals ensure that people have the necessary skills and knowledge, and they assist the leaders who are managing the change. They also provide team building for groups and individuals who require attention even after the implementation of change. They contribute to developing employees so they can maintain an optimum level of performance as significant changes occur in the work environment.

- *Develop rewards and recognition systems:* Rewards and recognition systems are often modified to motivate people to participate in making the change occur successfully. People tend to work with more diligence when they are rewarded and recognized. The reward mechanisms that HR designs need to be closely aligned with the true intent of the change. They also find opportunities to celebrate successes to recognize accomplishments associated with implementing change.

Element #8: Roll-On—Measure Results, Share Learnings, and Continuously Improve

The roll-on element helps change leaders focus on the deliverables of the change and how to improve continuously. Implementation does not conclude until the company realizes the value from the change, as is evident through measuring its results. The learnings from the experience need to be shared, which allows the entire company to benefit from the change. Finally, changes do not occur and then remain static. The company's employees need to focus on continuous improvement with a readiness for the next change.

Measure Results

People tend to focus on delivering what is measured. The Implementing Change and Transition Process should have clearly defined measures with specific people accountable for the deliverables. When the process is functioning well, the company defines the measurement expectations at a very early element. Throughout the change, the company reviews the extent to which those metrics have been achieved. The end result of the change should be measurements that will not be a surprise to anyone. They should have known how they were performing throughout the change implementation.

The measurements define the following:

- How the change contributed to giving the company relative advantage against the competition.
- How the change enhanced customer value.
- Whether the change has actually taken hold and transformed the way work is done on a regular basis.

As indicated earlier, the ultimate measure of success for most change is that after the change is implemented, people recognize the change as the new way of operating on a regular basis. If the measurement demonstrates this, then you know that the change has been established.

Shared Learning

The culmination of the change process is to ensure that the benefits from the change are saved as part of the company's intellectual capital. It is a great loss for companies if they lose their intellectual capital. The intelligence gained in a change process needs to be harnessed and re-used for future benefit.

Chapter 5 describes the importance of shared learning. The implementing change process culminates with an expectation that the learning and knowledge gained from this change process will be shared with others and will become part of the corporate memory. HR has a very important role to play in ensuring that shared learning occurs.

Consider the alternative. Imagine a company in which people do not learn from previous experiences. The company has no collective memory, no shared learning, and no way to find wisdom that has already been developed elsewhere. Only those who know the right people can find out how things are really done. People in this kind of company feel they have to discover ways to do things that they assume someone else knows how to do already. The common refrain is, "We must have done this before," but no one knows whom he or she should ask about it.

Shared learning needs to become a core capability. Companies will discover changes more quickly, and implementation often will proceed faster and with greater efficiency. A problem with shared learning is that the people who benefit the most from the shared learning are often those who were not involved in the change process. The ones who worked on the change process believe they know what occured. They may not be motivated to put in the time and effort to share what they know only for the benefit of others.

Some compelling reasons that can motivate people to provide this information and knowledge are the following:

- The process of sharing learning can help the change team understand why they succeeded or had limited success.
- They recognize that when they face the next change, they can use their previous experiences and knowledge to their benefit.
- They believe that if they share their learnings with others, others will share what they have learned with them.
- Often, a prerequisite for engaging in shared learning is the belief that sharing what they learned from an unsuccessful initiative will not affect them negatively.

- Sharing what they have learned should be a standard and required part of every change leader's and team member's responsibility.

HR professionals have an important role to ensure that shared learning takes place. Some ways they can achieve this include:

- Ensure that people are expected to have a debriefing session at the conclusion of each implementing change and transition project. Someone should be there to document the discussion of what they learned so that it can become a part of the company's intellectual capital.
- Publicize success stories that have been achieved through shared learning within the company. People then believe that the information they put into the system is actually being used, and they become more motivated to continue providing information for the system.
- Create a mentoring process in which people will be the custodians of shared learnings for the company. These people could be called upon when new changes are being implemented to share their experience and apply it to the new challenge.

Continuous Improvement

In this element of the implementing change and transition process, a number of insights emerge about how the change can be improved. The measurement identifies the areas in which the change has succeeded and where it has not. The shared learnings identify what has worked and what has not worked as expected. The measurement and shared learning often lead the change team to recognize that there are areas in which continuous improvement can still occur.

At the conclusion of the Implementing Change and Transition Process, the company makes clear recommendations for the next steps to be undertaken for continuous improvement. These recommendations identify how the change can be further refined to achieve the expectations identified early in the process.

Companies need to avoid the idea that once the change is implemented, they do not have to think about it anymore. This kind of approach can produce changes in which the benefits erode quickly. People regress to the old way of doing things, and the change does not produce the anticipated results. Even after the implementation, the company needs to continue to persevere to make the change a success. HR professionals have a role in highlighting the importance of continuous improvement and developing recommendations to further evolve this change.

Finally, with the development of the continuous improvement recommendations, the executive sponsors hold a Gate 2 meeting. At this review, they consider the extent to which the objectives of the change have been achieved. They measure success, learn what has been gained from this process, and explore the opportunities for continuous improvement to further achieve the preferred future.

HR Applies the Implementing Change and Transition Process to Its Own Changes

As described in previous chapters, HR has to be willing take the medicine it has applied to other parts of the company and use the Implementing Change and Transition Process themselves. HR professionals will lose credibility if they are unable to implement their own changes successfully. In addition, HR professionals' experience in initiating their own area's changes will benefit them in assisting other company areas. As a result of its role in the Implementing Change And Transition Process, HR becomes a very important strategic asset that helps business transformation to occur.

Summary

- The term *implementing change and transition* focuses the process on its primary purpose, which is to make the change occur and to have people commit to it willingly.

- This chapter explores each of the elements of the implementing change and transition process and defines how HR can contribute strategic value to each.

- Element #1 is *Understand competitive forces and customer value*. Understanding competitive forces and customer value is the foundation for deciding which change initiative to choose and determining the urgency for the change.

- Element #2 is *Select change leaders and define accountabilities*. HR professionals are involved in establishing the selection criteria and identifying the change leaders and the members for the change team. In addition, they assist in selecting the executive sponsor(s) who has the overall responsibility for the team's work.

- Element #3 is *Identify the preferred future and the urgency for the change.* In this element, the change team defines what they believe is the change's preferred future and why it is urgent for this change to occur. The three variables for a compelling change are defining the preferred future, identifying the sense of urgency, and identifying the first step. The HR professional has some important roles to play regarding these variables, including: being a facilitator, leader of an organizational change diagnosis, communicator of ideas on best practices, and the change leader's coach.

- Element #4 is *Engage key stakeholders and identify their interests.* Stakeholders' opinions should be solicited early in the process to increase the likelihood that they will accept the change. HR professionals can help identify the stakeholders who should participate. They can harness managers' and employees' opinions by using surveys, focus groups, and informal employee relations contacts to anticipate the interests of these groups and use the information to identify the best way to communicate the urgency an to implement a new change.

- Element #5 is *Plan the change in detail and anticipate contingencies.* This element focuses on defining how the company will implement the change and develop the necessary contingency plans in the event the implementation does not proceed as envisioned. For more complex change projects, sometimes it is useful to engage in simulations or pilot studies to pre-test the changes before they are fully implemented. To avoid some of the pitfalls, HR professionals coach change leaders as they implement pilots. The change leader needs to know when a change initiative is not proceeding well and, if it is not, recommend that it be abandoned or adapted. HR professionals can support the change leader in this role.

- Element #6 is *Roll-out: Communicate, train and help people adjust to gain commitment to the change.* Many good changes fail because people skip Element #6 that focuses on excellence in communication, training and helping people adjust. HR professionals often have a particularly astute understanding of this element and can contribute a great deal of value to the change leaders as they attempt to make change happen successfully. When change is introduced, there is often a need for training and development, which contributes to helping employees be ready and able to accept the new ideas and put them to use. HR professionals should also consider conducting team-building activities both before and while the change is introduced. A conscious effort needs to be made to help people adjust to a change. It is a change leader's responsibility to help people adjust, and HR professionals should be skilled at guiding and coaching the change leader in this role.

- Element #7 is *Roll-in: Implement the change and make it business as usual*. The implemented initiative is successful when it is the way work is done and is not perceived to be an initiative anymore. HR professionals contribute to this element in a variety of ways which includes: defining roles, accountabilities, and interdependencies; developing rewards and recognition systems; redefining the processes (such as performance measurement systems) to reflect the change in environment, and measuring progress in people development.

- Element 8 is *Roll-on: Measure results, share learnings, and continuously improve*. Implementation is not complete until the value from the change is realized, as is evident through the measurement of its results. The learnings from the experience need to be shared, which allows the entire company to benefit from the change. The measurements define the following:

  - How change contributed to giving the company strategic advantage against the competition.

  - How the change enhanced customer value.

  - Whether the change has actually taken hold and transformed the way work is done on a regular basis.

- HR professionals will lose credibility if they are unable to implement their own changes successfully. HR has to run its own area as well as provide input to other areas to help them apply the implementing change and transition process effectively.

CHAPTER TEN

ନ୍ତ

Insure a Return
on Investment in
Human Capital

In the current business environment, executives are watching the cost
and productivity of human capital very closely. Each cost in the organization has a direct impact on the company's profitability, on the
bonuses paid to people, and on the strategic value the company can
contribute to customers.

In one company the president regularly criticized the HR professionals because they could not tell him the number of employees in the
company and how much they were being paid. He consistently challenged HR about this issue. Until HR could give him answers to employee numbers and costs, he would not approve any innovative attempts
at organizational change. While the president's *style* was questionable,
his *request* was reasonable. HR could not respond to that need.

HR professionals have demonstrated the ability to understand the
cost of human capital when they participate in union-management
contract negotiations. To do these negotiations successfully, HR determines and forecasts the costs for most aspects of labor, often predicting
costs for the next three years. The analyses are sometimes so precise that
HR can recommend a reduction of wages as a concession and link it to
the condition that labor will recover some of its concessions if there are
productivity gains.

When no labor contract issue is involved, however, HR professionals often do not focus on the cost of labor and the issues related to the investment in human capital. It appears that HR is unaware of the need or are reluctant to be accountable for identifying the return on investment in human capital. The reluctance appears as follows:

- HR engages in analyzing the return on investment in human capital only when it has no other choice.

- HR professionals may have the capability to do this kind of analysis (or at least manage it); they just do not want to develop it or do not believe it is part of their role.

If HR wants to be a business within a business, it must manage its own finances. This means they need to know the costs and the profitability of those investments. In addition, HR's responsibility for the return on investment in human capital helps move it from the "softer" organizational side of the business to the "harder" business transformation side. HR finds ways to realize a better business and productivity outcome from the investment in people and their talents.

The following provides a more precise explanation of the terminology the *return on investment in human capital* (RIHC: pronounced "rick"):

- *Return*—reflects comparative analyses of the company's current human capital performance versus the investment and whether this performance is aligned with company strategy.

- *Investment*—reflects the amount of money and effort it takes to cultivate human capital. The term "investment" reflects my preference towards viewing people and human capital as an investment rather than as a cost.

- *Human Capital*—Chapter One defined "human capital" as the money and effort it takes to cultivate people and their talents. It reflects the economic value of the knowledge, skills, experiences, creativity, and innovations of people in the company that help make the company productive and that give it a competitive advantage.

The Strategic Value of the Return on Investment in Human Capital

HR must add strategic value to the company to help it achieve relative advantage against its competition. Taking accountability for delivering a return on investment in human capital is an important potential source of competitive advantage and eventual benefit to the external customer. Here are three examples of how companies have benefited from knowing the extent to which they have invested in human capital.

- *Example #1:* Consider the situation referred to at the end of Chapter Six of a company in the throes of a major acquisition. From the president's perspective, the cost of human capital was a compelling reason to include HR on a due-diligence team for the company about to be acquired. The HR vice president had the ability to analyze the return on investment in human capital and, therefore, was asked to be part of the due-diligence team. The HR vice president identified that the skills mix and "know-how" in both companies were equivalent and the purchased company had the cost of human capital advantage. Therefore, he recommended that the best investment in human capital was to re-deploy specific work that had been done in the purchasing company into the acquired company. The recommendation provided the company an almost immediate return on investment on the purchase.

- *Example #2:* In another company, the information HR collected about the investment in human capital was treated with such priority that the only people who could access the data were the HR professional and the president. The president had a "hot line" phone directly to HR. He called the HR professional almost daily on RIHC issues to provide information and strategic advice about how to deploy new products and new processes in new environments. The president felt that the company finally had a major asset (human capital) that entered into the domain of the "definable." HR set up the people database so that they could analyze any cross-section of individuals in the company. They provided data and interpreted the data by division, department, work unit, age group, gender, time in the company, and experience in the industry. HR was able to provide the data in almost any combination the president requested.

- *Example #3:* In a third company, HR was formally a cost and expense center that was an indirect cost to the business. Traditionally, if the businesses were upset with service, they just cut costs. After HR developed a focus on the RIHC, it changed its approach entirely. The HR vice president hired a Chartered Accountant within HR who helped him develop the economic models and the HR reporting. They implemented an economic model in which 85 percent of the HR budget became direct charges to the line businesses. The HR vice president was able to say what he was spending on the businesses, who was allocated to each business and the value they were providing. He can now have business and financial discussions with clients. If clients want to change their human capital budget, the HR professionals are able to identify the implications for the HR services they will receive. The new financial capability and analysis has guided the HR recommendations of how and where business transformation can occur within the company.

The Implications for HR

HR needs to assume accountability for identifying and measuring the RIHC. HR professionals should be required to produce information about the quality of the investment in human capital and the measurements of the productivity outputs that show the return on investments. HR needs the knowledge and ability to provide strategic advice about how to invest wisely in human capital. HR's role includes the following:

- Assist in determining the metric of human capital and its cost. With this information, HR will also be able to contribute more information to the company's annual report and strategic plans.

- Have ongoing strategic input on business and financial issues related to the return on investment in human capital, on how to increase the overall human capital in the company, and provide guidance regularly.

- Be part of a due-diligence process for any new acquisition to determine whether the investment in human capital in the company to be purchased is cost effective and to assess cultural and leadership issues.

When HR focuses on the numbers and the return on investment, as any business would do, companies have more reason to think of it as an "HR business within a business." The Finance department's business within a business is accountable for understanding the financial capital throughout the company. HR's internal service business is accountable for understanding the human capital throughout the company. HR becomes the expert in people as an asset and in how to re-deploy them so that the company can derive the best productivity and return on investment possible. HR sets the priorities and is in control of its own destiny with reference to people valuation; makes business recommendations about the critical issues of incentives, rewards, recognition, and for the overall budget associated with people.

Identifying a Metric of Human Capital

Many companies have developed slogans that "People are our number one asset." Some have the facts to back up these statements, but many do not. If executives want to know whether people are really their number one asset, they need to know the economic value of their people. They can make this claim with greater integrity and clarity if they can identify a metric that represents the company's overall human capital.

This section focuses on the challenging question of how to define a metric of human capital. In addition, this section considers some specific interventions that may have a greater probability to enhance this metric.

Recently, I explored the metric of human capital with an executive in a major financial institution in Canada. The focus of this effort was to explore if there is a preferred way to deploy training and development of employees that will increase human capital. Similar questions can be asked about other investment strategies in human capital such as better selection, retention strategies, enhanced technology, etc. Later in this section, these ideas will be considered briefly.

We began by attempting to define loosely a metric of human capital using the current measures that exist in the company. We considered that a metric of human capital for an employee is probably a reflection of some variables that already exist in the company database. These include:

- education level
- years of service in the company
- specific experiences and qualifications
- current and recent past performance-appraisal ratings
- assessment of the promotability and portability of employees
- bonus/profit share that the employee received
- the manager's results on 360° surveys

The measures listed above were the ones that were available on the database in this company. Other measures could be considered (such as creativity level, innovations, etc.); however, these may be more difficult to ascertain. We decided to focus on two of the variables—each employee's performance appraisals and promotability/portability ratings—for a brief experiment. A sample of employees was then identified from a large group of employees. All of the employees had been working in their current area for over one year.

We proceeded to speculate about which employees would most likely benefit the most from intensive training and development. We ranked them based upon the answers to the following questions:

- Is the employee motivated to learn new information and skills?
- Does the employee have the basic knowledge required for the program?
- Does the employee have the skills and abilities to do the work of the program?
- Once in possession of the knowledge and skills from this program, what is the likelihood that this employee will use the new knowledge and skills?
- Will the employee provide a return on investment from the program?

Afterwards, we rated each of the employees in the sample as a "key resource," "promotable", or "well placed" based on their existing ratings on the performance appraisal forms and their promotability/portability ratings. Employees who were high on both ratings were "key resources." Employees who were high on one rating were "promotable." Employees who were acceptable on both ratings were "well placed." No employee in this group was unacceptable on either rating.

It became evident from this analysis that the employees who we designated as "key resources" were the ones we believed would benefit the most from more intensive training and development. It suggested a hypothesis, that companies should "invest in the best." The hypothesis implies that, if limited funds are available, the best return on investment of training and development dollars will likely occur for the employees that represent a higher metric of human capital. In the terms used in this book, the hypothesis suggests that if a company wants to increase its human capital and it can provide training for "key resources" or "well-placed" employees, the "tie goes to training and developing the key resources."

We also considered that other groups have immediate and pressing needs and would benefit from targeted training and development. These include:

- New employees in the company.

- Employees who have been or will be assigned new work or will be expected to contribute to a new initiative.

- Employees who are not performing well because they lack training and development in a particular area.

- Employees who have been recently promoted/transferred or are about to be promoted/transferred.

We then speculated that if we can identify a metric of human capital for an individual, then we should be able to identify one metric for a team or a division or even for the entire company. If the theory holds true, that "all things being equal, companies should invest in the best" then higher training and development investment should be made for the teams that have the highest human capital value. The associated expectation is that the higher the metric of human capital for a team, the higher should be the performance expectations for that team.

We also considered that there would be no benefit to a manager to artificially elevate or reduce the human capital metric that they reported for their team. If the manager artificially makes the overall metric of human capital higher, then the investment will be greater and so will the expected team performance. If the team does not perform, it will reflect poorly on the manager. If, on the other hand, the manager artificially makes the metric of human capital lower, the employees on the team will likely be unhappy with their team's overall assessment. In addition, the team will not receive the investment in training and development that they would be eligible to receive.

As indicated earlier, the human capital metric analysis can apply to other areas in addition to training and development. For example, if a company believed it would be strategically wise to increase its overall metric of human capital, they might consider the following:

- Investing more in selecting employees to increase their metric of human capital as they enter the company. Some approaches can include raising standards for employment, pre-employment assessments, etc.

- Developing retention strategies to keep the key resources with high metrics of human capital. Some approaches are suggested in Chapter Four.

- Using technology and virtual teams to access employees with higher metrics of human capital who will work primarily from remote locations.

Calculating the Investment Made in Human Capital[1]

The approach to calculating the human capital investment will follow the wise counsel of perhaps the most important economist in the twentieth century, John Keynes. He advises people who engage in these kinds of analyses that "it is better to be roughly right than precisely wrong." HR does not determine the RIHC as if it is an engineering laboratory that puts in specific inputs and can identify one-to-one relationships with specific results. The process HR uses is not that precise. HR presents trends and broad analyses of the input investments in human capital and identifies the outputs represented by broad performance and productivity indicators.

Examples of this broad analysis already exist in marketing departments, which tend to analyze the investment and productivity of their customer base in broad terms. Most of their analyses involve segmenting the customer base to identify how to do more effective targeted marketing. They regularly identify their investments and the anticipated productivity of those investments. The principle of customer segmentation can be applied as well to internal employees and the internal analysis of the investment in human capital. Employee segmentation can help identify where investments are uneven and which areas require special attention. It also helps HR determine the areas in which future difficulties may occur.

Who Are the "Humans" in the Human Capital that Is Measured?

This section identifies the people who are included in a calculation of human capital. (Note that the term "headcount" is not used because it delivers a negative message that implies a lack of appreciation and respect.)

Many HR professionals consider only the full-time employees on the payroll when they count people. Unfortunately, this count does not reflect the actual workforce. As discussed earlier in this book, whenever possible or economical, external service providers should be engaged to do the company's non-strategic work and these external employees

---

[1] This section "Calculating The Investment Made In Human Capital" (p. 234–238) and a later section "Assessing the RIHC for Selection and Orientation" (p. 239–243) were written in collaboration with Moshe Gilat, M.B.A. Mr. Gilat is a labor economist who works with Teva Pharmaceuticals. He is also an international consultant on the topics of cost of labor and determining the return on investment in human capital.

should be counted in the people count. This approach provides the company with the elasticity and flexibility it requires.

Essentially, what the company has achieved through contracting to individuals and large scale outsourcing is to place full-time employees under the care of an outside vendor. However these external employees are still working for the company. The company just has a different cost structure (supplier fee vs. salary, less facility demands, etc.), different expenses associated with pension and benefits, and different management accountabilities to this employee group. Nevertheless, their cost should be included in the tabulation of the cost and productivity of human capital.

The analysis of the RIHC includes the following groups:

- Full-time internal employees (e.g., employees who work an agreed-upon percentage of the time for your company).
- Part-time internal employees (e.g., employees who work less than the agreed-upon percentage of time or less for your company).
- Part-time or full-time external contractors working on the company premises (e.g., full-time computer technologists who are employed by another company but come to work daily for your company).
- Part-time or full-time employees employed by an external service provider outside the company premises (e.g., an external service provider that is managing your company's payroll).

Rather than micro-managing the counting process, this section suggests that some level of imprecision is appropriate. The following example gives the kind of broad indications that are adequate: One company had approximately three times as many part-time employees as full-time employees. They counted the people who work over 50 percent of the time for the company (either internally or for an external service provider) as "one person." All employees who work 50 percent of the time or less for the company (either internally or for an external service provider) are counted as "one-third." The only employees who are not included in the analysis are the external service provider employees who are not paid on the basis of time (e.g., cleaning, security).

This definition covers employees and employees' substitutes and provides a way to control the true total number of people because it includes all workers whether they work inside the company or for external service providers. It also allows for more comparisons between business units and sites and comparisons with other companies and benchmarks. For example, a recent development in banks with branches is the outsourcing of tellers. External companies select, train, and pay tellers who work as external service providers for the bank. If the bank decides to compare its total employees and its investment in human capital with another bank but does not count the outsourced tellers as resources, the information will be misleading.

What Is Included in the Investments Made in Human Capital?

The essence of *human capital* is that investments are made so as to improve the company's productivity and increase its strategic advantage. As described earlier, a *metric of human capital* can include the knowledge, skills, and experience, as well as employees' creativity and innovations. The *investment in human capital* covers all investments in employees and not just direct costs paid to employees (salaries and benefits).

An analogous situation is the way that a purchasing department defines its costs, which is the purchasing price paid to the supplier. However, that does not reflect the true total cost. A better definition is the total cost from sourcing the product, to purchasing, to warehousing and finally to delivering the product to the production floor. A similar robust measure of investments can be used for employees. Investments associated with employees are far more than their salaries and benefits. They include other factors that support the person to do their work, such as resourcing, training, development, rewards, and other expenditures such as their office, cars, and cellular phones. This larger investment per employee reflects the cost of each individual employee.

The investment in human capital can be divided into money invested that the employee receives directly, money that is paid to third parties on behalf of employees and investments in employee development. The total invested in human capital is then reduced by the amount of any employment subsidies received.

- *Money invested that the employee receives directly:* This category includes both money paid to employees for time worked and for work they did not do directly.

  - *Pay for time worked*—Basic time plus overtime, shift differentials, other premiums and regular bonuses, incentives, and cost-of-living adjustments. For employees of external service providers, this includes payments to agencies to pay employees, payments to the self-employed, and payments to "consultants" as a substitute for payment for time worked.

- *Pay for time not worked*—Vacations, holidays and other leave, tuition, child allowance, seasonal or irregular bonuses, stock options, other special payments, and allowances.

- *Provisions and accruals*—Based on the prevailing accounting principles, provisions and accruals due to cover obligations (e.g., severance, vacation, and stock options).

• *Money paid to third parties on behalf of employees:* Includes non-wage payments that are either legally required or optionally covered as described below. It also includes amenities for work usually associated with an employee's position in a company and other general benefits the company offers to employees.

  - *Legally required non-wage costs*—Includes employer expenditures for payroll taxes and health insurance in some jurisdictions.

  - *Other non-wage costs*—Includes employer expenditures, contractual, and private benefit plans (e.g., pension and benefits).

  - *Amenities for work usually associated with an employee's position in a company*—Includes cellular phones, more elaborate desktop phones, portable computers, flights, hotels, meals, company cars, repairs, insurance, etc. As a general rule, the more expensive an employee is in terms of salary and benefits, the more money the company allocates to that person for other amenities to support their work. For example, the highest-paid employees in a company often receive the most expensive cars and often fly business class. In one company, the cost of those extras associated with the employee plus their benefits doubled their base salary.

  - *General expenditures directly related to all employees*—Includes employee transportation, cafeteria, health center, employee assistance programs, relocation fees, lockers, athletic facility, and advertisement.

• *Investments in employee development:* Includes all resourcing, training, development, rewards, and recognition within the company or through external service providers.

  - *Resourcing and securing talent costs*—Includes costs of advertising, recruitment agencies, creating key resource employer of choice positions in the labor market, and pre-employment assessments.

- *Internal training, learning and development costs*—Includes training programs, executive forums, and distributed learning initiatives. (These costs do not include time off the job.)

- *External training and development costs*—Includes university tuition paid for employees, payments to an external organization for an employee to take a course, professional association memberships, management developmental assessments, coaching and career transition. (These costs also do not include time off the job.)

- *Rewards and recognition costs*—This area reflects the costs of the plans to motivate and inspire employees to know what is important and to focus their attention on helping the company implement its strategic direction. It includes rewards for employees and teams for high-quality ideas submitted to employee suggestion programs, "spot awards" offered by managers to employees and teams for extra effort, and recognition programs offered to employees and teams for their special contributions to the company.

Knowing these expenditures is essential to identifying the actual investment in human capital. In most cases, HR can use existing data in their systems to collect the information. This includes hiring information, educational background, salary information, other financial data, performance information on annual, and other periodic reviews and career progression information. The information may already exist in most systems to calculate most of the investment in human capital. Often, the problem is the lack of ability to access the information in its proper form and merge the data to produce aggregate information and analysis.

Implications of RIHC for the HR "People And Organizational Processes"

HR can contribute to business transformation with its RIHC recommendations. In addition, HR needs to assess its performance on RIHC for its own initiatives.

Some examples of how HR is measured overall include the following:

- In one company, HR is utilizing common business metrics that are used with the rest of the company and is being assessed on them. It also is measured on the overall company employee attitude survey results as well as the employee attitude results within HR.

- In another company, HR is expected to be a role model and have results on employee surveys at least two percentage points higher than the average company results.

- In yet another company, HR is measured on how well it operates as a business in support of the line managers' goals and objectives. In this company, direct linkages are being established between line manager success in the achievement of business objectives and the extent to which the HR function contributed to that success.

HR should also have the ability to analyze the quality of the investment in human capital made in core people processes and organizational value-add processes. The next few sections explore some of the ways HR can assess the RIHC for these types of initiatives.

Assessing the RIHC for Selection and Orientation

The "best" investment in selection and orientation for any company will be based on the company's needs. The three needs (or drivers) that influence the company's investment in human capital for selection are:

1. The competitive position.
2. The external labor market.
3. The internal equilibrium.

For example, the competitive position may be the major business imperative for some companies. Others may focus their investment in human capital on the external labor markets to keep the best source of talent available to them. Still other companies may be most interested in internal equilibrium considerations of internal equity and balance.

Traditionally, HR has been more concerned with internal company equilibrium implications and with the labor market. The introduction of the company's competitive position is a somewhat newer concept for HR and has been emphasized in this book continuously. The idea that there is a point of balance among these three areas that is often temporary and circumstantial will be another aspect to consider.

- *The competitive position as the company driver for selection:*
  An example of a company that drives its investment in human capital by its competitive position is a company in Phase Three of the growth curve that is trying to transform because of competitive pressures incurred through the process of globalization. The

investment in human capital in selection will be designed to support and create distinctive capabilities for the company to compete. In addition, the investments need to facilitate the organizational elasticity and cultural flexibility that will enable the company to adjust to the new global challenges.

If the primary driver is the company's competitive position, HR has some important resourcing considerations in order to develop the "best" investment in human capital. They include:

- Is the investment in human capital aligned with the company's current or desired strategic direction?

- What level of expertise do we need to compete? Do we need the best? What is the potential damage of a shortage of excellent people or of mediocre performers?

- Do we have financial resources within the company to meet resourcing needs or do we need to explore external alternatives?

- What level of employment flexibility and cost flexibility is required to compete?

- *The external labor market as the driver for selection:*
  An example of a company that will be driven by the external labor market as it invests in human capital is a high technology growth company. In Phase Two of the growth curve, a company's major concern is attracting outstanding technical talent from a tight labor market. The ability to attract talent will enable it to secure financing and new customers.

Some of the most important resourcing issues to consider when assessing the best fit of human capital investment with the external labor market driver are summarized below:

- Who are our rivals for talent in the market? What is the competition's level of intensity? Is the competition on a local, national, or international level?

- Are we an important player in the market? Are we used as a training ground?

- Do people want to work for us? Are we attracting the best talent? Do people accept our offers of employment?

- What is our relative compensation? Are we requiring general or specific skill sets?

- Are outsourcing possibilities or strategic alliances available to enable us to secure the talent?

- *The internal equilibrium as the driver for selection:*

  An example of a company that will be driven by internal issues such as labor relations, structure, hierarchy, and culture is the Phase Three mature company. This company is often internally focused and more concerned with its own internal pay structures than either its external labor market competitiveness or its overall competitive position as a business. It evaluates its investment in human capital on the basis of maintaining the status quo in the formal and informal structure, sustaining the cultural norms, and motivating employees.

  Another example would be a government-owned utility monopoly. Since its competitive advantage rests on its monopoly status, the utility is often focused on internal equilibrium. To satisfy any discontent among the employees, the company needs to ensure fairness within the system. Collective bargaining negotiations often focus on the comparative status and wages of different employees. Once the monopoly status deteriorates, the utility has to shift towards the competitive driver. This requires a major adjustment within the company, and it creates a profound shift in the definition of what should be considered the new investment in human capital to meet the new competitive challenges.

  Some issues to consider for the internal equilibrium-driven company that is in the process of resourcing include the following:
  – Is there a gap between our internal compensation, hierarchy, and structure and the benchmarks in similar industries?
  – What has determined our internal compensation hierarchy, and structure in terms of cultural norms, union relationships, or business demands?
  – What are the implications of our policy on cost, attraction, turnover, retention, productivity, and turnover?
  – Is there a gap between our internal compensation hierarchy and structure and the business demands? Why?
  – How easy and willing are we to change the current compensation system, hierarchy, and structure? Who are the stakeholders who have a vested interest in the status quo?

- *The company driven by mixed forces for selection:*

  Most companies are driven by a combination of two or more of the drivers. The combination is not fixed but is dependent on changes in the drivers and on their relative weight at any point of time. For example, consider a high-tech firm that has already entered Phase Two growth and needs to compete in the tight labor market for software specialists (external labor market driver). However, it may find it will also pay higher salaries than the market to other employees such as mechanical engineers, since it has to keep its internal equilibrium (internal equilibrium driver) as it grows rapidly.

More than one driver may occur due to other factors as well. These include:

- *Country Differences:* Companies in a specific industry in different countries may have various drivers since different countries tend to have different cost structures.

- *Business Unit Differences:* A business unit may have different drivers than another business unit in a company. In most cases, the overall RIHC chosen for the company will be sub-optimal for each of the business units. The struggle will be between the forces that drive the internal equilibrium over the unique needs of the individual business units. Sometimes this phenomenon convinces the senior executive that the company needs to spin off certain business units that do not fit the company's business drivers. In a pharmaceutical company, the over-the-counter products business unit was driven by a very different set of issues than the prescription drugs business unit. These differences compelled the company to make compromises in their investment in human capital that they did not want to make. The company decided to sell the over-the-counter business unit so that the entire company could align around common drivers. The result was better overall company performance and a more focused competitive position in the marketplace. It also permitted a better strategy for the investment in human capital across the business units.

- *Jobs of Similar Importance but in Different Labor Market Segments:* The same drivers do not fit all kinds of jobs even if they are of equal importance to the company. This difference may occur if the jobs belong to different segments of the labor market. An example of this is a company that markets and services cellular phones. Its success depends on two key jobs: salespeople and technicians, but the labor market conditions and the learning curve for the two skill sets are extremely different. As a result, the company has installed two different reward systems and separated the salespeople from the technicians.

The company's justification for their action is intriguing. Because the labor market is not a tight market for technicians (external labor market driver), the company is able to pay them at a lower rate than it pays salespeople. However, to avoid the salary comparisons (internal equilibrium driver) that may arise if the salespeople work with the technicians, the company has decided to keep these two professional groups separate from each other.

The Assessment of the RIHC for Performance Development

This chapter explored earlier how a company could identify a metric of human capital and deploy training and development to increase the overall metric. This section focuses on some methods to identify the return on investment of training and development.

The return on investment in training and development has been a struggle for many HR professionals for a long time. Some have been able to identify some measures. They have done this by requiring participants in programs to demonstrate a return on investment of the training as part of the tuition to attend the training program. In some cases, HR has asked people who participate in training follow-up questions to identify what they have implemented. This feedback is then used to try to quantify the return on investment of those training programs.

Some HR leaders have chosen alternative measures for their programs that give broad indications of the return on the investment in human capital. For example, a training director in a financial services company attempted to influence the executive leadership to purchase alternative learning approaches based on multi-media learning tools. The argument against the purchase was that it was too expensive. However, the training director succeeded in convincing the executives to invest in the technology for instrumental learning (learning a skill). She based her argument on the idea that 1) it would generate greater return because of its capability to be re-used and 2) that it would increase the employees' ability to apply what they learned because the learning would occur when they needed it, any time, anywhere, and any place.

If the training and development program is focused and has immediate application, it will often have a dollar return that is evident quickly. HR professionals will need to track the benefits to show that the participants are doing things differently and are applying what they learned. They may have to assign a value to the benefits even if their measures are imperfect.

Here are three examples of this kind of measure of return on investment for people development:

- *Example #1:* A global training session on developing innovations and breakthroughs brought together senior managers from worldwide operations. The participants were encouraged to develop a joint breakthrough to create more international collaboration. During the training, two senior managers decided to launch a new product simultaneously in Canada and in the Caribbean (under normal conditions, the launch in the Caribbean would have occurred one year after the launch in Canada). As a result of the trust that developed between these two managers, the simultaneous launch was successful and netted a return of $70,000 that would not have occurred otherwise.

- *Example #2:* A European company held a training session on international negotiation. The participants were taught about the value of focusing on the interests of the other party. One insight offered was that knowing the other party's interests would help you give them only what they need and not more. They learned that it is useful to negotiate "without waste." In between the two-day session, participants were encouraged to apply what they learned. One participant decided to change a proposal he was submitting by indicating that he would charge for a review process (rather than his traditional approach of giving that review process for free). He recognized that the purchaser was willing to pay for the review process. The change in approach and the return on the learning for that person was $30,000.

- *Example #3:* The balanced scorecard[2] approach (a performance management measure) has enabled companies to measure the return on investment in human capital. The performance management approach aligns individual and team objectives to the overall company objectives. It also aligns with the key stakeholders of the company (i.e., usually the shareholders, the customers, and the employees). These measures have been used to assess the effectiveness of employee contributions to a company's overall goals for each of their stakeholders.

[2] Robert S. Kaplan and David P. Norton, *The Balanced Scorecard*, Havard Business School Press, 1996.

Assessing the RIHC of Internal HR Process Improvements

The investment in human capital also can be applied in the area of identifying the cost benefit analysis of HR process improvements and efficiencies. To make any change within HR, costing should be done to develop the business case in the same way it is done in the Implementing Change and Transition Process (Chapter Nine). In order to justify their actions effectively, HR professionals should have the capability to talk about financial performance and costs on all strategic initiatives and transformations within HR.

For example, consider a situation in which HR wants to focus on strategic business process outcomes and organizational value-added work. They decide to abandon (dump, delay, distribute, and diminish) much of the core people processes. To expedite those changes, they consider whether the people processes will be done by external service providers, or through an insourced shared services provider or not done at all. Here are some questions HR professionals may ask as they consider their RIHC choices of how to proceed:

- What is the cost of moving to a shared services infrastructure and the cost of outsourcing? How do the costs compare with each other? (Take into account the reduced cost associated with system upgrades, which are often at the expense of the external service provider rather than the company's expense.)
- Could some of the work be distributed to the line? Is there a potential quality cost associated with distributing the work to the line managers? (Perhaps they will not do the work because they do not see it as part of their responsibility, and as a result quality will drop.)
- Perhaps HR can continue to do the core people process work themselves. What opportunities are lost if HR does basic non-strategic transactions that distract them from doing strategic work?

HR Prepares Dynamic Reports on the Return on Investment in Human Capital

HR professionals should be able to prepare reports for line management that help them run their businesses and contribute to effective people-related decisions. They sometimes include specific demographic information such as numbers of employees, educational level, etc. In addition, the reports include information directly related to the line managers' business such as absenteeism, turnover, production downtime, lost time accidents, short-term and long-term disability, etc.

In the future, HR will also need to prepare dynamic reports that will provide strategic business information and will analyze the productivity of the investment in human capital. For example, with the analytical capability and the data, HR can do the following:

- *Present the sales per employee:* This measure takes on new meaning if the employee count is used as described in this chapter. Many companies believe they are increasing their sales per employee by outsourcing. Essentially, they remove the outsourced employees from their employee count and, therefore, they increase their sales per employee. This counting method reduces a company's ability to compare itself with companies that do not outsource as much.

- *Produce dynamic simulations:* This includes conducting "what if" analyses and predicting what would happen if the company invests in human capital in a different way and its potential impact on profitability. They also run computer simulations to predict the best way to invest and the most cost effective place to put work for the company based on productivity and cost of human capital.

- *Forecast the areas of best return on investment in human capital:* Identify if any opportunities have been missed or if opportunities can be discovered. For example, this forecast may include an analysis of the impact of raising salaries for specific groups and the cost of securing specific strategic employee skill sets.

- *Conduct comparisons of data:* Compare the data by locations, departments, types of jobs, education, age, seniority, etc. for the individual, team or organization to determine the best opportunities for cost effective internal investments.

Here are two examples of analyses that HR might conduct:

- *Example #1:* Consider a company that defines the metric of human capital simply by the educational level of employees. They have employees with an average of twelve years of education (high school graduates). The HR report suggests that a return on investment can be achieved if the company executives decide to increase their overall metric of human capital to achieve an average educational level of 14 years. They include a dynamic simulation of the impact of the investment in human capital on the company's productivity and customer satisfaction measures. The dynamic report recommends that the increase in the overall metric of human capital can be achieved by targeted recruitment, turnover, and educational upgrading.

- *Example #2:* In another company, the HR vice president uses their version of the RIHC information to predict future required investments in human capital. She defines the metric of human capital by demographic data such as age, marital status, education, professional expertise, number of children, and gender. She combines her analysis of the investment made in human capital, with the demographic and industry trends. She uses a forecasting model to do simulations to predict within a 5 percent error rate the anticipated number of people who will leave the company in the next five to ten years. She then recommends the required investment in human capital to keep the metric of human capital at its desired level.

As HR's credibility continues to increase, HR professionals will be able to respond to questions about how potential management decisions will affect investment in human capital. Executives will look to HR as the source of the analytical information and recommendations on RIHC. HR's strategic role will also become very evident in these companies.

The HR Competencies Needed to Support RIHC Analysis

The traditional HR professional is usually not trained to do RIHC analyses. To achieve the necessary skills, most HR departments will require the services of a labor economist or an accountant. Some of the competencies required for a person who will be in charge of this responsibility include the following:

- *The person clearly has to have a strong financial and/or labor economics background so that he or she can model this information effectively:* The individual needs to be able to generate accurate data that can be included in an overall financial report. Two sources of talent to explore for this role are individuals who are well-grounded finance or labor economists. Another source might be industrial relations professionals in unionized environments who calculate the cost of labor as part of the process of negotiating a collective agreement.

- *The person has to have the ability to handle abstract ideas:* The ability of the person to think abstractly and have a systems orientation to the business will be a critical competence for this role. Some of the financial considerations involve simple mathematics; however, some of the numbers and the dynamic analyses are probability-oriented and more abstract. They also need to have the ability to convert data into information and knowledge.

- *The ability to communicate complex ideas in simple language:* Extremely clear and precise communication skills are a must for this individual. He or she needs to know the right questions to ask and be able to provide information that will help others make appropriate decisions. To be understood correctly, the individual must be able to speak in the language of the person he or she is assisting. If the person is unable to communicate simply, then people will not understand and will not be able to derive the maximum benefit from their analyses.

- *The ability to transfer expertise:* This person can not hoard ideas or information but must be someone with whom others are willing to collaborate. He or she must be willing and able to use the information to formulate recommendations and identify the RIHC. The individual must also enable others to do this kind of activity independently.

- *A strong sense of ethics and confidentiality:* This person will be the holder of very private and strategic information about human capital. Often the only people who have direct access to this information are the company's executives and perhaps one or two other people. Therefore, this individual has to be extremely trustworthy. For this reason, this role usually does not exist without executive support and approval.

- *Ability to use technology to analyze the investment in human capital:* Most of the analysis will be done through computer software programs. The person needs to be comfortable with systems and programs that will yield the required information. He or she will also benefit from a creative approach to computer programming to conceptualize alternate ways of accessing data that may be in diverse locations in the company.

Benefits for HR When It Takes Accountability for RIHC

HR and the company reap many benefits when HR takes accountability for RIHC seriously:

- *RIHC becomes an area in which HR can provide expert guidance to senior executives, which enables HR to:*
  - Furnish human capital information to executive leaders that is essential to running the business.
  - Use its knowledge of RIHC to contribute to discussions about the company's overall productivity.
- *HR recommends the best utilization of people based on data (and not hunches) and benefits the company by being able to:*
  - Identify the best place for people if the work can be done equally well in multiple locations.
  - Determine whether the company is doing better in its investment in human capital with current practices or in alternative ways.
  - Identify work that is wasteful and, therefore, not a good investment and determine the under-utilized potential in the company.
  - Use the RIHC analysis as part of the recommendation of whether to outsource or not.
- *HR's overall perception and position changes in the company, providing the following benefits to HR:*
  - It gains the responsibility, authority, and influence on this "hard" issue (money), which helps it position and sell softer recommendations.
  - It has a much better case to convince business executives to support its recommendations if it can identify some level of return on investment in human capital for initiatives such as selection, training, ongoing learning, and retention.
  - It will be able to justify process improvements and suggested changes within the HR function. Invariably, as a result of HR's success in process improvements and determining the cost of human capital, other areas in the company will look to it to help them with their people and process investments.
  - It becomes a center of expertise concerning the meaning of and projections about the RIHC. For example, if HR says salaries should be frozen, it may be more highly credible than a finance recommendation because HR will have based its recommendation on a balance of the RIHC and the impact on the motivation and performance of people.

 – It teaches and reinforces an ongoing awareness about RIHC among leadership so that it becomes part of any business decision.

Barriers to HR in Leading the RIHC Business Transformation

Even if HR wants to lead the RIHC process, some of the company's leaders may not welcome this and, in some cases, may resist HR's role in calculating the return on investment in human capital.

For example, some senior managers or executives may feel threatened if HR knows the investment in human capital and they, as the leaders of the area, do not have these numbers. They may feel HR has information that may threaten their control-oriented leadership. Others may not want to use the data they receive from HR, or they may not know how to use the data they receive. Still others may have a stereotyped image of HR and may not respect HR's capability to discuss financial matters even if they are about human capital issues.

HR employees may also have some resistance to HR's focus on RIHC. For example, some HR professionals may avoid this work because they lack the skills or confidence to do dynamic analyses of human capital investments. These people will need to align with expert resources, such as labor economists or professionals within the company's financial services area to help them. Some other HR professionals may believe that this kind of work is not the domain of HR and will avoid it if they can.

Notwithstanding the above potential barriers, companies that move in this direction have found that HR is able to contribute to their company's business transformation by (1) providing strategic advice and recommending decisions on how to deploy new products and processes and (2) determining the specific environments in which they should be deployed. HR moves from an important internal service to an essential service business that is highly strategic and important to the competitive success of the company.

Summary

* For HR to be a business within a business, one of the process outcomes it must understand is the *return on investment in human capital* (RIHC).

* HR needs the knowledge and ability to provide strategic advice about how to invest wisely in human capital.

* In calculating the investment in human capital, HR presents trends, broad analyses, and key performance and productivity indicators.

* The investment in human capital covers all matters that are invested in employees and not just direct costs paid to employees (salaries and benefits).

* The investment in human capital can be divided into money invested that the employee receives directly, money that is paid to third parties on behalf of employees, and investments in employee development. The total invested in human capital is then reduced by the amount of any employment subsidies received.

* When HR is able to contribute value to RIHC, the expectation will also increase concerning its ability to analyze the quality of the investment it makes in HR core people and organizational processes.

* To determine the return on investment in human capital for selection, HR must be intensely aware of the company's strategic direction and its desired future outcomes. The balance between the drivers can vary due to many factors including country differences, business unit differences, and jobs of similar importance but in different labor market segments.

* HR professionals should have the capability to talk about financial performance and costs on all strategic initiatives and all transformations within HR so that they can justify their actions effectively.

* The traditional HR professional is usually not trained to do RIHC analyses. Sometimes HR will require the services of a labor economist or accountant to provide some consulting assistance and to transfer learning to the HR professionals.

- HR and the company reap many benefits when HR takes account-ability for RIHC seriously:
  - RIHC becomes an area in which HR can provide expert guidance to senior executives.
  - HR recommends the best utilization of people based upon data, not hunches.
  - The overall perception and position of HR changes in the company.

PART FOUR

The Way Forward

CHAPTER ELEVEN

HR Structure, Roles, and Relationships

Structure is the way work and people are organized to enable the business to fulfill its accountabilities. The previous chapters defined much of HR's work—the people, organizational, and business process outcomes. This chapter describes how HR's work can be organized so that it can be delivered efficiently and effectively.

The structure of HR's work can be rather simple in small companies. This chapter focuses on larger, more complex companies. In these environments HR serves many internal clients in different areas such as in multiple business units, geographical locations, customer segments, and functions. In these elaborate work environments, the challenge is to design a comprehensive structure for HR to enable it to deliver its mandate. In companies that are less complex, this discussion will still be of benefit. HR professionals in smaller and simpler companies can glean ideas that will fit their business context and strategic direction.

An Approach to Organizational Structure for HR

This section describes a model for an HR structure. The model functions as a guide and not as the definitive answer. As described in Chapter Five, an organizational structure should not become rigid, resulting in the structure governing the work, rather than the work governing the structure. A pragmatic approach to organizational design should prevail to ensure alignment with the current reality in the company.

The proposed model for an HR structure is based on the organizational design work of Bartlett and Ghoshal (*Managing Across Borders,* 1989)[1]. The authors provide a frame of reference that can guide HR professionals to identify the structure that meets their specific needs. Their proposed model creates a balance between local responsiveness and global efficiency. In a similar sense, the HR preferred organizational structure is based on a balance between local client responsiveness and company-wide (i.e., global) efficiency and effectiveness.

Achieving Internal Client Responsiveness

HR professionals have to meet unique internal client needs regularly. In these situations one company-wide policy and standard does not fit local client requirements. For example, consider a marketing and sales department that needs to develop a better working relationship and a common set of goals. The HR professional needs to tailor the approach to this specific need. A company-wide process may not help this marketing and sales department resolve its issues.

Some of the forces that may drive the HR business to be locally responsive are the following:

- External environment issues
  - local skills shortages
  - local legislation
  - cultural and linguistic issues
- Local business needs
  - specific business unit goals and objectives
  - unique stage of organizational development
  - unique resource requirements and developmental needs
- HR responsiveness needs
  - local presence to gain acceptance by line management
  - ability to influence local strategy development

---

[1] Christopher A. Bartlett and Sumantra Ghoshal, *Managing Across Borders,* Harvard Business School Press, 1989.

- ability to influence RIHC investment locally
- ability to respond to unique organizational and cultural needs

Achieving Company-Wide Efficiency and Effectiveness

Some HR work may not have to be tailored as much to specific internal clients because the needs in the different client groups they serve are the same or very similar. For example, when HR deploys technology in this kind of situation, the same technology systems can be used in all the business areas. The internal client base can be considered as one "company-wide" client for the technology deployment, service, and support. The HR services can become a center of excellence in one place with a limited representation in the specific client business areas.

An example of the forces that may drive an HR business to structure centrally to achieve company-wide efficiency and effectiveness include the following:

- Lower production and service costs
  - derive economies of scale for HR expenditures
  - reduce cost on company-wide HR products and services
  - expand commonality and standardization of HR systems
- Financial management
  - identify company-wide "Return on Investment in Human Capital"
  - develop common financial reporting on RIHC
  - insure more financial accountability over HR services
- HR efficiency and effectiveness
  - company-wide delivery of core people processes
  - company-wide values and strategic alignment
  - company-wide succession planning and talent pool management
  - company-wide shared learning and knowledge management

Balancing Internal Client Responsiveness with Company-Wide Efficiency

Companies that require a comprehensive service delivery from HR often require an organizational structure that strikes a balance between the specific needs of internal clients and the needs for company-wide efficiency and effectiveness. In many cases, the balance required for this kind of HR structure is somewhat analogous to the "mass-customization" in a manufacturing environment. This is a process that enables a manufacturer to mass produce a product that the local customers *experience* as customized to their needs. The customers want the global efficiency characteristics of high quality at a low cost and at a fast speed and, at the same time, want the product to be highly personalized so that the services and products are precisely what they need. Mass customization allows production processes to both customize to the "local" needs of the individual customer or market and to do it in such a way that the product can be "globally" produced in a mass production manner.

In companies that expect to achieve a balance between company-wide efficiency and specific local client responsiveness, HR is compelled to mass customize as well. They need to achieve the following:

- *Local Client Responsiveness:* HR professionals contribute to the development of the internal clients' business strategy, providing expert guidance related to people and organizational processes. They are responsive to the internal clients' business to help create a flexible culture, align strategic initiatives, and help implement change and transition. They are active in organizational consulting assignments, support the creation of a shared learning work environment, and handle specific employee relations issues that can not be handled by the line managers. They also share their knowledge and expertise with other HR professionals who are supporting other internal clients to facilitate alignment of their approaches within the company.

- *Company-Wide Efficiency and Effectiveness:* HR professionals are accountable for the company-wide core people processes to achieve economies of scale, commonality of systems, and the return on investments in human capital. The HR company-wide efficiencies are needed for the core people processes such as selection and orientation, performance development, compensation and recognition, employee service and retention, and termination approaches. In addition, the company-wide HR services include the implementation of HR technology and its applications, as well as accountability for insuring the "return on investment in human capital."

Figure 11.1 shows an HR governance structure designed to balance local client responsiveness with company-wide efficiency. Work that does not achieve local client responsiveness or company-wide efficiency should be abandoned.

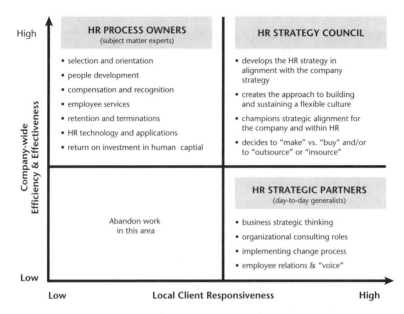

Figure 11.1: A Model of an HR Structure

Three primary roles for HR professionals are presented in Figure 11.1. These are:

1. *Strategic partners:* This HR role is a "local internal client responsiveness" role. The role of HR strategic partners is described in Chapter Two and Chapter Six.

2. *Process owners:* This HR role is a "company-wide efficiency effectivenss role." HR process owners are responsible specifically for the HR processes and not other company processes (such as the process for billing).

3. *HR Strategy Council:* The HR strategy council includes process owners and strategic partners. The objective of the council is to balance the need for local internal client responsiveness with company-wide efficiency and effectiveness. Often this group includes some of HR's key clients in the company as well.

Roles and Relationships for the HR Strategic Partners

This section focuses on the strategic partner role as it relates to process owners, the HR strategy council, and other strategic partners.

Strategic partners must work in alignment with the other HR professionals. The following are suggestions for strategic partners to optimize their relationships with the process owners, their colleagues on the strategy council, and their other strategic partners.

- *Relationships with the process owners:* Strategic partners must be closely linked to the process owners. Many of the support services that strategic partners recommend will be delivered through groups dealing with people processes. Strategic partners will be liaisons with the process owners on the development of service-level agreements, working with them to meet the clients' needs for core people process services. Strategic partners also must have a general working knowledge of all the people processes and operate in accordance with those that have been developed. Successful strategic partners also take responsibility for the marketing and communications link to the client and support the development and implementation of the people processes.

- *Relationships with the HR strategy council:* Strategic partners are usually members of the HR strategy council and, therefore, have a vested interest in both its success and the ability to implement the strategies they develop. The HR strategic partners need to be open and candid in HR strategy council meetings and discuss the following:
  - Emerging strategic business issues and their HR implications.
  - How they meet local business needs and at the same time be in alignment with the overall people strategy.
  - Alternative approaches to their clients' pressures to deliver service when their client's direction differs from the HR strategy council's direction.
  - Successful and unsuccessful interventions in response to the needs of their clients.

- *Relationships with other HR strategic partners:* Strategic partners share what they learn in their business environments with the other strategic partners. When they are working in alignment, HR strategic partners are able to achieve the following:
  - Develop a working knowledge of the issues their colleagues are facing with their clients.
  - Develop the capability to fill in for another strategic partner when the need arises to ensure continuity of service to the client groups.

- Assist other strategic partners when they lack specific skills. For example, some strategic partners are skilled as organizational consultants, while others are not. Other strategic partners may have more skills in complex employee relations' issues, while others may not. The strategic partners that have specialty skills should be available to other client groups in addition to their own clients.

- Find ways to create economies of scale among the strategic partners so that services to several internal clients can be achieved at the lowest possible cost while not sacrificing quality service and timeliness.

Roles and Relationships for the HR Process Owners

The role of the process owners is to manage the delivery of the company-wide services and process outcomes. These include HR's core people processes (as described in Chapter Four), the implementation of technology and its applications (Chapter Five), and the role of making the best investment in human capital (Chapter Ten). A great deal of their work is done through automation, external service providers, and the collaboration with other internal resources. In their process areas, they are expected to deliver cost-effective solutions with timeliness, quality and expertise.

HR process owners are also accountable for continuous improvement and communication. They promote and launch the people processes in the organization. They are responsible for training and motivating managers and employees throughout the organization to ensure that they are appropriately involved and do their part to deliver the process outcomes.

The HR process owners also have accountabilities to the internal clients, and they work with them in collaboration with the strategic partners. They are accountable for those standard parts of the process that often do not require participation of strategic partners. For example, process owners would handle directly junior-level recruiting and orientation as well as handling complaints directly if they arise. They also identify alternative options of delivering the service in order to remain competitive. This includes keeping informed about how their company's performance compares with the external competition's performance.

Being an "owner" means that HR is accountable for the entire process, even though the HR process owner does not control all the parts of the process. Some examples include the following:

- *Example #1:* Determining the return on investment in human capital (RIHC) requires the participation of Finance, Information Technology, and managers to collect and produce accurate information. HR process owners are accountable for the delivery of the RIHC analysis even though they do not have all the parties reporting to them.

- *Example #2:* Another example is in the area of selection and orientation. The process owners need the participation of others in order to be successful at selection and orientation. The roles of other professionals in the company include the following:

  - *Managers* are expected to forecast their recruiting needs, understand the work requirements, participate in behavioral interviewing, and take an active role in the new employee orientation.

  - *Other internal service functions* are expected to collaborate with the people process owners so that as a new employee arrives for work, all the pieces are in place. This includes the ability to pay the employee (by Finance); provision for the office, desk, and technology to be available for the employee to work (by Facilities and Information Technology); and announcement to the other employees that the new employee has arrived (by Communications).

  - *External service providers* are often involved, including recruiters and perhaps specialists who do pre-employment assessments.

HR process owners need competencies in the following areas:

- *Influence Skills:* Ability to influence others. For example, they have to directly or indirectly influence line managers to deliver their part of the people process.

- *Relationship Building:* Form excellent alliances with HR strategic partners in the business areas to help market, communicate, and implement many elements of the people processes.

- *Numerical Skills:* Produce specific, quantifiable process outcomes that can be measured to determine a return on investment of the people processes.

- *Technical HR Skills:* Be the process experts in the area over which they have "ownership."

- *Organizational Skills:* Ensure efficiency, effectiveness, and economies of scale.

- *Conceptual Skills:* Think from the perspective of the entire company and be very open to mass customizing the standard approach to meet local client requirements.

HR Process Owners' Relationships with External Vendors

HR will undoubtedly use some vendor assistance in providing service to the company. The external assistance will be necessary for HR to succeed in abandoning some traditional core people process roles. Excellence in vendor relations and management of those relationships will be an essential competency for the HR process owners.

HR's approach to vendor relations is similar to the approach that many companies are taking in their procurement departments in the process of purchasing supplies. Most purchasing departments have recognized the value of reducing the number of suppliers and creating preferred supplier relationships. These relationships are characterized by a selection process that identifies the company's special needs and specific service agreements that are renewed annually or every few years. HR also needs several preferred suppliers (rather than many) to ensure that the vendors understand the company strategy, vision, and norms so they can align their services to the company's unique needs.

HR process owners' success as vendor managers is usually based on their information technology infrastructure that allows them to manage the purchases and inventory they receive. They can then discuss issues more intelligently with the external service providers. They do not rely on the preferred supplier's accounting and technology but, instead, rely on their own data, comparing it with the data the preferred supplier provides them. HR process owners, therefore, need internal technology controls so that the vendors data matches their own. Furthermore, the preferred suppliers need to develop service agreements that parallel the agreements the process owners developed with their internal clients.

The external service provider also has other roles in addition to supplying products and/or services:

- Give research and development intelligence on the up-and-coming technologies and innovations to consider in the near future
- As a follow-up consulting service, help HR and the internal client refine the service or product to more precisely meet the needs of the business.

HR process owners are expected to create standards of performance for vendors in the same way they would create standards for internal service deliverers. For example, one high-technology company used preferred suppliers for many of its services. They outsourced recruiting, training and even the sales roles to external vendors. The company was a major customer (a strategic customer) to the preferred supplier and was able to exercise more controls over the supplier because of the company's special position in the supplier's portfolio of customers.

The company was concerned that they might lose quality control over the personnel and quality processes the preferred supplier was using. The supplier agreed to:

1. Participate with the company in joint selection and orientation of new recruits and staff within the supplier company,

2. Have the supplier staff spend time in the company learning about the company's objectives and values, and

3. Get to know more closely the people with whom they would work in HR and sales service. The high-technology company believed that their attention to managing the relationship, values, and staffing in the preferred supplier company was a major reason the preferred supplier relationship worked as well as it did.

HR process owners should make the effort to relate to the outsourced suppliers as members of their team who work for them under different conditions of employment and perhaps for different amounts of time. This point was suggested earlier (Chapter Ten), that external service providers should be counted as part of the company's people count as if (and in fact since they are) part of the team as well.

Furthermore, many of the HR administrative staff may have been hired by the external service provider's company to provide the administrative services for them. This pattern already is occurring in Information Technology in which programming in many companies has been outsourced and part of the outsource contract includes hiring the programmers who were with the company and were replaced by the outsourced firm. Companies have found that the same people who worked for them in the past are now working for the external service provider and delivering service on a part-time or full-time basis to their former companies.

Often, special relationships need to be established with other external sources that are somewhat different from the relationships with outsourcing firms. For example, HR often needs to develop strategic relationships with universities to help ensure that the company has an adequate supply of educated people. The business takes students and provides them with internships and may engage in a recruiting program to secure the best graduates from the programs. In exchange for the commitment to the university, the company often has an influence on shaping the university curriculum in their business area. For example, some companies have strategic partnerships with universities to have their executives teach classes for them in their business schools. Other companies have decided to offer joint company and university business degrees. Still others have decided to locate near the university for more immediate access to university research and for university recruiting.

Process Owner Relationships with Other HR Professionals

To be successful, HR process owners need to develop excellent internal relations within HR, including relationships with HR strategic partners, the HR strategy council, and the other HR process owners.

- *Relationship with the HR strategic partners:* HR process owners are in a triangular relationship between themselves, internal clients and HR strategic partners. Sometimes clients will want to give strategic partners the responsibility for jobs and, at other times, will give responsibilities directly to the process owners. Some of the process owners' duties include:
  - Update HR strategic partners of upcoming changes in a process.
  - Collaborate with the strategic partners to develop specific process requests and conditions of satisfaction, (i.e., developing service agreements).
  - Take and give "early warning signals" about future needs for the core people processes.
  - Keep HR strategic partners informed of line managers' requests when they receive them directly.
- *Relationship with the HR strategy council*: Most HR process owners are usually members of the HR strategy council and, therefore, have a vested interest in its success. Regarding their relationship with the HR strategy council, their duties include:
  - Recommend any major change to their processes with a business case for all to consider.
  - Escalate critical incidents and emerging issues.

- Receive input, feedback, and share the results from their metrics.

- Escalate cost issues concerning the people processes before they spiral out of control.

• *Relationship with the other HR process owners:* It is very important that HR process owners view themselves as part of the larger HR business team and that they work closely with the other HR process owners in delivering service. HR may be implementing and/or considering several interventions that involve many process owners. These processes all have specific expected outcomes but are not discrete processes. For example, process owners of a recruiting and orientation process will need to collaborate with those responsible for the performance development process and the rewards and recognition process.

To align their work with the other processes and with the strategic partners, HR process owners should have a general knowledge of the other processes, develop cross-process solutions, consolidate their metrics to assess their overall performance, and coordinate their communications. To avoid overwhelming the client with too many HR changes at one time, the process owners should consider having a master project management chart for all their interventions.

Roles and Relationships for the HR Strategy Council

The total alignment of the HR service business coalesces at the HR strategy council. The council is usually chaired by the HR vice president, who is accountable for the overall HR process outcomes. In some cases, the members of the HR strategy council have portions of their bonus tied up in the overall success of the HR strategy and in its successful implementation.

The HR strategy council focuses on the strategic process outcomes of importance to the company such as ensuring a flexible culture, achieving strategic alignment, implementing change, and securing a return on investment in human capital. The council considers the efforts to balance local client responsiveness and company-wide efficiencies. They also are stewards of the core HR people processes and ensure that efficiencies, costs, and quality service are delivered. Finally, they usually decide whether to "make" a service rather than "buy" a service and whether to use external service providers or to do the work within HR.

The HR strategy council insures that the people strategy is aligned with the company strategy. They function as a kind of "Board of Directors" of the HR People Strategy. In this role they do the following:

- Understand the business strategy and align the people and organizational process outcomes to it.
- Identify which stategic business process should be the focus for HR.
- Measure, analyze, and integrate HR people, organizational, and business process outcomes and make recommendations to the executives on HR's future direction.
- Ensure collaboration between the HR process owners and the HR strategic partners. Share learnings and transfer knowledge freely.
- Develop the overall HR strategy budget as part of the company budget.

The HR strategy council usually includes some key internal clients. It also may have an advisory group of senior managers that can be called a "clients council." The clients council provides perspective on company-wide governance issues and stimulates discussion on vision, values, and organizational structure issues. It contributes to defining the policy framework in areas such as code of business conduct, succession planning, and termination guidelines. The clients council also may test out ideas that the HR strategy council develops to increase the likelihood of implementation success and commitment to them.

The HR strategy council develops the HR strategy. They deal with the trade-offs among the processes and between the HR process owners and the strategic partners if necessary. They also handle potential dissatisfaction in one division if they implement a company-wide decision that disadvantages an area. Finally, they sponsor the roll-out of multiple HR people and organizational processes.

"Make" Versus "Buy" Approach

The HR strategy council must decide whether to make (design and implement) or buy (outsource) its core people services. The decision should be based primarily on whether the core people process is strategic or not. If it is not strategic, but still must be done, HR can buy services if they are affordable and do the minor modifications necessary to tailor the services to the company's needs. HR can then spend its energy and resources on delivering the strategic business process outcomes rather than developing unique capabilities in non-strategic core people processes.

In the past few years, HR has become a major buyer of the expertise of external service providers. Many companies have recognized that HR functions as a *distributor* of services rather than as a *creator* of HR services. HR buys the people processes provided by external services, develops them, and then distributes them to the clients.

HR may also buy rather than make services where organizational value-add and strategic business process outcomes are concerned. HR often does not have the research strength to design the organizational value-add and strategic business process outcomes services from scratch. HR should then collaborate with specific preferred supplier consultants who operate as external resources with sufficient knowledge of the company to help deliver the company's strategic business processes quickly and efficiently.

Outsource Versus Insource Approach

HR strategy councils often struggle with the question of whether to outsource or insource services for core HR people processes. For a number of years, the solution seemed to be to outsource, which gave HR the opportunity to quickly upgrade service delivery to industry standards.

More recently, though, the pendulum has started to swing back to the creation of "shared services," particularly in large complex companies with multiple divisions, businesses, etc. There has been recognition that it may be cost effective to develop services equivalent to those provided by an outsourced firm but to do it internally. In essence, shared services is a client-driven process of "insourcing" services rather than "outsourcing." It works well under the following conditions:

- When the company has multiple levels of complexity.
- Where an external outsource firm cannot be expected to tailor to the specific needs of the company as well as the HR function can.
- Where shared services can reduce the costs to a more manageable level than the cost for the outsourced firm's services.

Unfortunately, shared services has often been misunderstood and is a source of confusion for many internal clients. Some refer to shared services as another term for centralizing HR. Others believe it is a method to share services for some core HR people processes among several businesses and not for all the businesses in a company. Some companies will say that shared services is driven by economies of scale and compromises to their unique business needs and often do not result in quality service to their local business area.

This confusion is most acutely felt during the introduction and transition phase to a shared services model. It may be due to inadequate communication to the internal clients about why shared services is being introduced and inadequate back-up during the transition to ensure quality service. If there are early lapses in quality service, it can paint the shared services approach as a cost-cutting exercise that will reduce quality service. Any potential deficiencies in the transition process need to be carefully anticipated so as not to sacrifice the credibility of the shared service and the entire HR service business.

External service providers are attempting to operate as multiple-company shared services, which means they are sharing the services among many companies rather than strictly within one company. This solution will fit more easily for less complex organizations that do not want to or do not have a need to invest in building their own shared services. The outsourced servicez provider functions as the center of excellence for many companies. Also, the cost of ongoing research and infrastructure is the provider's rather than the company's cost. If the relationship works well, HR is able to focus more intensely on the strategic business process outcomes rather than on the core HR people processes.

In larger multi-business organizations, shared services is introduced to achieve administrative operational excellence with a more personalized approach than most outsourced firms could provide. Shared services are driven by client service agreements in the same manner as an external outsource firm and has the added advantage of being able to focus on linking and aligning all company services. To succeed, shared services must demonstrate superbly executed, cost-effective administrative services that achieve commonality of systems and economies of scale. It also has to be able to give fast and immediate response to HR operational effectiveness needs.

The HR Strategy Council Manages the Risks to the HR Business

As with any organizational design, risks may occur that need to be anticipated and managed. Here are some of the risks that may be encountered and some suggestions for reducing them:

- *Risk #1—The HR strategy council will develop strategies that are not aligned with the company imperatives and direction:* The risk that this will occur is greater if the HR vice president is not accepted as a full member of the executive team. In this case, the likelihood of becoming disconnected increases. The development of a client's council can be an alternative way to insure that senior HR people meet with clients from time to time and align their services to the client's needs. Also, the HR strategic partners can be an alternative access route to aligning with the internal clients one at a time.

- *Risk #2—The HR business will not be financially supported to implement its strategy:* Sometimes funding issues emerge because the company lacks capital resources. Other times it may signal a lack of confidence that HR can deliver on its promises. The HR strategy council can reduce the risk by introducing the budget in a gate review process as described in Chapter Nine. By lessening the cost commitment and by introducing decision points, the HR strategy council reduces the anxiety over the investment and the degree of financial exposure at any given time. In addition, it is far more effective to ask for money based on successes rather than on a promise of success. The HR strategy council finds opportunities to show small successes as they make their case for budgetary support. Finally, they may want to identify some quick hits that will give some immediate return on investment in the HR strategy.

- *Risk #3—The HR strategic partners and the HR process owners will become disconnected and unaligned:* This problem has become a major issue for HR as it has moved to the structural model described in this chapter—especially when the HR process owners are coordinating an internal shared service. Essentially, the strategic partners respond to the needs of their local clients and the process owners respond to the needs of the total company. These two groups of professionals do not always have the same perspectives, which produces an HR business that is not internally aligned when they need to work with each other. In some cases they become fragmented.

Here are two ways that this risk has been overcome in companies. These are:

1. The HR strategy council consists of both strategic partners and process owners. Through their dialogues with one another, the strategic partners and owners can make explicit attempts to develop mutual accountabilities and share learning with each other. Increased alignment will be the result.

2. Some companies expect HR strategic partners to be the project leaders on at least one core people process project at any given

time. The logic is twofold. First, it utilizes the most senior people for the most challenging assignments (in most cases the process owners and the strategic partners are the most senior people with the most experience to handle such an assignment). Also, it forces the HR strategic partners to do a company-wide project so that they will have to get out of the internal client's cocoon and understand the larger business needs to deliver the project.

For example, in one company the HR professional who is the process owner for selection and orientation is also the strategic partner with the Information Technology area of the company. Another HR professional who is the HR strategic partner with the Sales clients also collaborates with the HR process owner accountable for compensation and recognition. These dual roles are chosen because they relate to each other (i.e., selection is very important in this company to the Information Technology area, and compensation is a critical issue for Sales). In addition, it forces the HR professionals to think both from a local client perspective and a company-wide perspective.

- *Risk #4—It may be unclear whether the strategic partners are really adding value to their internal clients:* The strategic partners often work in isolation with their internal clients. Sometimes, little mentoring occurs. Clients may give feedback about their performance after the problem has become too severe, and it is too late to salvage the situation. One company reduced this risk by involving the HR vice president, who took an active mentoring role with each of the strategic partners. This mentoring role currently includes quarterly joint visits with the internal clients and the HR strategic partner to discuss how the HR business services are being received.

The HR Strategy Council Models the Way

The HR strategy council must demonstrate commitment to modeling team effectiveness and successful decision-making. They need to work collaboratively and demonstrate a flexible culture within HR and align all HR initiatives to each other and to the company vision. They need to be strategic implementers (not just idea people) who take accountability for delivering the HR strategic business process outcomes. They insure that the core people and organizational value-add processes are delivered with excellence even if it is done by an outsourced firm or distributed to the line or by shared services.

Summary

- Structure is the way work and people are organized to enable the business to fulfill its accountabilities. Previous chapters defined much of HR's work—both core and strategic work. This chapter describes how HR's work can be organized so that it can be delivered efficiently and effectively.

- A structure is proposed that balances company-wide efficiency with local internal client responsiveness. It is composed of three major roles for HR: strategic partners, process owners, and HR strategy council.

- Strategic partners must be closely linked to HR process owners, on the development of service agreements and working with them to meet the needs of the clients for core people and organizational processes.

- The role of HR process owners is to manage the delivery of the company-wide services and processes. These include HR's core people processes (as described in Chapter Four), the implementation of technology and its applications (Chapter Five), and the role of determining the return on investment in human capital (Chapter Ten).

- HR will undoubtedly use some vendor assistance in providing service to the company. The external assistance will be necessary for HR to succeed in abandoning some traditional core roles. Excellence in vendor relations and management of those relationships will be an essential competency for the HR process owners. HR process owners are expected to create standards of performance for vendors in the same way they would create standards for internal service deliverers. HR process owners relate to the outsourced suppliers as members of their team who work for them under different conditions of employment and perhaps for different amounts of time.

- The total alignment of the HR service business coalesces at the HR strategy council. The council is chaired by the HR Vice President, who is accountable for the overall HR service business outcome.

The council focuses on the identified strategic process outcomes, such as ensuring a flexible culture, achieving strategic alignment, implementing change, and securing the best return on investment in human capital.

- The HR strategy council considers the efforts to balance local business responsiveness and company-wide efficiencies and effectiveness. The council develops the HR people strategy business plan. They also are stewards of the core HR people processes and ensure that efficiencies, costs, and quality service are delivered.

- An HR strategy council must make a decision about whether to make or buy its core people services. Many companies have recognized that HR functions as a "distributor" of service rather than as a "creator" of HR internal services.

- HR service businesses often struggle with the question of whether to outsource or insource services for core HR people processes. More recently, the pendulum has started to swing back to the creation of shared services, particularly in large complex companies with multiple divisions, businesses, etc. In essence, shared services is a client-driven process of "insourcing" services rather than "outsourcing." External service providers are attempting to operate as multiple-company shared services, which means they are sharing the services among many companies rather than strictly within one company.

- As with any organizational design, risks may occur that need to be anticipated and managed. Each of these risks must be mitigated to insure that HR has the credibility and ability to fulfill its mandate. The risks are:
  - Risk #1—The HR strategy council will develop strategies that are not aligned with the company imperatives and direction.
  - Risk #2—The HR business will not be financially supported to implement its strategy.
  - Risk #3—The HR strategic partners and the HR process owners will become disconnected and unaligned.
  - Risk #4—It may be unclear whether the strategic partners are really adding value to their internal clients.

- The HR strategy council must demonstrate commitment to modeling team effectiveness and successful decision-making.

CHAPTER TWELVE

The Solution after Next: Integrating Internal Service Businesses

Consider a large company in which HR, Information Technology, Finance, Communications, Facilities, and other internal service businesses focus on delivering aligned services to the internal client in order to add value to the external customer.

Although this may seem to be an uncommon scenario, think about the many companies that have undertaken a similar process in service of the external customer. At one point, these companies realized they functioned in what was popularly known as "silos." This mentality focused their businesses more on their products and services and less on the customers' and the company's needs. Technology, customer demands, intense competition, and even global market pressures forced convergence of different company capabilities. Companies were compelled to break up the silos and instead design their structures based on their customers' needs and expectations. Essentially, the solution has been to focus the company on business processes and customer needs.

In many companies, internal service businesses are considering a similar re-alignment. HR, Finance, Information Technology, Communications,

Facilities, and others have their unique functional areas and services. Often, they do not work together. But the same forces that have driven changes in other areas of the company are compelling changes in the fundamental expectations of internal service as well.

In addition, as more internal service areas adopt the structure, roles, and relationships recommended for HR (in Chapter Eleven), they will find their services to the internal client overlapping. For example, consider that in a certain company both Information Technology and Human Resources decide to structure in a similar way. Both design their own shared services that overlap with each other's service business areas (especially in the technology area). In essence, internal clients have two strategic partners, one from HR and another from Information Technology. Each strategic partner sets up service agreements, each wants time with the internal client to understand the client's needs and each wants to be an active participant on the client's senior management team.

If only two internal service businesses like these want to go down this path, it may be manageable. However, consider that the other areas catch the vision. The financial area starts to see itself as a financial services business, the communications function develops strategic partner relationships, and other internal service areas consider this approach as well. The internal client may become overwhelmed with all the attention and may not be able to give the necessary time to all these "well intentioned" professionals. As a result, the internal service businesses will not work effectively.

There are some potential troublesome scenarios that may create the urgency to adopt an integrated internal services approach:

- *Scenario #1:* The internal clients realize they need the internal service businesses to help them develop strategy, but the process is cumbersome. Too many people in the many service businesses are trying to be strategic partners with the clients. The clients are overloaded with requests for information from the different internal service businesses as they transform independently. The problem is even more difficult because the strategic partners from the various internal service businesses are not communicating with each other and are not motivated to do so.

- *Scenario #2:* The clients are concerned that the internal service businesses are not aligned with each other, and they know that their needs for service require the internal service businesses to collaborate. They are finding that they are working too hard trying to coordinate the efforts of the internal service businesses and the timing of specific initiatives that will be introduced into their business.

- *Scenario #3:* The clients complain that too many people are trying to develop service agreements. Each of the agreements appears in a different form, compounding the problem. In addition, each strategic partner is asking the internal client the questions that the previous strategic partner asked. The strategic partners are not talking to each other or sharing information and knowledge.

Internal clients want and need total intergrated solutions. The internal service businesses will need to collaborate to manage the relationship with the internal clients. Major quality improvements, cost-savings, and efficiency gains are possible outcomes.

Of course, it is important to identify the extent to which that integration can take place. The transformation of all the internal service businesses will need to be coordinated in alignment with internal clients' needs and with the objective to benefit external customers.

Five Levels of Integrating Internal Service Businesses

The intended outcomes of integrating internal service businesses are:

- Enhanced quality client service across internal service businesses and
- Improved efficiencies, cost savings, and shared learnings.

As one leader said, "Most companies are not rich enough to afford uncoordinated service." When internal service businesses do not work well together, the possible result is re-work, client dissatisfaction, and inefficiencies. The work has to be done right the first time, every time. Sometimes the internal service businesses will have to integrate some services to deliver the required quality. Figure 12.1 depicts five levels of integrating the internal service businesses. These are:

1. Shared learnings among internal service businesses
2. Joint planning and project management
3. Common processes and approaches but still operating separately
4. Collaborative work for specific initiatives
5. Structural integration of internal service businesses based on client needs

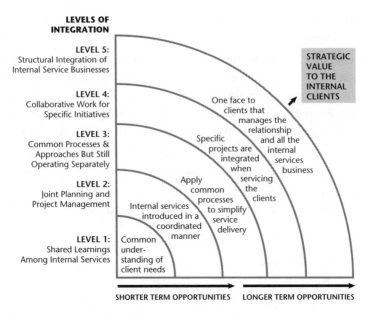

LEVELS OF INTEGRATION

LEVEL 5:
Structural Integration of Internal Service Businesses

LEVEL 4:
Collaborative Work for Specific Initiatives

LEVEL 3:
Common Processes & Approaches But Still Operating Separately

LEVEL 2:
Joint Planning and Project Management

LEVEL 1:
Shared Learnings Among Internal Services

STRATEGIC VALUE TO THE INTERNAL CLIENTS

One face to clients that manages the relationship and all the internal services business when servicing the clients

Specific projects are integrated

Apply common processes to simplify service delivery

Internal services introduced in a coordinated manner

Common understanding of client needs

SHORTER TERM OPPORTUNITIES   LONGER TERM OPPORTUNITIES

Figure 12.1: The Five Levels of Integrating Internal Service Business

The folowing are some of the features of the model in Figure 12.1:

- *Each higher level of integration assumes that all levels below it have taken place:* Although the integration does not have to occur sequentially, the lower levels of integration often take place before a higher level of integration to have the best chance of succeeding.

- *Identifies proposed timelines for implementation at each level:* Levels 1 through 3 are easier to accomplish and often can be implemented in the shorter term. Levels 4 and 5 are more complex because they intervene in the actual work of each internal service business, often resulting in a longer implementation time.

- *Provides examples of the strategic value to the internal clients.* An example of the strategic value to the internal client is identified for each level of integration. The remainder of this chapter presents additional ways the internal clients receive strategic value from integrating internal service businesses.

Level 1—Shared Learnings among Internal Service Businesses

At level one, the various internal service businesses are implementing change initiatives that are different from the others. They are having discussions with the internal client about their strategy and their needs. Their objective is to keep each other informed so that all are aware of what the client has said to any of the strategic partners.

Internal service businesses can save time and effort through shared information and learning by doing the following:

- *Use a successful idea from another area.* Often, all that is required is that an idea be modified, which saves the service business a great deal of time because they do not have to create the idea from scratch.

- *Learn from another area's mistakes.* A failure in one area can be a source of learning so that time will not be wasted making the same mistakes.

- *Use implementation pathways that have worked for other service businesses.* If a service business has successfully implemented a change, other service businesses can learn from their experience. It's possible that what they have done will work again or that similar implementation processes can be used.

Strategic partners can use a variety of methods to share information and learning. Many of these methods can be informal if their personnel networks will support the sharing and openness. The strategic partners can also access information through electronic means so that any service business professional will be able to get information about the internal client and the external customer anytime, anywhere.

Strategic partners in different service businesses may also find it useful to participate in a service business council. They can meet and discuss their work, share their understanding of the needs of their internal clients and external customers, and discuss the business strategy to deliver value to the external customer segments. The internal service businesses can help each other understand the business pressures and the customer demands more effectively.

The service business councils will also be designed to do the following:

- Provide a non-evaluative and non-threatening environment in which the strategic partners can learn from each other's challenges and best practices.

- Encourage strategic partners to use what they learn from others in their own situation and consider the cross-impact of their work on others.

- Reinforce the importance of strategic partners continually staying in touch with each other as changes are being introduced.

- Develop a common language to enhance understanding across the internal service businesses.

The Strategic Value of Level 1 for the Internal Client:

The client receives value from the integration of shared learnings (Level 1) in a variety of ways. These include:

- *Enhanced support:* Support is enhanced because the internal service businesses communicate well with each other about client needs.

- *Time and effort saved in communicating with strategic partners:* Clients have to repeat less of their background information to the strategic partners since the partners know it already from their shared information and learning.

- *A model for their business areas:* Internal service businesses can become the client's model for sharing information in their business areas.

Level 2—Integration through Joint Planning and Project Management

At the second level of integration, internal service businesses engage in a joint planning process and project management though they do not do any formal joint projects.

Joint Planning

The service business council (described in Level 1) could be used for the joint planning to discuss priorities and timing for communication and implementation of projects. The council could also help with the budgeting process for the internal service businesses. The strategic partners could discuss their priorities, consider what should be funded and to what level, and make consolidated proposals to the executives on budget allocations. It is important for strategic partners to recognize that their work on the council is essential and not an add-on project that is of less importance than their day-to-day work.

Joint planning provides opportunities for strategic partners from several service businesses to discuss their contributions to their clients and how they can align their services more effectively. The result can be a consolidated plan that tells the clients what they will receive from all the service businesses. In addition, strategic partners can plan the implementation of initiatives within a service business and explain potential barriers. Other ideas for joint planning include:

- *Segment clients:* Segmenting internal clients according to those that are more strategic can be just as important as segmenting external customers. This segmentation may mean employees or teams that are considered more strategic than others may receive a higher level of service. For example, client segments that have unique business requirements to help them satisfy their external customers may have special service offered to them. Client segments should be common to all internal service businesses as much as possible. Specific service standards can be developed for each client segment and be applied across the internal service businesses.

- *Develop a central database to create an inventory of internal client service projects:* A central database to track internal client service initiatives, problems, complaints, and successes can be developed. It can be used as a shared learning resource for all the internal service businesses and their clients. The database should be capable of being updated continually and be accessible to the widest possible audience through web-based technology.

- *Operate the joint service business council as if it is an internal board of directors:* The people on the council represent all the service businesses rather than just their own. The service businesses take ownership of *all* their internal services because that is the way their clients view it. The internal services businesses will also be advisors to each other on how to implement change and enhance the quality of service delivery.

Implement a Joint Project Management Process

The internal service businesses enhance company-wide efficiency by operating with one major project management process. They create an overall project chart that lists and prioritizes the initiatives the strategic partners plan to present to the internal clients. If initiatives are not jointly project managed, each service business will see its change as a priority, even though the clients are unable to give the same attention to each of the priorities. Project management helps keep the clients from being overwhelmed by the number of changes and increases the chance that initiatives will be implemented effectively.

Project management can also include staging new initiatives so that the clients are not overwhelmed by the plethora of changes. This process allows the clients to experience a systematic roll-out of major initiatives. This will mean that priorities will have to be established among internal service businesses to insure that the clients are able to manage the expected changes. In addition, the overall project management would be able to track the project as well as identify the metrics for each of the initiatives as it proceeds.

The Strategic Value of Level 2 for the Internal Client

The strategic value the clients receive from the integration of planning and project management (Level 2) includes the benefits identified for Level 1 plus the following:

- Clients are not overloaded with too many changes occurring at the same time.

- Clients have access to information and the status of all the internal service changes so that they can learn independently about change initiatives.

- Clients receive services based on "segmented" needs. This means that they receive services only if they need them rather than receiving them regardless of their need.

Level 3—Integration through Common Processes and Approaches But Still Operating Separately

Level 3 adds another feature to the integration of the internal service businesses—common processes and approaches. Here are two compelling reasons to develop common processes and approaches:

- They simplify the introduction of changes to the internal clients.

- They create opportunities for additional collaboration among the internal service businesses in the future.

Level 3 also includes common metrics that everybody will use, even though the internal service businesses will still be separate functions. For example, service agreements with clients will have a common format even though they will be established separately. The service business professionals can then combine the service-level data to generate their overall metrics.

Common processes and approaches will be helpful in these ways:

- *A common service agreement format and process can be developed:* All the service agreements use a similar format and process so that internal clients will save time and effort developing agreements. Also, the basic background information for the service agreements are shared among the internal service businesses so that the clients will not have to respond to the same questions from the various strategic partners.

- *A common "implementing change and transition" process can be used:* Most internal service businesses are introducing change into the business. These businesses need to agree on a process for implementing change and transition (as identified in Chapter Nine) to be applied to the implementation of any new change. The process must identify the specific elements that project leaders in each internal service business must follow. This common process for implementing change and transition will help reduce the number of unknown factors that may occur when a new initiative is unveiled. It will alleviate some anxieties for those who are expected to accept the new change. Managers and employees will be more accepting of the *process* of change even while not being familiar with the *content* of the change.

- *Coordinated communications and marketing processes can be developed:* Marketing materials that clearly state the service businesses' coordinated services are important so that clients understand all the services that are available to them. When clients have appropriate internal marketing materials, they are more apt to suggest additional collaborative efforts by the internal service businesses that will be helpful to them.

- *Common training programs for employees that address client service excellence can be designed and delivered.* Each of the service businesses needs to train staff on how to operate within a flexible service business culture. It may be useful if the training includes members of each of the internal service businesses so that they can learn about each other's work and improve their capability to work with one another.

- *A common evaluation process to assess the effectiveness of the service businesses in meeting client needs can be developed.* The internal service businesses can develop a common evaluation process to determine the extent to which changes actually achieve objectives. This process would necessarily include evaluation forms (possibly an "on-line" form) to be used in common by all the internal service businesses. The businesses would need to manage the timing of the evaluations so that the client would not be overwhelmed with excessive feedback requests.

- *Other common templates can be developed.* Other templates that the internal service businesses may consider include their approach to business plans, budgeting, business process improvements, costing, billing for internal services, and post project evaluations.

The Strategic Value of Level 3 for the Internal Client:

Internal clients receive the following additional benefits from level 3:

- *Changes are less difficult to manage by internal clients* because of the common processes, even if the content of the changes differs among the internal service businesses.

- *Communications are coordinated,* therefore reducing confusion when multiple interchanges and interactions have to occur between the various internal service businesses.

- *Training is coordinated*, focusing employees on learning how to implement the internal service changes.

Level 4—Integration through Collaborative Work For Specific Initiatives

Level 4 adds a new dimension of collaborative work among the internal service businesses. The company that chooses to explore this path will need to identify areas in which cross-service business collaboration is necessary. They can then create teams of multi-service businesses to service those needs.

In part, the convergence of the internal service businesses is dependent on technology that is robust enough to allow for convergence. Also, the nature of the solutions clients require necessitates integrated services to meet their needs. The clients are not asking silo questions. HR, I/T, Finance, and others need to collaborate to develop total solutions that meet their clients' needs.

For example, consider a company that has a very high-growth business area that needs to recruit several hundred professionals within a short time. The internal service businesses agree to collaborate on this recruitment process to ensure that they find people who could be fully functional as quickly as possible. This initiative includes the ability to recruit the people; sign them up, be ready to accept them with space, furniture, telephones, personal computers, salary, and benefits; and orient them to their new responsibilities.

It requires extensive collaboration among the internal service businesses. Human Resources does the recruiting, orientation, benefits, and payroll. Information Technology insures the delivery of the telephones, computers, software, and education on how to use the system and the technology orientation. Finance arranges to pay the bills through accounts payable, defines metrics, and tracks the costs of this process. Facilities arranges to have the facilities available for the new hires. To move quickly and gracefully, the internal service businesses need to coordinate these efforts. They establish a cross- service business team for this initiative so that the client experiences them as one team and not as several internal service businesses.

Consider another example that involves a company that decides to consolidate its four office locations into one center. The service businesses are asked to collaborate to help the company with this initiative. They develop a joint coordinating team to manage the process and divide up the roles according to areas of expertise. HR takes responsibility for the organizational analysis to find duplication, to manage the selection of people, and to develop metrics. Information Technology is accountable for consolidating and changing specific technology platforms to be able to run the business out of one office. Finance measures the savings from this initiative and monitors the overall costs. Facilities participates in the organizational analysis to insure that the move can be made efficiently and quickly.

Internal service businesses are encouraged to merge their service delivery for specific initiatives such as the above examples. Other examples include:

- *Administrative services synergies:* Administration overlaps occur among the internal service businesses (Finance, I/T, HR, Communications, PR, Legal, etc.) that could be merged to service them all.

- *Common call centers for employee questions and issues:* Multiple call centers often confuse employees. In one company, the HR department alone had three call centers. As much as possible, the call centers should be combined to deliver one-stop shopping for information and advice to employees.

- *Integration of internal services for some core people processes:* Integrate some of the critical life-cycle events for employees at work in which enhanced collaboration among the service businesses can take place. These can include the following:

  - *Employee point of arrival.* When new employees arrive, they need to have services from Information Technology, HR, Finance, and Communications. These services can be implemented collaboratively among service businesses.

  - *Annual performance review process.* HR and I/T can partner to deliver performance reviews electronically.

- *Integration of internal services during major organizational changes:* Often multiple services businesses are involved in both internal organizational changes as well as major business changes, such as mergers and acquisitions.

Consider Selecting a Pilot Area for Integrating Internal Service Businesses at Level 4

Piloting the integration of internal service businesses in a specific area may be an excellent way to explore the potential for service businesses to collaborate. The following are some potential criteria for selecting a pilot area:

- The area is one that people experience as a problem or a "sore spot."
- Someone within the internal services businesses wants passionately to get the initiative done and will sponsor it personally.
- The leadership of the selected area agrees to the pilot for cross-service business collaboration.
- The collaborative work in the area is do-able.
- The results can be measured.

The Strategic Value of Level 4 for the Internal Client

Clients receive the following additional strategic value in Level 4:

- *Implementation is integrated:* At specific critical moments (especially employee life-cycle events), internal clients receive integrated implementation among the internal service businesses.

- *Clients can access integrated internal service administrative areas:* Some of these areas are integrated, such as shared services and call centers.

- *The costs for internal services can be combined for the client:* This enables the client to identify the overall cost for internal service work and allows for cross comparisons among the internal service areas.

Level 5—Structural Integration of Internal Service Businesses

The fifth level includes the previous four levels and adds structural integration of the different service businesses. Essentially, the service business silos are broken up and reconfigured into a more unified internal service business that helps internal clients meet the needs of external customers. Although the structure merges, areas of professional expertise in HR, I/T, etc., still remain but within an integrated organizational structure.

This model already exists in small firms that do not want to hire many internal resources. They expect people to be multi-skilled and to be able to deliver value in multiple internal service business areas. Larger companies have been more reluctant to move in this direction. The most significant area of resistance to Level 5 is often in financial services. Some companies will never structurally integrate Finance because of its critical importance to the senior executives and to company shareholders.

In larger companies, total integration of internal service businesses may be impractical. However, it is worth exploring. For example, internal clients may be interested in a "super" strategic partner that plans *all* their internal service needs and helps develop integrated solutions. If HR focuses on strategic alignment (Chapter 8) they will be well suited for this role as service businesses integrate.

The "super" strategic partner works with the client to identify needs and expectations and then develops a clear statement of the expectations of each internal service business. The partner also identifies the budget and resource requirements and what actions will be taken when and by whom to help the client deliver value to the external customer.

It is probable that a back room of professionals (with, for example, HR, IT or Finance expertise) would be identified to deliver parts of the integrated solutions. Their skills may be used individually for specific specialty areas or they may work as a team to deliver integrated solutions to the client. Each area of internal service expertise will be accountable for the entire integrated internal service business. Each will be as concerned about the other internal service businesses' issues as they are about their own.

The Strategic Value of Level 5 for the Internal Client

Internal clients receive the following additional benefits from Level 5:

- *One point of contact with a "super strategic partner"* for most of the internal service business needs.

- A *higher quality intervention* because of access to the expertise of all the internal service professional disciplines.

- *Reduced complexity of working with a variety of vendors* because of one point of contact with a strategic partner and also because of a simpler management of the internal client's service needs.

- *Potential lower overall costs of internal services* as new synergies are found among the former service businesses to deliver less expensive service of a higher quality.

The difficulty that some companies find with Level 5 is the assumption that one individual can function effectively as a super strategic partner for multiple internal service business areas. It is still unclear whether it is within the capability of one person to have meaningful conversations with clients about all their internal service needs. Further research on the viability of Level 5 would be appropriate.

The Extent to Which Internal Service Businesses Can Be Integrated

In the process of integrating internal service businesses, the internal clients' needs and values must be included in the design. It cannot be done in isolation. Figure 12.2 presents ten questions that will help a company assess whether its internal service businesses are ready to begin to integrate and to what extent it will be possible. These ten questions can be tested against the five levels of integration.

Figure 12.2

Ten Questions to Assess a Company's Readiness to Integrate Internal Service Businesses

1. What are the business needs that are driving the integration of internal service businesses?

2. What are the potential cultural synergies and barriers to integrating internal service businesses and what could be done to overcome the cultural barriers?

3. What are the risks and benefits of proceeding down this path?

4. What are the projected returns on investment of integrated service businesses?

5. To what extent do internal service businesses collaborate on projects with other service businesses? Is there an open dialogue among the leadership of the internal service businesses?

6. Are the communications between the internal service businesses and the internal clients effectively helping them support this change and manage their expectations?

7. What is unique to each of the internal service businesses that will probably not be integrated into an internal service business?

8. What "quick hits" can be implemented easily and quickly to start the integration of the internal service businesses?

9. What will be the optimum structure to operate the integrated internal service businesses?

10. Will the financial resources be available to support the integration as it proceeds based on a compelling need for change?

Epilogue: High Performance HR Professionals Lead the Transformation

High performance HR professionals have an opportunity to take a leadership role in helping their company focus on strategic initiatives that relate to people, organizations, and business processes. HR professionals must continually strive to enhance their credibility and acceptance as facilitators of the strategic business process outcomes. At the same time, HR professionals must balance their focus on strategic business process outcomes without losing sight of core people and organizational process fundamentals. These fundamentals will continue to be important to executives, who will still ask if HR is hiring people who can do the work and whether they are integrating and orienting them into the company and training and developing them.

The transformation of human resources will have implications for the company's managers, employees, and customers. Line managers will take responsibility for people as an integral part of the manager's function. HR will provide the guidance, training, coaching, and specific tools. Employees will take ownership for their work, behaviors, careers, contribution to the company, and their own personal well-being. They will be assisted by their managers and HR to fulfill their potential. The managers and employees will contribute to creating a business culture and organizational design that is focused, flexible, and fluid. Customers will be delighted with the attention and service they will receive from all parts of the company.

HR's transformation will also challenge the university educational system outside the company. Universities are accountable for preparing HR students for the new roles they will be expected to accept. The university programs will need to expand beyond day-to-day HR skill development to include a strategic focus for HR. As the role definition and the work of HR professionals continues to evolve, universities will need to expand what they teach and develop an enhanced university curriculum for the aspiring high performance HR professional.

Finally, HR must commit to a continual development of its professionalism as a field of discipline. HR professionals need to be able to describe clearly and deliver the value they can offer the company, the employees, the clients, and the customers. The professional field of HR provides many opportunities for personal growth for HR professionals as they focus on contributing strategic value to the company, their clients, and the customer.

Summary

- As more internal service businesses with a company adopt the structure, roles and relationships recommended for HR (in Chapter Eleven), they will find their services to the internal client overlapping.

- The following are the five levels of integrating internal service businesses:
  1. Shared learnings among internal service businesses.
  2. Joint planning and project management.
  3. Common processes and approaches but still operating separately
  4. Collaborative work for specific initiatives.
  5. Structural integration of internal service businesses.
- Strategic partners in different internal service businesses may find it useful to participate in a service business council. The strategic partners meet and discuss their work, share their understanding of the needs of their internal clients and external customers, and discuss the business strategy to deliver value to the external customer segments.
- At Level 1 of integration, the various internal service businesses form a relationship with one another that enables them to learn from each other. Internal service businesses can save time and effort through shared information and learning through the following:
  - Using a successful idea from another area.
  - Learning from another area's mistakes.
  - Using implementation pathways that have worked for other service businesses.
- At the Level 2 of integration, internal service businesses engage in a joint planning process and project management, though they do not do any formal joint projects. The internal service business council could be used for discussions about priorities and timing for communication and implementation of projects. Joint planning provides opportunities for strategic partners from several internal service businesses to discuss their contributions to their clients and how they can align their services more effectively. The result can be a consolidated plan that tells the internal clients what they will receive from all the internal service businesses.
- Level 3 adds another feature to the integration of the internal service businesses—common processes and approaches. Common processes and approaches will be helpful in these ways:
  - A common service-level agreement format and process can be developed.

- A common "implementing change and transition" process can be developed.

- Coordinated communications and marketing processes for all the internal service functions can be developed.

- Common training programs for employees that address internal client service excellence can be designed and delivered.

- A common evaluation process to assess the effectiveness of the service businesses in meeting client needs can be developed.

- Other common templates can be developed.

- Level 4 adds a new dimension of collaborative work among the internal service businesses. Internal service businesses are encouraged to merge their service delivery for specific functions and events such as mergers and acquisitions. Other examples include:

  - Administrative services synergies.

  - Common call centers for employee questions and issues.

  - Integration of internal services for employee life-cycle events (point of arrival, annual performance review process, point of departure).

  - Integration of internal services during major organizational changes.

  - Common areas of accountability.

- Level 5 involves structural integration of the different service businesses. In larger companies, total integration of internal service businesses may be difficult to achieve, however, it is worth exploring. Even where there is structual integration, it is likely there will be specialized centers of excellence for HR, I/T, Finance, and other professional disciplines.

- HR has the opportunity to take a leadership role through exploring how to integrate internal service businesses; however, it should start by first transforming its own organization, with the focus on the strategic value that HR provides to the company and to the customer.

An Interview with David S. Weiss

STRATEGIC HUMAN
RESOURCES MANAGEMENT:
CHALLENGES AND OPPORTUNITIES[1]

What external pressures are having the greatest impact on human resources management?

Organizations are facing quite a few pressures at the present time. I will refer to three key challenges.

1. *Alternative competitive forces.* New competitive forces are creating new pressures for companies to respond to service and product delivery in very different ways. These competitive forces place tremendous demands on companies to embrace technology and alternative relationships, sometimes with competitors.

2. *Customer expectations and values.* Customers have become very demanding; they expect responsiveness, quality, and bundling of services, so that the services they receive are total solutions rather than just parts of the solution. This is creating significant challenges for companies that see themselves as the delivery agents of only one service.

3. *Access to capital.* Companies often have great difficulty responding effectively to these pressures because of the lack of available capital. As a result, we are seeing very significant mergers and acquisitions. These pressures are driven by the need for both new competencies and additional capital to meet the external challenges.

---

[1] This interview was originally published by IRC Press of Queen's University in 1999. The interview was conducted by Mary Lou Coates. It is reprinted here with permission.

How are these pressures driving both business strategy as well as human resource (HR) strategy?

These external pressures are creating a tremendous challenge for HR professionals to enhance their business acumen, their understanding of the business issues and the needs of the external customer. For some HR professionals, their understanding of this goes beyond what they would typically be expected to know and do. HR is also being challenged to develop strategies to create an organizational culture that allows people to be more flexible during dramatic changes. As the changes are introduced, HR professionals have developed excellence in implementing change and ensuring that transitions are effective. Finally, HR strategy is being driven by the need to create an overall business alignment of HR practices with the many initiatives in the company.

Can you briefly describe what the current role of HR should be in today's organization?

The HR role should focus on three major areas.

1. *People processes.* People processes refer to the employment life cycle that employees engage in from when they are brought into the company, developed, paid and receive ongoing assistance and support, to when they eventually leave. HR's role is to ensure that there is excellence throughout this cycle. Many of the people processes, especially the more administrative ones, are now being done by external suppliers. However, HR is expected to ensure excellence will continue even if HR is playing a vendor management role.

2. *Organizational processes.* The second area covers value-added organizational processes. For example, HR is expected to contribute to the organization by creating a learning process where people can share their experiences of what works and what does not work. HR is also expected to enable employees and managers to be more resilient through the application of technology and self-management processes. Finally, there is a strong expectation for HR, through coaching and consulting, to enable organizational capability and effectiveness. These roles may not be strategic, but they are value-added.

3. *Business transformation.* In this area HR works at the strategic level. They help the company deal with issues and gain its competitive position within the marketplace. There are a number of strategic alternatives that HR may focus on, such as, organizational culture, change management, alignment between business and HR, the

return on investment in human capital, etc. Typically, most Human Resources organizations have the bandwidth to tackle only one or two of the strategic issues that are most pertinent to the organization. The challenge for today's HR then will be to determine which of the organization's strategic initiatives it will address.

What does strategic HR mean?

It is important to have a common understanding of the word 'strategic.' Something is strategic if it allows the organization to gain competitive or relative advantage against the competition. In private sector companies, relative advantage may be evident because they are in a competitive mode. But even non-profit and government agencies need a competitive mindset. They deliver a service or a product that is compared to standards and benchmarks. If they are going to capture the hearts and minds of those people who are receiving the service or product they also must identify how they can develop the strategic capabilities to give them that relative advantage over the 'competition.' Strategic HR managers, then, are able to deploy the people and organizational processes that enable competitive advantage to occur. They are very focused on what provides that strategic advantage, and at the same time, they are excellent at creating the systems to deliver that advantage.

Recently, I introduced the concept of strategy as competitive advantage to an HR leadership team. When I asked, 'Who is your competition?', they explained that the competition is the people external to the company who could replace them.

I then asked the line executives the same question: 'Who is the competition for HR?' They gave an entirely different answer. They said that the competition for HR in their company is the value created by HR professionals in their competitors' companies.

Apparently, the executives are not concerned about whether the HR professional is an employee in the company or external. Rather, they want to deploy HR services that surpass the value their business competitors receive. In their terms, the external HR professionals are not the competitors of their internal HR professionals, rather they are their partners. The internal HR professionals and the chosen external professionals work together to deliver strategic value and provide the company with relative advantage against the competition.

What is HR's role in achieving alignment between business strategy and HR strategy and ensuring that the HR activities themselves are mutually reinforcing and integrated?

There are two parts to your question. The first part is the relationship between business strategy and HR strategy, and the second part is HR strategy within itself. There are two other alignment issues for HR, as well. HR should also be considering its relationship and alignment with other internal service providers and how that ultimately contributes value. Finally, HR must consider how it can contribute value in areas that are not HR-related but are business-to-business alignment issues within the organization or company.

1. *Alignment between business and HR.* HR needs to partner with business in order to identify what the customer needs and to design people and organizational solutions that help the business satisfy those customer needs.

2. *Internal HR activities.* There is a strong demand that HR develop an overall approach that is internally coherent when they deploy their HR strategies. When they do an organizational intervention, it should align with their people processes. Each process should be mutually reinforcing to allow them to achieve the overall objective of the strategy.

3. *Alignment of HR and other internal service providers.* Many line managers are looking for solutions that are more than HR solutions. They are looking for the internal services to bundle their capabilities to give them a complete solution. The alignment of HR with information technology, finance, communications, real estate, and other functional areas is becoming more important. For example, if a company decides to move an office from one place to another, there will be HR issues, technology issues, financial issues, communication issues, and real estate issues. Alignment will be needed to give a complete solution to the internal client. They will then bundle solutions to deliver value to customers.

4. *Business-to-business alignment within the company.* Since HR is one of the areas that has people deployed throughout the entire company, they have knowledge across the entire organization, and can contribute value to the overall alignment of all the strategic initiatives. For example, in a private sector company, the marketing, manufacturing, and development areas may all have individual initiatives. There is an assumption that the executives are accountable for ensuring that the individual initiatives align. That does not always occur, because the executives are often driven by their objectives. HR has

people deployed within each area. In a number of companies, HR has the mandate to ensure the alignment of all of the initiatives to achieve the overall company direction. The same could be said for a non-profit or a public sector organization. They would need similar kinds of alignment among the multiple services that they offer.

When we talk about HR becoming a strategic business partner, what does that mean?

There are two areas to consider. First, human resources professionals who work as strategic business partners, work with, not for, their clients within the company to deliver value to the customer. (When I refer to 'customer,' I mean the external customer, not the internal customer. I use the term 'client' to refer to the internal customer.) This means that human resources professionals, as strategic business partners, will have the capability to redirect solutions or initiatives that are not in the best interests of the customer. HR professionals are the experts on the people and organizational solutions, while the line manager has the best data on the nature of the problem. Together they have the capability to discover the right answer that delivers the best service and that will enhance customer value.

Second, on most occasions, HR gets involved with a client at the point when the problem is identified. As a strategic business partner, HR is part of the development of the strategy and is able to anticipate problems before the need arises. They help develop the strategy rather than simply respond to needs. They also are able to contribute to the business- and customer-related issues by providing the special expertise on people and organizational processes.

In most organizations, business strategy drives HR strategy. Are there cases where an HR strategy can become a business strategy?

Yes. For example, one HR leader was successful in guiding the company to include a core strategy to create a strong positive culture. The strategic initiative focused on the development of core values and the associated behavior for employees. HR also designed the rewards and recognition to enable the strategic culture initiative to occur.

How can HR contribute to bringing about needed changes in organizations?

HR needs to have an active role in bringing about change in the organization. Let's consider three ways they can do this. First, HR must have the ability to understand what is driving the business and its customers, so that they grasp the company challenges in a meaningful way. With that understanding, HR can create organizational change in alignment with the customer drivers and the business challenges.

Second, HR professionals need to have a broad knowledge base to provide them with the information to be idea merchants. They need to continuously develop their unique database of solutions and willingly share it. When they enter into conversations with clients, they can then play an expert and facilitative role in bringing about change in the organization.

Third, HR professionals need to find ways to have their 'other' required work done. If HR is inundated with administrative work or with employee relations problems on a regular basis, they will not have the time to invest in introducing changes to the organization. Human Resources professionals need to be outstanding in the process of disciplined abandonment; they will have to redeploy certain roles and determine which things do not need to be done anymore. A rigorous exercise of disciplined abandonment is essential to create the time to focus on bringing about organizational changes.

Traditionally HR was viewed as the conscience of the organization and the employee advocate. Now HR is expected to be a strategic business partner to the CEO and partner to line management. Are these conflicting or competing roles?

Let's consider the conscience of the organization and employee advocate role. When HR individually takes on that role, it segregates itself from the other leaders, creating some limitations on the willingness of the others to involve them in strategic issues. The preferred approach is that line managers, who work directly with the employees, should have the role of employee advocate. Human Resources professionals would operate as the enablers, ensuring that line managers work effectively with their employees to address their needs, enhance their potential, and deliver value to the company and the customer.

What kinds of HR responsibilities or activities are being outsourced and/or delegated to line management?

Human Resources professionals need to determine what activities are strategic, (i.e., activities that provide competitive advantage), and what activities are not strategic but need to be done. They should consider whether to outsource or delegate the non-strategic activities so that they are not burdened with delivery. They are often still held accountable for vendor management for those activities and will need to develop excellence in that area. Many of the non-strategic activities are often done better by specialized external service providers in support of HR professionals.

Some examples of work that HR can outsource include:

- payroll, benefits, and pension responsibilities, with the third party managing the entire infrastructure;
- the employee call/response centre, which is a centralized method of direct access to HR for information and advice;
- technology deployment and delivery, which can be either outsourced or delegated through an alliance with the IT professionals within the company.

HR should also be delegating many of the day-to-day employee relations issues to line managers. The old model where line managers are responsible for the work and HR is responsible for the workforce is very problematic; it forces HR professionals to spend almost all their time working on employee relations. Instead, the managers within the company function as the local 'HR' professionals, and the Human Resources professionals operate as the centre of excellence to deliver value to the line managers. In many cases, HR professionals need to be the last, not the first, point of contact on employee relations issues.

Being an enabler to line management?

HR professionals function as both partners to and enablers of line management. For example, if there are 1,000 people in the company and 180 are managers, the Human Resources professionals partner with and enable the 180 managers to help them manage the other 820 people. This is how HR has increased its ratio from what used to be a low number to in some cases 1:200. The HR professionals are not really dealing with 200 people. It's not a correct assumption. What they are doing is working with the 30 or 40 managers that are servicing those 200 people. That becomes a manageable number. The ratios are also higher because there are many people who are doing HR services from outside the company. In reality there are many more people who are doing HR services than those low numbers would suggest because line managers are doing some of it and external vendors are doing some of it.

What are some of the paths or directions human resource management might follow in terms of HR's roles and priorities?

HR management practices often reflect what the company executives envision for HR. The HR priorities will likely result from not only customer demands but also the extent of the openness of the executives to allow initiatives to occur. For example:

- Some companies are open to alternative HR strategies and are *early adopters* of new initiatives. In these companies, you will find very experimental HR management roles and priorities. You will often see culture as part of their strategy. You will see efforts to create systems of change management and determine alternative ways of working. The direction will often be reflected in the competencies of the person hired as, for example, VP of HR.

- Other companies are *late adopters* of innovative practices with people and organizations. When they are late adopters they often hire people who are more responsive and less driven to introduce new changes.

- Some companies see Human Resources as an *administrative function* and have little time for HR to enter into business issues.

In other words, although the human resources roles and priorities should be determined by competitive challenges and customers, they will be directly affected by what the leadership of the company wants to see within Human Resources. They will likely select people within HR accordingly.

There will also be some financial roles that HR will be expected to deliver. For example, HR will be expected to ensure that the company is making the best investment possible in people and organizational processes, i.e., the human capital investment made to allow the business to do what it needs to do. The challenge for Human Resources is to introduce the financial component, which determines the value received from the activities and interventions that are being promoted by the company and within Human Resources. It's happening already in a number of different industries and sectors and it will continue to increase. The Human Resources capability to use economic models to determine the economic value of their interventions is something that HR professionals will be asked to do. It may take HR a little outside of their comfort zone. I envision that in the next five years or so, we will see labour economists or accountants with the specialized ability to analyze and present the return on the investment in human capital within the HR function.

There are other challenges that I have mentioned previously that Human Resources will likely face, such as culture, alignment, and change management.

Would the HR professional who has been able to move beyond the traditional HR role and become more knowledgeable about the business be better able to face this challenge of determining the value of the return on investment on human capital?

Clearly. One question Human Resources professionals have been asking is, 'How can we get to the executive table?' The assumption that being bright and having HR professional expertise is enough to get to the executive table is incorrect. They will not get there if they do only people processes and organizational value-added. The HR professional will get to the executive table if they can deal with the strategic risks of the company. They must get involved in the business transformation that contributes value to the company and value to the customer; then they can be part of the conversations with executives about strategic questions.

If Human Resources has the capability to talk about the return on investment in human capital, then when there is a transformation within the company, their ideas and input will be sought and they can make recommendations with confidence. The need to go beyond the traditional HR role becomes even more obvious when a company engages in an acquisition. HR often wants to be part of the due diligence team to assess whether the company should be purchased. They often argue that culture and leadership are the reasons why they should be brought in. However, that is often not a sufficient reason to bring HR in early. It will bring them in after the acquisition. However, if they have the knowledge of what the best investment in human capital is and can assess whether their company or the acquired company will have the capability to deploy people with the best investment and to give the best return, then Human Resources becomes an essential part of the due diligence process and they become strategic. That contribution, I believe, will become more and more common. It has started to happen in some companies that have HR online information and data programs generating return on investment analyses of human capital and people and organizational processes.

What implications does the new strategic HR have for unions, industrial relations issues, and collective bargaining?

The realization by companies that there is a relationship between employee satisfaction, customer satisfaction, and profitability has become more and more evident. In many cases, adversarial industrial relations hurt employee commitment. Employee satisfaction, then, will suffer if there is a difficult environment within the company, regardless of whether there's a union or not.

This is evident with employees who have direct contact with customers. If they are not happy, there will be an immediate effect on how they interact with their customers. For those people who work in manufacturing facilities and are removed from customers, particularly in companies that have a great many quality control mechanisms and standards, it may not be as obvious that employee satisfaction will generate a certain level of customer satisfaction. It seems, however, that it does.

The relationship between employee satisfaction and profitability may lead companies to consider alternative approaches to labour-management relations that contribute to both business imperatives and positive employee relations. It leads companies to consider a version of cooperative approaches that I discussed in my first book in 1996, *Beyond the Walls of Conflict.*

Many have realized that a competitive approach with the union is somewhat dysfunctional. Companies need to compete with the competition, not with their own workforce. However, for some companies and some unions, being totally cooperative is unrealistic. So, I have coined the term, 'contextual negotiations'—which is a balance between the two.

Contextual negotiations is a pragmatic approach that is driven by practicality rather than a belief in cooperation. They apply mutual gains when it is in the interest of the parties and where there are business imperatives driving the decisions. Mutual gains is recognized as part of the repertoire of choices of how to negotiate rather than the only way to proceed. Unions and management are more accepting of contextual negotiation since it is pragmatic rather than based on a belief system.

You have referred to 'organizational capability.' What does it mean to build organizational capability and what role does HR play?

The term 'organizational capability' became popular through the work of David Ulrich in his 1990 book, *Organizational Capability.* It, of course, has evolved to have many different definitions. A company with organizational capability has an outstanding state of readiness to implement changes reliably, quickly, and with quality, and is, therefore, very responsive to needs. When a company that has organizational capability merges with another company, they are able to see the benefit almost immediately of that merger. While that may be an unlikely scenario, it is a goal towards which organizations strive. HR then has an important role in creating organizational capability. They must align different parts of the organization to achieve an outstanding state of readiness. They build a flexible culture that can be responsive to the challenges as they occur. They must also create the ability to implement change and to help people transition into these changes with the speed and agility that allows the organization to be successful.

You talked earlier of HR's challenge in determining which strategic initiatives to pursue? Would having this organizational capability enhance the ability to decide which strategy should have priority?

Organizational capability will help HR determine and implement strategic initiatives. However, for many people, organizational capability is difficult to grasp. It's not tangible. You don't see organizational capability. Rather, it is a 'readiness to act,' the energy that allows certain things to occur.

When Human Resources professionals say 'our job is to create organizational capability,' many people do not understand what they mean. But, if they talk about it in terms of the deliverable—for example, 'we create a flexible culture,' or 'we create an aligned organization and business,' or 'we create the ability to implement change and help people through transition' or 'we create an organization that can determine quickly the return on investment in human capital'—people will be able to grasp the outcome effectively. The concept of organizational capability is outstanding. However, because many leaders struggle with that level of abstraction, the concept needs to be communicated in concrete terms that focus on the actual deliverable.

What are organizations using to measure or reflect HR's contribution to business performance?

I mentioned earlier the notion of the return on investment in human capital (RIHC) as being an important emerging measure that Human Resources is starting to consider. RIHC metrics are really important for Human Resources to determine so that they have a measure of human capital. They can help guide leaders on how to invest appropriately in specific areas versus other areas. It will also help HR determine the return on investments of its own initiatives.

There are two parts to the RIHC measure. These are:

1. *The economic analysis of the return on investment of human capital initiatives.*

2. *The alignment of specific performance objectives with the balanced score-card of the company.* A 'balanced scorecard' has been explained in the well-known book called The *Balanced Scorecard* (Kaplan and Norton 1996). It identifies the three or four key stakeholders to whom it wants to deliver value, such as the customer, the shareholder, the employee, and the community. They determine the metrics of overall company objectives for each stakeholder. Every employees' objectives are linked to those overall macro objectives of the company. HR professionals then anchor rewards, recognition, and bonuses to the performance on the balanced scorecard.

What value does benchmarking HR practices serve?

Benchmarking is a very helpful process for Human Resources. Benchmarking is a process by which you break apart a service into a series of sub-processes and you search for external or internal examples of those processes being done in a 'best practices' way. Then you reconfigure the service to follow the best of each of the processes you have benchmarked. You ultimately do the service better by compiling all of the best practices from the individual sub-processes that you studied.

HR can continuously improve by looking externally and internally at what is being done in an excellent way. Externally, HR can identify best practices that can result in continuous improvement in what HR delivers. Internally, HR can identify best practices on a regular basis. They can become an information source that allows the company to leverage its own internal best practices and benchmarks to enhance performance in other areas. For example, one company developed outstanding capabilities in servicing the external customer. They recognized the need to deliver value in this area and developed excellent technology to measure and assess the extent to which the customer is happy with the service. Human Resources professionals brought those capabilities into the company, using the same methods to measure their effectiveness and the satisfaction of their internal clients.

Unfortunately, this is not often done. If Human Resources did internal benchmarking, they could leverage success. However, it is unfortunate that often the only time companies find out that they are a benchmark is when another company comes to them and says 'I'd like to benchmark your process.' HR should identify their internal benchmark capabilities and leverage that for their own company's benefit, not just for someone else who wants to benchmark them.

Turning to the HR professional, what are organizations looking for today?

I would look for three things. These are:

1. *A higher level of professional expertise.* There is recognition that HR does have a unique database. It has its own science in which there are areas of specialty. When people are asking a Human Resources professional for their input, they will have an expert opinion to offer, because they have that knowledge base and have developed that database.

2. *Outstanding influence and consulting skills.* They need to have the ability to influence, to communicate effectively, and to work through the organization for alignment and change.

3. *A much broader understanding of customer needs and business acumen.* They will have the expertise to engage in conversations that demonstrate that they appreciate both the challenges within the business and the demands of customers. The Human Resources professional will be seen as a business professional with an HR expertise. They will have the capability to influence people about the changes that are required to meet people and organizational needs.

What skills or knowledge or competencies are necessary for successful HR leadership?

First, *HR professionals will need the ability to build alliances.* There will need to be alliances with line managers to become strategic business partners. In addition, there's a need for alliances with other professionals within the company who are doing human resources-like activities but are not within the Human Resources function. Many companies have line people who may be responsible for change management or for continuous improvement or other activities that could very well have been within the HR function. Those alliances, and the ongoing conversations that result, make sure that people are proceeding in the same direction. There's also a need to build alliances with the other internal service areas. Human Resources would then have the capability to bundle their solutions and deliver a complete answer to their client, an answer that would include, for example, an information technology component, a communications strategy, etc. As a result the client will not have to ask three or four different sources to put a solution together.

Second, *HR leadership needs to understand the business drivers and customer needs.* HR will need to partner with marketing to hear the 'voice of the customer' clearly. This understanding will enable them to develop and design the appropriate people and organizational processes to meet customer needs. They also have to have a systemic view of HR services. They need to be outstanding at recommending appropriate solutions and architecture that will allow the business to do what it needs to do to be successful.

Third, *HR leaders need to have excellent skills in mobilizing people into action.* Their good ideas need to be put into effect. They must have a delivery mindset, where things get done in a timely, high quality manner.

Let's take an individual who has been working in the HR field for several years. How can he or she retool for the future?

First, many human resources professionals have recognized that lifelong learning is something they want to promote for all the workforce, as well as themselves. They need to be educating themselves and learning constantly. Whenever there's an opportunity, they should expand their knowledge base and their understanding of what they are trying to contribute, both as HR professionals and as business partners. They need to be looking at the strategic HR issues, at best practices, and at implementing them within their companies. Some have used external coaches, such as consultants, as a one on one learning experience to help them think through business issues. That relationship, whether it's visible or invisible to others, helps the HR professional to generate the best solutions and gives them the ability to do it independently and with confidence the next time. Of course, the Human Resources professional should be reading books and attending courses and conferences to be exposed to new ideas and to achieve lifelong learning.

Second, the focus on the customer will challenge HR professionals to hear the voice of the customer directly. In addition to partnering with marketing, HR professionals may want to consider having direct contact with customers from time to time. It would be intriguing for the HR professionals to have conversations with the HR professionals in the customer organization. Also, the HR professionals should be in contact with the Human Resources leaders within the supplier organizations.

Human Resources professionals need to expand their horizons. They need to continually develop and retool through different kinds of conversations that will enable the company to succeed and enhance the employability of the HR professionals themselves.

What changes are needed in industrial relations (IR) and human resources management programs, and business schools if they're going to prepare students adequately for a career in HR or IR?

IR and HR programs need to be studied closely to determine whether the challenges that I have described, if they believe they are valid challenges, are truly reflected in their curriculums. For example, are alternatives offered in the IR curriculum that reflect the variety of choices a professional entering into a business context or organizational context may face? Will that professional be able to make wise choices about whether to use a cooperative or a more traditional approach? In Human Resources, the traditional programs likely focus on people processes, which are very important, but the curriculums need to be reviewed to see if the new emphasis on how Human Resources can contribute to organizational value-added processes and business transformation processes are covered in the course offerings.

The IR and HR programs need to reflect the business context and customer value and how HR and IR professionals actually contribute value to those issues. They need to help students put their role into context and understand how they are positioned within the company, and how they can deliver value.

I believe that there will also be a demand for new kinds of programs and perhaps new kinds of degrees as a result of the redefinition of HR and IR. The normal MBA program, where the students take some organizational courses or a specialty program, may not suffice in capturing the full expertise that will be required of HR and IR. It also may not suffice if HR really wants to be a discipline unto itself. A focused degree, such as a Master of Human Resources (MHR), may be required. An MHR might actually capture some of the more in-depth expertise that will be required of HR professionals as they enter the workforce now and in the future.

There is also going to be a need for continuing education for people on the job. They will need courses or technology-distributed learning to develop their expertise in the field. Whether colleges and universities will be the ones that respond to this need is unclear. If not, I suspect there will be other private sector organizations that will respond to the need and will deliver. But, without question, the colleges and universities have the highest credibility to deliver HR continuing education.

Lifelong learning requires immediate access to learning. Never-the-less, people will still attend seminars because they not only transmit certain knowledge, but they also provide informal networking opportunities that should be encouraged. In this way HR professionals can expand their thought processes and have a better understanding of the business challenges that exist within many companies.

What areas of HR will take on greater importance as we approach the new millennium and beyond?

We have already discussed several areas of great importance to HR. These include creating a flexible culture, organizational capability and alignment, and implementing change. Other areas for HR include the following:

1. *Technology drivers that create opportunities for Human Resources.* The Year 2000 technology problem (Y2K) became a blessing in disguise for Human Resources. Many HR professionals used the Y2K problem as an opportunity for a business case to buy the new technology that is Year 2000 compliant. The new technology gave them the capability to foster employee self-reliance and allow managers to become HR leaders

through the technology support. Human Resources professionals will need to know how to leverage and get maximum value from the technology in order to deliver on their promise to the company.

2. *The return on investment in human capital which will demonstrate the financial value of human capital investments.* I suggest that this will be an important driver in the future.

3. *Retaining the key resource employees to support a strong positive culture.* This will continue to be an issue of great importance to HR as it proceeds forward.

4. *The capability to manage vendors.* As they deploy work to external services, or, in some cases, to internal services, they will need to know how to manage those services and guarantee quality. HR will need to develop vendor management skills, through technology and through relationships with the supplier organizations.

You have a new book entitled High Performance HR: Leveraging Human Resources for Competitive Advantage *(Weiss 1999). Can you briefly describe what it is about and what your intentions were when you decided to write the book?*

The Human Resources field is in the process of dramatic change. Three or four years ago, people were talking about the demise of HR and asked whether it was really necessary. What has emerged from research and debate is a redefinition of HR. HR is now being positioned to contribute to business transformation in new ways based on the competencies of HR professionals.

Almost all the books in the HR area are what is called 'contributor' books. These are books that have topic areas, and a variety of authors write the chapters. The editor then brings the pieces together into one book. The individual authors give their own perspectives and, in many cases, are operating from their own independent models. There have been very few HR books where there has been one voice and an integrated view of what HR should do.

I was concerned about the ability of Human Resources professionals to really understand how they can leverage their organizations for competitive advantage. With that concern in mind, I believed it was important to have a book written with one voice, with it's own internal coherency, that would allow people to understand what it means to become excellent in people processes, in organizational value-added processes, and in business transformation processes. In addition, HR needed to know what to abandon and what is crucial to the strategic direction of the company.

I also became aware of the need for Human Resources professionals to shift their attention from thinking about internal customers to focusing on delivering value to the external customer as part of their primary mandate. That thought needed to be communicated very clearly. The implications for the way HR should be configured, should be governed, and should deliver services needed to be understood.

As a result, I wrote the book as a guide to Human Resources professionals so that they will understand conceptually and practically what they need to do. There are many practical insights into how HR professionals can become strategic business partners and also deliver the basic services expected of them. The book will show HR professionals how to get to the table and become strategic business partners.

In addition to the guidance and framework that it provides Human Resources professionals, the book will help executives and senior leaders understand what HR is about in their own language. Many executives do not understand the business contribution that gives strategic value to HR. It's my hope that a book such as *High Performance HR* will help executives appreciate the value that Human Resources can offer. The book may also stimulate change within organizations and define the strategic expectations of Human Resources leadership.

Finally, there is an important need to look at the curriculum of Human Resources within universities and other educational institutions. *High Performance HR* will provide university professors with a text for curriculum and courses that will train future Human Resources professionals. The book will hopefully make a meaningful contribution to the field of HR and to the future of HR professionals.

Is there anything else you want to add or comment on?

It is a very exciting time for Human Resources professionals. Just a few years ago it was a very frightening time; it seemed that there was not a clear mandate of what Human Resources professionals could contribute. The opportunities are there now for Human Resources professionals to add strategic value to the company. And they can do it. If they choose to discover the path that really adds value for competitive advantage and customer service, Human Resources can be major catalysts for the success of the company. HR professionals can bring their expertise and knowledge to help companies and employees fulfill their potential and succeed. The future of Human Resources is waiting to be created; HR professionals can seize the opportunity.

References

Kaplan, Robert S. and David P. Norton. *The Balanced Scorecard: Translating Strategy Into Action.* Boston: Harvard Business School Press, 1996.

Ulrich, David and Dale Lake. *Organizational Capability: Competing From the Inside/out.* New York: Wiley, 1990.

Weiss, David S. *Beyond the Walls of Conflict: Mutual Gains Negotiating for Unions and Management.* Chicago: Irwin Professional Publishing, 1996.

Weiss, David S. *High Performance HR: Leveraging HR for Competitive Advantage.* New York: John Wiley & Sons, 1999.

A COMPREHENSIVE READING LIST FOR HR PROFESSIONALS

Adizes, Ichik. *Corporate Life Cycles: How and Why Corporations Grow and Die and What To Do About It.* Prentice-Hall, 1988.

Alex, Lynne. *Mergers and Acquisitions: A Survival Guide.* Thomson Professional Publishing Co., 1997.

Ashkanas, Ron; Ulrich, Dave; Jick, Todd; Kerra, Steve. *The Boundaryless Organization: Breaking the Chains of Organizational Structure.* Jossey-Bass Inc., 1995.

Bartlett, Christopher A.; Ghoshal, Sumantra. *Managing Across Borders: The Transnational Solution.* Harvard Business School Press, 1989.

Bens, Ingrid. *Facilitation With Ease!* Participative Dynamics, 1997.

Berger, Lance A.; Sikora, Martin J. *The Change Management Handbook: a Roadmap to Corporate Transformation.* Irwin Professional Publishing, 1994.

Block, Peter. *Flawless Consulting: A Guide to Getting your Expertise Used.* Pfeiffer & Co., 1981.

Block, Peter. *Stewardship: Choosing Service Over Self-Interest.* Barrett-Koehler Publishers Inc., 1993.

Block, Peter. *The Empowered Manager: Positive Political Skills at Work.* Jossey-Bass Inc. Publishers, 1987.

Bosemen, Glenn and Phatak, Arvind. *Cases in Strategic Management.* John Wiley & Sons, 1998.

Bridges, William. *Managing Transitions—Making the Most of Change,* Addison-Wesley Publishing Company, 1996.

Buckingham, Marcus and Coffman, Curt. *First Break All The Rules: What the World's Greatest Managers Do Differently.* Simon & Schuster, 1999.

Burack, Elmer. *Creative Human Resource Planning and Application.* Prentiss-Hall, 1988.

Butteris, Margaret. *Reinventing HR: Changing Roles to Create High Performance Organizations.* John Wiley & Sons, 1998.

Cascio, Wayne F. *Costing Human Resources: The Financial Impact of Behaviour in Organizations*. PWS-Kent Publishing Co., 1991.

Conger, Jay A. and Benjamin, Beth. *Building Leaders: How Successful Companies Develop The Next Generation*. Jossey-Bass Inc. 1999.

Davis, Stan; Davidson, Bill. *20:20 Vision: Transform Your Business Today to Succeed in Tomorrow's Economy*. Simon & Schuster, 1991.

De Bono, Edward. *Lateral Thinking*. Penguin Books, 1970.

Dotlich, David L. and Noel, James L. *Action Learning: How The World's Top Companies Are Re-Creating Their Leaders And Themselves*. Jossey-Bass Publishers, 1998.

Edvinsson, Leif and Malone, Michael S. *Intellectual Capital: Realizing Your Company's True Value By Finding Its Hidden Brainpower*. HarperCollins Publishers, Inc., 1997.

Fisher, Roger and Uri, William. *Getting to Yes: Negotiating Agreement without Giving In*. Penguin Books, 1981.

Fitz-enz, Jac. *The ROI of Human Capital: Measuring the Economic Value of Employee Performance*. American Management Association, 2000.

Fombrun, Charles; Tichy, Noel M.; Devana, Mary Anne. *Strategic Human Resource Management*. John Wiley & Sons Inc., 1984.

Gale, Bradley T. *Managing Customer Value: Creating Quality and Service That Customers Can See*. The Free Press, 1994.

Gubman, Edward L. *The Talent Solution: Aligning Strategy And People To Achieve Extraordinary Results*. McGraw-Hill Companies, 1998.

Hamel, Gary and Prahalad, C.K. *Competing for the Future*. Harvard Business School Press, 1994.

Hammer, Michael and Champy, James. *Reengeering the Corporation: A Manifesto for Business Revolution*. Harper Collins, 1993.

Hammer, Michael and Stanton, Steven A. *The Reengeering Revolution: A Handbook*. Harper Business, 1995.

Hargrove, Robert, *Masterful Coaching*, Jossey-Bass/Pfeiffer, 1995.

Hays, Richard D. *Internal Service Excellence: A Manager's Guide to Building World-Class Internal Service Unit Performance*. Summit Executive Press, 1996.

Jaques, Elliott. *Requisite Organization: The CEO's Guide to Structure and Leadership*. Cason, Hall & Co. Publishers, 1989.

Kaplan, Robert S. and Morton, David P. *The Balanced Scorecard*. Harvard Business Press, 1996.

Katzenbach, Jon A. *Teams At The Top: Unleashing The Potential of Both Teams And Individual Leaders.* Harvard Business School Press, 1998.

Kepner, Charles H.; Tregoe, Benjamin B. *The New Rational Manager.* Kepner-Tregoe Inc., 1981.

Kouzes, James M. and Posner, Barry Z. *The Leadership Challenge: How to Keep Getting Extraordinary Things Done in Organizations.* Jossey-Bass Publishers, 1995.

Kriegel, Robert J. and Louis Patler, *If It Ain't Broke...BREAK IT!,* Warner Books Inc., 1992.

Kübler-Ross, Elisabeth. *On Death and Dying.* MacMillan Publishing Co., Inc., 1969.

Lajoux, Alexandra Reed. *The Art Of M&A Integration: A Guide To Merging Resources, Processes & Responsibilities.* McGraw-Hill, 1998.

Lipman-Blumen, Jean and Leavitt, Harold J. *Hot Groups: Seeding Them, Feeding Them, And Using Them To Ignite Your Organization.* Oxford University Press, 1999.

McNeil, Art. *The "I" of the Hurricane: Creating Corporate Energy.* Stoddard Publishing Co., Ltd., 1987.

Mirvis, Philip H. and Marks, Mitchell Lee. *Managing The Merger: Making It Work.* Prentice Hall, 1992.

Naybey, Christopher; Salaman, Graeme. *Strategic Human Resource Management.* Blackwell Business, 1995.

Odenwald, Sylvia B.; Methany, William G. *Global Impact: Award Winning Performance Programs from Around the World.* Irwin Professional Publishing, 1996.

Ohmae, Kinichi. *The Borderless World: Management Lessons in the New Logic of the Global Marketplace.* Harper Business, 1990.

Ostroff, Frank. *The Horizontal Organization: What The Organization Of The Future Actually Looks Like And How It Delivers Value To Customers.* Oxford University Press, 1999.

Pasternack, Bruce A. and Viscio, Albert J. *The Centerless Corporation: A New Model For Transforming Your Organization for Growth And Prosperity.* Fireside, 1998.

Peppers, Don and Rogers, Martha. *The One-to-One Future: Building Relationships One Customer at a Time.* Doubleday, 1993.

Pfeffer, Jeffrey. *Competitive Advantage Through People: Unleashing the Power of the Workforce.* Harvard Business School Press, 1994.

Pfeffer, Jeffrey. *The Human Equation: Building Profits By Putting People First.* Harvard Business School Press, 1998.

Porter, Michael A. *Competitive Strategy: Techniques For Analyzing Industries And Competitors.* The Free Press, 1998.

Pritchett, Price, Robinson, Donald, and Clarkson, Russell. *After The Merger: The Authoritative Guide For Integration Success.* McGraw-Hill, 1997.

Renckly, Richard G. *Human Resources: Emphasizing Practical Problem Solving and Day-to-Day Operating Details.* Barron's Educational Series Inc., 1997.

Robinson, Dana Gaines and Robinson, James C. *Performance Consulting.* Berrett-Koehler Publishers Inc., 1995.

Senge, Peter M. *The Fifth Discipline: The Art and Practice of the Learning Organization.* Doubleday, 1990.

Senge, Peter; Kleiner, Art; Roberts, Charlotte; Ross, Richard; Smith, Brian. *The Fifth Discipline Field Book: Strategies and Tools for Building a Learning Organization.* Doubleday, 1994.

Slywotzky, Adrian J. *Value Migration: How to Think Several Moves Ahead of the Competition.* Harvard Business School Press, 1996.

Stewart, Thomas A. *Intellectual Capital: The New Wealth Of Organizations.* Doubleday, 1997.

Ulrich, Dave. *Delivering Results: A New Mandate For Human Resource Professionals.* Harvard Business School Press, 1998.

Ulrich, Dave. *Human Resource Champions: The Next Agenda for Adding Value and Delivering Results.* Harvard Business School Press, 1997.

Ulrich, Dave; Losey, Michael R.; Lake, Gerry. *Tomorrow's HR Management: 48 Thought Leaders Call for Change.* John Wiley & Sons, 1997.

Ulrich, David and Lake, Dale. *Organizational Capability: Competing from the Inside Out.* John Wiley & Sons Inc., 1990

Von Oech, Roger. *A Whack on the Side of the Head: How You Can Be More Creative.* Warner Books, 1983.

Weiss, David S. *Beyond the Walls of Conflict: Mutual Gains Negotiating for Unions and Management.* Irwin Professional Publishing, 1996.

Weiss, David S. *High Performance HR: Leveraging Human Resources For Competitive Advantage.* John Wiley & Sons, 2000.

Wright, Philip C; Mondy, R. Wayne; Noe, Robert M. *Human Resource Management.* Prentice-Hall Canada Inc., 1996.

INDEX

๛